A WAR
★ ★ ★ WITHOUT ★ ★ ★
RIFLES

THE 1792 MILITIA ACT AND THE WAR OF 1812

JAMES N. GIBSON

Archway Publishing books may be ordered through booksellers or by contacting:

Archway Publishing
1663 Liberty Drive
Bloomington, IN 47403
www.archwaypublishing.com
1 (888) 242-5904

ISBN: 978-1-4808-3245-9 (sc)
ISBN: 978-1-4808-3246-6 (e)

Library of Congress Control Number: 2016909211

Print information available on the last page.

Archway Publishing rev. date: 1/31/2017

CONTENTS

INTRODUCTION

The War of 1812 is one of the least studied of America's conflicts. Though it's understandable that it would produce less interest than, say the American Civil War or World War II, even the Spanish–American War gets more attention than the first conflict America fought as an independent nation. This is tragic because the issues that caused this war have such a similarity to the current world problems. Far better than Vietnam, this conflict shows the constitutional and human limits of governmental power, as well as the lengths some people will go to overcome these limitations.

The War of 1812 was the first war in which the United States fought outside of its official borders. Even the earlier Indian wars were fought on land recognized as part of the United States, not as lands controlled or governed by another government. This war was also the first to involve the militia set up under the 1792 Militia Act—the law that required every man to own a military weapon. Finally, because the war did not go as planned, it was the first conflict in which a proposal was made to draft men into the Federal Army.

Today, the history of this war has been written and rewritten to suit the political needs of various groups or special interests. Theodore Roosevelt wrote one of the best-known works when he was only twenty-three years old. His manuscript's glowing descriptions of the fledgling US Navy has since become the standard for navy historians on this period. Since the 1950s and 1960s, National Guard historians have also written their histories of this time, with emphasis placed on the value of the special militias that would become the paternal ancestors of many present National Guard units. US Army historians have also written histories on this conflict that attack the common militia for its lack of discipline and unreliability. By default, these histories promote the value of a large, professional, standing army over any type of militia, including the National Guard.

The Supreme Court of the United States has probably done more to rewrite the history of the 1800s than any other group. In its 1918 ruling on the legality of conscription, the court said,

> Except for one act formulating a plan by which the entire body of citizens (the militia) subject to military duty was to be organized in every state (Act of May 8, 1792, c. 33, 1 Stat. 271) *which was never carried into effect*, Congress confined itself to providing for the organization of a specified number distributed among the States according to their quota, to be trained as directed by Congress and to be called by the President as need might require."

Seventy years later, in *Perpich v. the Department of Defense*, the court expanded on this history by stating that the Militia Act of 1792 was not enforced for over one hundred years prior to its repeal in 1901. Of course this means the Supreme Court doesn't recognize that the common militia existed after the year 1792, even though the aforementioned army and guard histories of the War of 1812 state the common militia existed twenty years later.

Thus, we get to the point of this book: to document the history of a militia law that the Supreme Court says was never enforced and that political activists say was never implemented. To document the effect of this law's caliber clause on the presence of rifles in the militia leading up to this war, and how the lack of riflemen affected the outcome of some of the major battles of this conflict. To then document the other laws passed during the period before the war to assist in the implementation of this act. Finally, to show how the war affected this law and what policy changes were made regarding rifles post conflict.

CHAPTER 1

The Years before 1812-
The Silent Wars with Europe

The War of 1812 has long been associated with certain issues: the ending of European support for the Native American tribes, the conquest of Canada, the seizure of American sailors and ships by England, and the American demand to be respected as an independent nation.

Of these four issues, the most prominent was the United States' desire to be distinguished as a powerful country in North America. In this regard, the outcome of the war saw the United States become a true nation and not just an association of small, quasi-independent states.

Figure 1: Native American Warfare

The Native Americans

The conflicts between the Native American tribes and the United States had been Britain's thorn in America's side since the revolution. It was part of Britain's foreign policy to supply arms and support to Native American tribes along the Great Lakes—land England ceded to the United States by the Treaty of Paris, which ended the revolution. These tribes would be England's proxies, preventing the United States from truly occupying the territory.

And England wasn't the only country doing this. France, which still held visions of reclaiming portions of North America, maintained trading posts along the Mississippi and Missouri Rivers. In these areas, French forces gave arms and powder to Indian tribes to prevent the United States from expanding to the Mississippi River. Rounding out the European presence was Spain, who claimed Florida and all the territory bordering the Gulf of Mexico.

Conflicts with various tribes extended the length and breadth of the new nation. In the south, the Chickamauga Cherokee and other tribes raided Georgia, South Carolina, and Kentucky from their base in northwestern Georgia. In the great Northwest Territory, which would eventually become the states of Ohio, Indiana, and Michigan, Chief Little Turtle of the Miami tribe led his people, along with the Shawnee, Hurons, and Delawares, in several battles with units of the United States Army and Militia.

Of course, the European powers' reasons for doing this were hardly noble: By using the tribes as proxies, they were destroying the tribes while also weakening the United States. In the Europeans' minds, over time the fighting would leave both sides too weak to prevent a European move back into those territories.

However, before the United States could engage this European and Native American alliance, another conflict had to be settled—namely, the internal US conflict over who owned the territories in question. Following the revolution, the states argued with each other over who had the better claim to various western territories. This issue stalled the westward expansion until 1785 and even prevented Maryland's ratification of the Articles of Confederation[1] until 1781. The following map shows many of these conflicting land claims.

One of the best examples of the various land claims is the territory we now call Vermont. Originally it was part of French Canada, but following the French and Indian Wars, Vermont became a British possession. Almost immediately three northeast colonies laid claim to the territory. Massachusetts laid claim based on the Massachusetts Bay Colony charter of 1629. New York laid claim based on a land grant issued by the Duke of York in 1664. New Hampshire finally laid claim based on a decree from King George II in 1740.

England could have avoided this power struggle if King George II had decreed the territory New Hampshire's. Instead, in 1741 he fixed the boundaries of Massachusetts, leaving New York and New Hampshire to fight it out with each other over who owned Vermont. The result was a land war, with both colonial governors issuing land grants and titles on the same Vermont property. By 1770 the situation had reached such a level that Ethan Allen[2] formed his legendary Green Mountain Boys to protect the New Hampshire settlers from New York settlers.

Early in the revolution, the disputed territory became the Republic of Vermont. This didn't settle the claims held by New Hampshire or New York, but both colonies had other, more pressing problems. After the war, Vermont became a sort of Casablanca for men trying to

---

[1] The initial government document for the United States. Passed during the revolution, it set forth powers and limitations for the congress and the states. In 1789 it was replaced by the much stronger Constitution of the United States, which included a president and a supreme court.

[2] Ethan Allen was a veteran of the French and Indian War who later served as a lieutenant in the American Revolution. He seized the British fort of Ticonderoga but failed in his later attempt to take Montreal. Following release from British custody, he lobbied for Vermont to be recognized as an independent state.

escape the law. One of these was Daniel Shay, leader of the legendary Shay's Rebellion of 1786 and 1787 (see chapter two).

The Vermont situation was of such prominence that it is mentioned in Federalist Paper Number 28, "A National Army and Internal Security," by Alexander Hamilton.

> If, on the contrary, the insurrection should pervade a whole State, or a principal part of it, the employment of a different kind of force might become unavoidable. It appears that Massachusetts found it necessary to raise troops for repressing the disorders within the State; that Pennsylvania, from the mere apprehension of commotions among a part of her citizens, had thought proper to have recourse to the same measure. Suppose the State of New York had been inclined to re-establish her lost jurisdiction over the inhabitants of Vermont, could she have hoped for success in such an enterprise from the efforts of the militia alone?

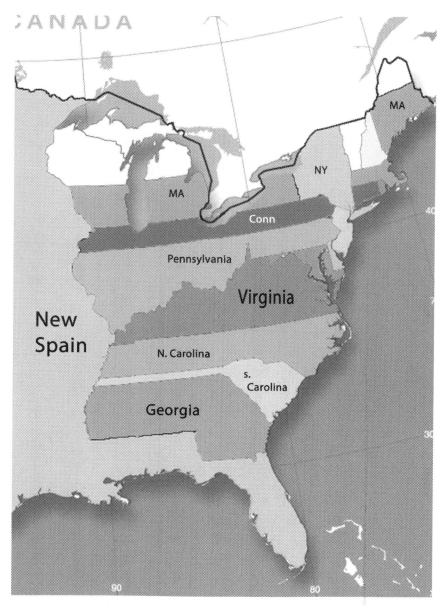

Figure 2: State Land Claims, 1780.

Granted, this comment by Hamilton was written to gain the support of the people of New York for the new constitution, not the people of Vermont or New Hampshire. Yet these words also show the strength of emotion these land claims prompted in the people of the various states. Thus, until 1785 there was no western expansion and therefore few confrontations with the tribes. After 1785, however, the gloves were off, and with the passage of the Northwest Ordinance in 1787, confrontation between the United States and Native American tribes was inevitable. The following letters make the point.

Letter from Colonel Benjamin Wilson to Governor St. Clair, Harrison County, October 4, 1789. On the 19th of September last, a party of Indians killed and scalped four persons, and captured four; the family of a certain William Johnston, within about nine miles of Clarksburg. On the 22nd, the Indians killed John Mauk's wife and two of his children, and burnt his house; the same evening, burnt Jacob Flotzer's house; the family hardly escaped. On the 23rd, burnt Jethro Thompson's house; and on the 26th, burnt John Simm's house; and on the 28th, stole from Randolph county, ten or eleven horses. The number for horses taken from this county, is not yet truly ascertained: but certain, five horses taken—cattle, sheep, and hogs killed. Some part of this mischief done eleven or twelve miles in towards the interior parts of this county. Sir, be assured, the people of this part of the county are much alarmed and much confused; and in my humble opinion, if something more than treaties made with part of the Indian tribes, is not done shortly, it will be with difficulty the frontiers of this county can be kept from evacuating their settlements.

Letter from the Governor of Georgia to Edward Telfair, Secretary of War, April 29, 1793. From the deposition of Benjamin Harrison and Francis Pugh, and from the information of Joseph Dabbs, there is little expectation of avoiding a general war with the Creeks and the Cherokees. Blood has been spilt in every direction on the extended frontier of this State, and one man killed in the State of South Carolina. I have directed fourteen block-houses to be erected, each to be garrisoned by one commissioned officer, two sergeants, and seventeen Privates.

Figure 3: On the left, *The murder of Miss Jane McCrea, 1777* by N. Currier, 1846. On the right, General Anthony Wayne.

Battles, raids, ambushes, and skirmishes were an ever-present part of life in the western lands from 1780 to 1796. One such example was Fort Nashborough, the foundation for today's city of Nashville, Tennessee. For fourteen years, from 1781 until the Treaty of Tellico Blockhouse in 1794, the fort was under regular attack by the Chickamaugua Cherokee. The beginning of the end for the southern tribes was the establishment of the states of Kentucky in 1792 and then Tennessee in 1796. With these states firmly established the United States now controlled the south bank of the Ohio River to the Mississippi, as well as a major section of the eastern bank of the Mississippi.

In the Northwest Territories, military expeditions sent by President Washington to put down the native resistance twice ended in dismal failures. Of the two, the force lead by Arthur St. Clair would produce the Battle of Wabash on November 4, 1791—the worst military defeat the United States Army would suffer for the next one hundred years. Of his 1,120 troops, St. Clair lost 97 percent to Little Turtle's warriors. On hearing the news, President George Washington was said to have lost his temper and sworn out loud. Washington's next general would not let him down.

Mad Anthony Wayne wouldn't be as rash as his predecessors, and under the cover of peace negotiations, he prepared his troops throughout the winter of 1793. Using a new concept called a legion, he formed his forces into four groups. Each group consisted of four companies of musketmen, two companies of riflemen, one company of artillery, and one troop of cavalry.

Wayne didn't fight in the European style but in a manner similar to Emperor Trajan of Ancient Rome. As he advanced from Fort Washington (now the city of Cincinnati), he built forts and blockhouses along the way. These ensured a strong line of supply and communication while denying the Indians more and more territory. One such fort was Greenville, site of present-day Greenville, Ohio. Other forts built by Wayne's order were Fort Recovery (built on the site of St. Clair's defeat in 1791), Fort Defiance, and Fort Loramie. Including Forts Jefferson and Hamilton (built by St. Claire), Wayne had many strong defensive positions to use to maintain supplies and men.

Figure 4: *Charge of the Dragoons at Fallen Timbers,* By R. T. Zogbaum.

After several skirmishes and a major attack on Fort Recovery in June, Wayne's legion finally confronted 1,300 Indians at a place called Fallen Timbers (near Toledo, Ohio) on August 20, 1794. Here Wayne administered a crushing defeat using his combined force of artillery, cavalry, and infantry. In 1795 the defeated Western Indian Confederacy signed the first Treaty of Greenville, putting an end to the conflict over the Ohio Territory and setting the stage for statehood in 1803. The treaty distinguished a clear border between Indian land and settlement land.

The end of Little Turtle's war did not end the disputes between Native Americans and the United States. There was still the issue of the Michigan and Indiana territories with the tribes, particularly the Shawnee. Then in 1803, Jefferson purchased the Louisiana Territory from France. Now the territory of the United States did not stop at the eastern bank of the Mississippi. New Spain was pushed back to just south of the Red River and then westward to the Rocky Mountains. The border then went northwest along the mountains to Montana.

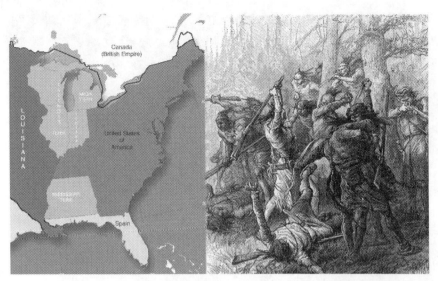

Figure 5: Extent of the United States, 1803 and the fighting at Tippecanoe

The purchase of Louisiana reinforced the need to properly control the Mississippi, Michigan, Indiana, and Illinois territories already claimed by the United States. Standing in the way in the north was Tecumseh and a new confederation of tribes supported by the British. In the south were the Creeks and Seminoles, supported by Spain.

The first confrontation would be in the north against Tecumseh's Indian alliance. Tecumseh had been battling US expansion since he was born. Tecumseh's father had been killed in 1774 battling the forces of the royal governor of Virginia. In 1780, US Army troops destroyed his childhood home. After that, his older brother, who fought with the Chickamaugua Cherokee, raised Tecumseh until his death during a raid on American settlers. Following this, in 1790 Tecumseh returned to Ohio, where he fought at Fallen Timbers as part of the Shawnee contingent serving under Little Turtle.

Tecumseh is said to have not signed the treaty of Greenville in 1795; given his estimated age of twenty-seven, it is hard to think of him as a chief. After 1795 he moved to what is today Greenville, Indiana. There, with his younger brother (the prophet), he began a nativist religious revival movement to build tribal alliances against white expansion. These activities brought them into conflict with Chief Black Hoof of the Shawnee, who was trying to maintain peaceful relations. The conflict eventually forced Tecumseh to move further west to the Wabash and Tippecanoe Rivers in 1808, where he established Prophet Town.

Figure 6: Chief Tecumseh and *William Henry Harrison* By Rembrandt Peale, 1813.

The governor of the Indiana Territory, William Henry Harrison, set the stage for open conflict. Harrison wanted to build the population of Indiana as quickly as possible in order to qualify for statehood. To do this, he needed land for settlement, and in 1809 he succeeded in getting the tribes to cede 2.5 million acres in Illinois and Indiana to the United States. Called the Treaty of Fort Wayne, it was supported by Chief Black Hoof of the Shawnee but was violently opposed by Tecumseh.

Tecumseh threatened to kill all the chiefs who signed the treaty. He traveled around the territory urging warriors to renounce the chiefs who sought peaceful negotiations with the United States and join his coalition. He then went south to gather support from five major Indian nations: the Cherokee, Chickasaw, Choctaw, Creek, and Seminole. It was while he was away that Harrison decided to launch a preemptive strike.

Fearful of the growing tribal alliances Tecumseh was putting together; in August of 1811 Harrison launched an all-out war against the unofficial capital of the alliance, Prophet's Town. First he marched to the treaty line of 1809, where he built Fort Harrison to cover his lines of supply. There he received permission from Secretary of War William Eustis to enter Indian territory and engage the Indians. With this approval, Harrison marched north, and on November 6, 1811, he camped outside of Prophet's Town. The next morning found the two sides engaged in battle, with the Indians defeated by that afternoon. Harrison's forces then razed the town and returned to Vincennes before the winter set in.

The Battle of Tippecanoe was essentially the first battle of the War of 1812. Tecumseh was politically hurt, but he wasn't dead—he wasn't even there. He withdrew with his remaining followers to Canada, where they received support from the British government. His activities in the south would also lead to the Creek civil war, where the Red Sticks and the Creeks from the Upper Towns would rise against both the United States and friendly Creek tribes after the start of the War of 1812.

The Conquest of Canada

The conquest of Canada is probably the least understood of the reasons for why the United States went to war in 1812. For many years, it was listed as simply the United States' desire for land that pushed for the seizure of Canada. But following the purchase of Louisiana in 1803, additional land was hardly on the minds of either the US government or the American people.

The issues that prompted the call for the invasion of Canada were more political in nature. These issues included securing the northern borders against British support of the Native Americans. Then there was the fact that Canada was originally a French colony taken by Britain during the French and Indian Wars.

Figure 7: Painting of an Indian village in Ontario, Canada, 1800. (Library and Archives of Canada).

Excerpt from the Congressional Record: Debate on a Bill for a Detachment of the Militia, June 1797. Mr Dayton: He did not, however, think we should have a war; and, if such an event were to take place, he

did not think there was a probability of an invasion.
Our situation in 1794, he said, was very different. We
were then not only depredated upon by the British
at sea, but Lord Dorchester[3] had issued his warlike
proclamation; the Indians were counted, and had
their tomahawks in their hands uplifted and ready
to strike.

The call for invading Canada is in fact older than the United
States. There were several invasions or forays into Canada during
the revolution, in an attempt to weaken the British hold and possibly
stimulate a French uprising. Then in 1777, the Continental Congress
signed the Articles of Confederation, the initial governing document
of the United States. Written in this document was the following
article.

Article XI. Canada acceding to this confederation,
and adjoining in the measures of the United States,
shall be admitted into, and entitled to all the
advantages of this union; but no other colony shall
be admitted into the same, unless such admission be
agreed to by nine States.

Thus, it was the view from the very foundation of the United States
that Canada was to be allowed to enter the union at any time, without
even the approval of any of the other states. This was a special privilege
that showed the strong desire on the part of the founding fathers to
have Canada as a state in the United States. It is more than possible that
after thirty-five years of wanting this, the remaining founding fathers,
Jefferson and Adams, may have become convinced that they could
force this union. Jefferson is reported to have said about the planned
1812 invasion of Canada, "The acquisition of Canada this year, as far

---

[3] Lord Dorchester was Guy Charleton, First Governor General of the Canadas.

as the neighborhood of Quebec, will be a mere matter of marching, and will give us the experience for the attack on Halifax,[4] the next and final expulsion of England from the American continent."

Regardless of this view, by 1812 the political situation in Canada was hardly conducive to Canadians wanting to join the United States. Though Quebec was still primarily French by nationality, they were hardly supporters of the French revolution. Many recent French immigrants to Canada had come to escape the terror of the republic. Also, the United States was primarily Anglican in religion, whereas Quebec was primarily Catholic. The British had not imposed Anglican traditions on them, but the French Canadians were well aware that the most radical of the Anglican denominations had gone to the American colonies. This, plus the attacks against the Catholic Church in France by the French Republic, an ally of the United States, made the French Canadians fearful of losing their religious rights if they left British control.

West of Quebec, Canadians citizens were primarily of British heritage. These recent immigrants to the Ontario region came from either Britain or were American Tories who'd left the United States following the revolution. It is estimated that forty-six thousand expatriate Tory Americans settled in Canada, ten thousand in Quebec and Ontario and the rest in Nova Scotia. Called the United Empire Loyalists, they were granted as much as two hundred acres of land to establish themselves in Canada. In addition, thousands of Iroquois, expelled from New York, had also settled in Ontario just west of Buffalo. Neither of these groups wanted anything to do with the United States, with the Tories' sentiment against unification with the United States being the strongest. Thus, by 1812 there was no support for a union with the United States in any section of Canada.

---

[4] Halifax in the 1800s was more a fortified military harbor than a city. Its true growth only began during the Napoleonic wars of 1797–1812, and that was due to the large military presence. Taking it in 1812 would have been extremely difficult regardless of Jefferson's assertions.

Another fact to be made regarding the call for invading Canada was that Canada was not the only territory that the United States wanted to invade. In truth, the invasion of Canada was also a call for invading New Spain in the west and Florida to the south. Because of various wars and agreements with Great Britain and France in the years since the revolution, by 1812 Spain possessed not only present-day Florida but the coastal sections of Alabama and Mississippi, with the City of Vicksburg in Spanish territory. The purchase of Louisiana created a gap in Spain's territories that exasperated the problems.

By invading these territories, the US government hoped to stop Spain's support for the southern Indian tribes, thus ending the Indian raids on US border towns in Georgia and Mississippi.

Message of President Jefferson to Congress, December 3, 1805

> With Spain, our negotiations for a settlement of differences have not had a satisfactory issue. Spoliations during a former war, for which she had formally acknowledged herself responsible, have been refused to be compensated but on conditions affecting other claims, in nowise connected with them. Yet the same practices are renewed in the present war, and are already of great amount. On the Mobile, our commerce passing through that river continues to be obstructed by arbitrary duties and vexatious searches. Propositions for adjusting amicably the boundaries of Louisiana have not been acceded to. While, however, the right is unsettled, we have avoided changing the state of things, by taking new posts, or strengthening ourselves in the disputed territories, in the hope that the other Power, would not, by a contrary conduct, oblige us to meet their example, and endanger conflicts of authority the issue of which may not

be easily controlled. But in this hope we have now reason to lessen our confidence. Inroads have been recently made into the territories of Orleans and the Mississippi; our citizens have been seized, and their property plundered, in the very parts of the former which had been actually delivered up by Spain, and this by the regular officers and soldiers of that Government. I have therefore found it necessary, at length, to give orders to our troops on that frontier to be in readiness to protect our citizens, and to repel by arms any similar aggressions in future. Other details, necessary for your full information of the state of things between this country and that, shall be the subject of another communication. In reviewing these injuries from some of the belligerent Powers, the moderation, the finness, and the wisdom, of the Legislature will all be called into action. We ought still to hope that time, and a more correct estimate of interest, as well as of character, will produce the justice we are bound to expect. But should any nation deceive itself by false calculations, and disappoint that expectation, we must join in the unprofitable contest of trying which party can do the other the most harm. Some of' these injuries may perhaps admit a peaceable remedy. Where that is competent, it is always the most desirable. But some of them are of a nature to be met by force only, and all of them may lead to it. I cannot, therefore, but recommend such preparations as circumstances call for.

Figure 8: President Thomas Jefferson. By Rembrandt
Peale, 1800

In addition to the Indian issue, there was also the issue of trade
down the Mississippi River (which Spain regularly blocked prior to
the purchase of New Orleans) and a port access along the Gulf of
Mexico at Mobile, Alabama. So unyielding had Spain been on river
trade that throughout the Washington Administration, there were
rumors that disgruntled Westerners planned to seize the ports from
Spain. In 1793, when Spain and France were at war, four French
agents found it very easy to recruit men in Kentucky and Tennessee
for an attack on New Orleans. However, Washington could not allow
this to happen, and in that same year he sent General Anthony Wayne
to Kentucky to erect and garrison Fort Massac just below where the
Tennessee River enters the Ohio River and just above where the Ohio
River enters the Mississippi River. This location was the perfect choke
point to prevent armed men from Tennessee and Kentucky from
traveling to New Orleans by boat.

Tensions with New Spain continued even after passage of the
1796 Pinckney's Treaty, which defined the borders of the United

States to the western Spanish colonies and allowed navigation to New Orleans and the right of deposit there. With the purchase of Louisiana in 1803, this treaty became obsolete, and the potential for open conflict increased drastically.

Spain viewed the Lewis and Clark expedition of 1804 as provocative and actually sent troops into the Louisiana Territory in the vain hope of intercepting the expedition. As the previous letter to Congress showed, by 1805 Spain was prohibiting US citizens from using the port at Mobile for the shipment of their produce. Then in 1806, President Jefferson was told that thousands of Spanish regulars had been deployed to the east Texas border to reinforce Mexican militiamen. Jefferson sent one thousand regulars to reinforce the militia at New Orleans, only to discover the story was false. Some skirmishes occurred along the Sabine River, but war was avoided, and a neutral zone was established between the Arroyo Hondo and Sabine River, which by 1812 had become the de facto border.

The Seizure of United States Ships and Sailors

Figure 9: British Captain inspects "New recruits."

Having discussed the first two reasons given for the War of 1812, we need to discuss the issue of US trade and the seizure of ships and sailors by England. To do this, we should discuss the European situation at that time, which could be summed up by one event: the French Revolution.

Following the French Revolution in 1789, French and US relations became quite strained. Jefferson, Madison, and Monroe supported strong French relations, even at the height of the period known as the Reign of Terror, but others such as Washington, Adams, and Hamilton were concerned about the new French attitude, particularly the extremism.

When war broke out between England and France in 1793, England began seizing all ships found heading to France or to French-controlled nations. As a result, from 1793 to 1794, over 350 US vessels were taken at sea, their cargoes and crews rerouted to England. The loss of so many ships had a serious effect on US trade and economy, forcing President Washington in 1794 to send John Jay to London to try to solve the issue diplomatically.[5] The result was the London Treaty of 1794.

Under the treaty, England got the most favored trading status with the United States, and America agreed to Britain's anti-French maritime policies. In return, the United States got Britain to finally abandon its forts along the Great Lakes, compensate US ship owners for their lost ships, allow US trade to India and the West Indies, and set the border between the United States and eastern Canada.

---

[5] As an example of how serious this situation was, in 1794 the government passed a statute placing eighty thousand militia on alert for possible war. This statute expired after two years but was then semi regularly renewed until the hostilities in Europe subsided in 1800.

Figure 10: Chief Justice John Jay, by Stuart Gilbert and President John Adams.

This treaty was a response to England's need to concentrate its efforts against France following the start of open warfare in 1793 and the defeat of the Indian tribes at Fallen Timbers in 1794. Yet this treaty also opened up a full-blown diplomatic crisis with France and set the stage for the creation of a new Democratic Republican party to counter the Federalist Party in the United States.

In response to the treaty, French warships began seizing US vessels in 1796, with nearly three hundred vessels in custody by 1797.[6] Federalist Alexander Hamilton preached war with France, but Federalist President Adams instead sent three diplomats to France in the hopes of a diplomatic settlement. Three French agents (code-named X, Y, and Z) met the diplomats on their arrival and promptly demanded a cash bribe for the French foreign minister, a huge loan

---

[6] The French government also sent agents to the Creek Indians in the Mississippi territory.

to support the French war effort, and an apology for statements made by President Adams as preconditions to any negotiations.[7]

When congress and US newspapers learned what happened in 1798, it set off a firestorm of anti-French feelings. The words "millions for defense, not one cent for tribute"[8] became the rallying cry for expanding the US Navy and the US Army. Congress gave Adams authority to build and field twelve twenty-two-gun warships, to expand the army, and to generally prepare for war. Treaties with France were then rescinded, and the US Navy began overtly searching for French privateers along US territorial waters and the Caribbean.

Excerpt from Congressional Debate over a Bill to Raise a Provisional Army of 20,000 Men, April 24, 1798

Mr Otis: "If what was said by the agents of that Government to our Envoys could be relied on, there was a direct threat to ravage our coasts. He hoped, however, no invasion would take place; but, when he said this, he calculated upon the French acting as reasonable beings, but perhaps he calculated delusively. Indeed, they are now threatening the invasion of a country, where one may suppose they would have as little chance of succeeding as this country."

Mr Harper: "If gentlemen did not think the army immediately necessary, and did not choose to leave it with the President to judge of the necessity, they might make it to depend upon a declaration of war by France, on an invasion, or in case Victor Hugues

---

[7] Today, this X, Y, Z affair sounds horribly like the 2006 nuclear weapons talks between the United States and North Korea.

[8] Attributed by American newspapers to the US envoys to France when confronted with the request for the bribes. In truth, the US envoys were more eloquent: "Not a sixpence."

were to bring his black troops, or send his threatened frigates against us, or if an insurrection should be excited by our enemy, then the President should be empowered to raise an army. (…)What, he asked, was the situation of the West Indies? Were they not told that Victor Hugues,[9] with 5,000 of his best troops, is ready to make a blow upon the Southern country, whenever the word of command shall be given?"

Called the Quasi-war because war was never declared, this conflict resulted in the creation of a thirty-ship US Navy, the temporary doubling of the US Army, and the formal creation of the Marine Corps. Most of the land forces would never see any service, but the navy and the marines were highly occupied. Several French privateers were taken, as well as several French warships. One of the most daring events was the landing of marines at Puerta Plata on Santa Domingo, where a French privateer was cut loose from its moorings and the harbor defense cannons were spiked. The conflict ended in September 1800.

During this buildup for war, congress also passed the Alien and Sedition Acts, a series of acts with the titles "Alien Friends Act," "Sedition Act," "Naturalization Act," and "Alien Enemies Act." The first law allowed presidential deportation of any resident alien considered "dangerous to the peace and safety of the United States." The second made it a crime to publish "false, scandalous, and malicious writing against the government or its officials." The third extended the duration of residence prior to becoming a citizen from five years to fourteen years. Finally, the last act (which is still on the Federal books) authorizes the president to apprehend and deport

---

[9] Victor Hugues was a French colonial who was the first Caribbean insurgent. By organizing free blacks, mulattoes, and French colonists, he succeeded in forcing the British out of Guadeloupe. In the following years, he exported his insurgency to all other French islands controlled by the British.

resident aliens if their home countries are at war with the United States. These laws proved to be extremely unpopular, particularly to people connected to the new Democratic Republican party.

Vice President Thomas Jefferson (Democratic-Republican) denounced the Sedition Act as a violation of the first and tenth amendments. The acts eventually became major issues in the 1798 and 1800 elections. Working closely with Aaron Burr of New York, Jefferson rallied his party in 1800 against the Sedition Acts and the new Federal taxes imposed to build the army and navy. The result was the election of Jefferson as president and Aaron Burr as vice president. Now, with the Democratic Republicans in charge of both the executive and legislative branches of government, the anti-French views were thrown out, and the pre-London Treaty, anti-British views were back in power, just in time to be used for personal gain by a French general recently nominated First Consul of France: Napoleon Bonaparte.

Napoleon Bonaparte dominated the world political situation from 1800 to the War of 1812. From 1793 to 1802, England and France were continuously at war with each other. During this time, Napoleon rose through the ranks and finally led a major military expedition to conquer Egypt. He failed in this, and on his return to France, he essentially took control of the nation and made himself First Consul. From that day forward, he would use the United States as a pawn in his various confrontations with Great Britain.

Napoleon had grand plans for North America—grand as in having the entire continent under a French flag. First, he negotiated a peace treaty to end the Quasi-war with the United States on September 30, 1800. The following day, he concluded a treaty with Spain to return control of the Louisiana territory to France. As part of the terms of the Treaty of San Ildefonso, Napoleon was to give the then infant Duke of Parma a kingdom in Italy (which France had just reconquered). The treaty was kept secret from the world in order for Britain to not take any overt action. Regardless of this secrecy, Jefferson became aware of it in 1801 and sent diplomats to Napoleon to secure the purchase of the city of New Orleans, thus insuring US trade through that city.

Figure 11: *Napoleon Crossing the Alps*. Painting by Jacques-Louis David.

Initially Napoleon rebuffed Jefferson's diplomats. His plans included the creation of a massive French presence in western North America, with the possible result of seizing Canada or even New Spain. All these plans, however, rested on the recovery of Haiti as a staging base for his military campaigns. When this operation failed in 1803, Napoleon had to abandon his grand plans for North America. As a result, Jefferson suddenly found himself being offered not just the city of New Orleans but also the entire Louisiana Territory for approximately fifteen million dollars.

The sale of Louisiana not only helped fund Napoleon's renewed war against Europe, but it put the United States in the French sphere of influence—which placed the United States in conflict with Spain and

Great Britain. With the start of a renewed European war came new shipping seizures. This time both British and French warships seized US ships, though Britain was adding fuel to the fire by impressing US sailors into British naval service.

The Barbary War

Figure 12: *Decatur Boarding the Tripolitan Gunboat*, By Dennis Malone Carter

The British and the French were not the only ones seizing US ships in the early 1800s. Since 1783, Moslem pirates working out of Morocco and Algiers had been threatening US trade into the Mediterranean.[10] Further, following the seizure of Malta by Napoleon in 1798, the knights of Malta were no longer able to keep the Algerian corsairs in check. Thus, attacks against US shipping by Moslem pirates had increased by 1800.

Having beaten the French privateers in the Quasi-war, many in the US government felt the navy was strong enough to take on the

---

[10] Though working out of these lands, they were being given sanction to operate there by the Ottoman Empire in Turkey.

Barbary pirates. All they needed was a really good excuse, which they got on Jefferson's inaugural. On that day, the Pasha of Tripoli demanded $225,000 from the new administration to prevent war. Jefferson refused, the Pasha declared war, and in 1801 Jefferson ordered several US Navy frigates into the Mediterranean with specific orders to seize the vessels and the goods of the Pasha. By 1803, the cream of the new US Navy was in the Mediterranean.

Battles were few; the Barbary corsairs had little interest in trying to tangle with the large US Navy frigates. Thus the biggest event was in October 1803, when the frigate *Philadelphia* ran aground in Tripoli harbor and was taken by the pirates. In a daring night raid four months later, US naval forces commanded by Stephen Decatur succeeded in burning the ship in the harbor before the pirates could take it to sea to attack US shipping. The daring attack even earned the praise of British Admiral Lord Nelson. The first Barbary war ended the following year.[11]

With the Barbary war ended and the US government feeling very proud of its new navy, the European situation came back to their attention. Britain had beaten both France and Spain at sea in the Battle of Trafalgar in 1805. The following year, Napoleon implemented the continental system to impose a Europe-wide embargo on British goods. The British responded in 1807 with "Orders in Council" that prohibited her trading partners from trading with France. This included the United States, who was still obeying the Treaty of London.

---

[11] The second Barbary war began right after the end of the War of 1812.

Figure 13: *USS Chesapeake.* By F. Muller, US Navy Art
Collection

Thus the stage was set for the worst incident of seizure and
impressment. In June 1807 the fifty-gun British warship *Leopard*
attacked and disabled the thirty-eight-gun frigate USS *Chesapeake* just
off Norfolk Virginia. The story is that several of the *Leopard*'s crew
deserted to the *Chesapeake* when the two ships were in Chesapeake
Bay; the British were blockading French ships in the harbor at the
time. Supposedly to recover the men, the British captain ordered his
ship to open fire, killing three and wounding eighteen sailors. Having
won the battle, the British captain boarded the US Navy frigate
and removed four men (one British, and three Americans who had
previously been impressed into British service). The British sailor was
eventually hanged, but the Americans were imprisoned in Halifax.

The USS *Chesapeake* was a warship, not a cargo vessel with
some New England merchant's goods, and so impressment was the
underlying issue. The insult was directly to the entire nation, but
Jefferson didn't want war. Instead, in December congress passed the
Embargo Act of 1807. This act was a total embargo prohibiting the
export of cargo from American ports. In recent years, it has been
ranked as the seventh worst mistake ever made by a US president. The
Embargo Act had no effect on Britain, who had a good harvest in 1808

and was already opening new trade routes. Further, the government in power in Britain was becoming fearful of the commercial growth of the United States and wanted to stifle it as much as possible—and if the US government wanted to help, more power to them. The immediate effects of the embargo was the near bankruptcy of northeastern shipping and the new textile companies that had just begun.

Exports from the United States dropped from $108 million in 1807 to less than $25 million in 1808. To keep from going under, many New England merchants began smuggling goods overland to Canada. Some more enterprising shippers would fill a ship with cargo "for a southern port," and then once out to sea, they'd meet a British ship at a pre-arranged location to transfer the cargo. By the election of 1809, the domestic political situation was so bad that just three days before the election, congress replaced the embargo with the Non-Intercourse Act. The new act lifted all embargos except those directly against Britain and France.

The Non-intercourse Act failed as miserably as the Embargo Act, as did the subsequent 1810 Macon's Bill Number 2. Thus, from 1807 to 1812, British naval officers had seized up to nine hundred ships and impressed into military service some six thousand US citizens.

However, the situation was beginning to bend toward the United States. With the invasion of Spain in 1808, Britain began fielding more and more troops against Napoleon. Further, Portugal (invaded the year before) had been the major producer of cotton for both Europe and Britain. Now with the cotton fields in a war zone, Britain and France were both looking for textiles. A poor harvest in 1812 also made Britain in need of food products.

Thus, on June 16, 1812 the British foreign minister announced that the blockade on US shipping would be relaxed. Unfortunately, given the speed at which messages moved at that time, it was too late to stop open warfare.

America's Position in North America

Obviously this last issue was political and emotional; it was nothing more than an attempt to express the feeling that the United States was important, a power equal to all the European powers and worthy of respect. As noted earlier, by 1812 the United States had forced Spain to cede territory to it. The navy had fought the Barbary pirates and won a form of victory. The navy had also fought French privateers in the Caribbean and won there as well. The army had beaten the proxy Native American forces of England and Spain several times, and there were other victories.

For years after the revolution, the governments of Europe had been wagering on how long the United States would last. England was consistently pessimistic about the chances of the nation holding together; they thought the country's westward expansion would eventually make the nation too large to be governed by the US system.

In this they were almost right. There had been numerous incidents where the United States almost came unglued. Starting with Shay's rebellion, there had been several crises generated by corrupt officials, courts, and other teething problems expected with a new nation. The later Whiskey Rebellion against Hamilton's tax on distilled spirits further tested the nation's ability to deal with itself.

As noted earlier, in 1793 the US government had dealt with attempts by French agents to embroil the United States in France's conflict with Spain. An earlier spy event involved George Beckwith, who had befriended Alexander Hamilton. Publicly, Beckwith was a gentleman seeking to recover land formally granted to him on the Ohio River. In reality, he was a British agent who tried to get the United States to launch an attack on Spain. During his conversations with several government officials, he privately assured them that if the United States asserted its rights against Spain to navigate the Mississippi, the governor of Canada could be relied on for assistance.

This was obviously an attempt to get the United States to declare war on Spain over the Mississippi River.

Beckwith was eventually unmasked, but instead of deporting him, Hamilton began using him. Beckwith became the unofficial bridge between the administration of George Washington and the British government. The meetings, as well as the subjects of the meetings, were so covert that Secretary of State Thomas Jefferson was not informed. The relationship lasted until 1791, following which Washington had all formal contacts suppressed.

The greatest conspiracy of all occurred in 1805 and was hatched by no less than former Vice President Aaron Burr. Working with the governor of the Louisiana Territory, General James Wilkinson, Burr is said to have been planning to take over the lands west of the Alleghany Mountains up to New Spain. Wilkinson was the key player because he controlled the largest US military force in that section of the nation.

Surprisingly, General Wilkinson was also a spy for the Spanish Crown—a fact that would come out years after his death. For decades he was working toward the interests of Spain and not those of the United States: Fifteen years earlier, Wilkinson had offered to forcibly seize Kentucky for Spain, only to be rejected by the Spanish Crown. During the Burr affair, it was Wilkinson's Spanish connections that forced him to inform Jefferson of the conspiracy in 1807.

In the end, by 1812 the United States had gone through many trials and was still holding together. Many in government, particularly the representatives of the western states, were ready for the United States to take its place on the world stage—and what better way to do that than to take on Great Britain and beat it? Thus, we have now covered the major reasons commonly given for why the United States went to war in 1812.

The political situation in the United States had greatly changed since the signing of the constitution. The following list shows the number of signers that were no longer alive when the country went to war and greatly tested the intents of various sections of the document.

Signers of the Constitution Dead by 1812

John Blair: 1800
George Mason: 1792
Alexander Hamilton: Killed in a duel with Aaron Burr in 1804
George Washington: 1799
George Wythe: 1806
John Rutledge: 1800
Thomas Fitzsimons: 1811
Benjamin Franklin: 1790
Thomas Miffin: 1800
Robert Morris: 1806
James Wilson: 1798
William Blount: 1800
Alexander Martin: 1807
Roger Sherman:[12] 1793
Richard Dobbs Spraight Sr.: Killed in 1802 in a duel with Federalist
John Stanly
Robert Yates: 1801
David Bearly: 1790
William C. Houston: 1788
William Livingston: 1790
William Paterson: 1806
Nathaniel Gorham: 1796
Abraham Baldwin: 1807
William Leigh Pierce: 1789
Daniel Carroll: 1796
Daniel Jenifer: 1790
John Hancock: 1793

---

[12] Roger Sherman signed the Articles of Association, the Declaration of Independence, the Articles of Confederation, and the Constitution.

CHAPTER 2
The 1812 Army and Militia

When the United States went to war in 1812, it seemed to have all the advantages according to contemporary documents. The United States had a population of 7.7 million people compared to a Canadian population of just over 500,000. The United States could, based on its population, field a militia of over one million men and had congressional approval for a regular army of 35,600 men. The US Navy had 20 vessels: 3 large, 44-gun ships, 3 large frigates, and 14 other smaller vessels, including gunboats. Canada had only 7,000 regular troops and around 75,000 potential militiamen. But numbers on paper can be deceiving.

The Regular Army

Figure 14: Depiction of an army surgeon, 1812. US Army image

Contrary to what the paperwork said, the US Army in 1812 was in terrible shape. Though the authorized strength was over 35,000, the actual manpower was 11,744 officers and men (6,744 on station). These men were in turn scattered along the boundaries of the United States at various forts, ports, and cities. Thus, concentrating enough troops to launch an attack meant stripping troops from other important locations.

Along the Canadian border were the following strategic forts: Fort Dearborn (53 men), on the site of the modern city of Chicago; Fort Mackinac (88 men), on the straits between Lake Michigan and Lake Huron; Fort Detroit (119 men), at the western approach to Lake Erie; and Fort Niagara, at the mouth of the Niagara River on Lake Ontario. In addition to these strategic forts, there were other forts in New York, Pennsylvania, and Ohio, as well as the Michigan, Illinois, and Indiana territories. There were forts like Fort Wayne in Indiana (85 men), Fort Recovery in Ohio, Fort Knox (not the modern one), Fort Kaskaskia in Illinois, Erie Pennsylvania, Buffalo New York, Fort Ontario (Oswego, New York), Sackett's Harbor, Ogdensburg, Plattsburg, and Fort Harrison in Indiana. But these forts were small, and duty to these isolated locations was viewed as the worst postings one could get in the US Army.

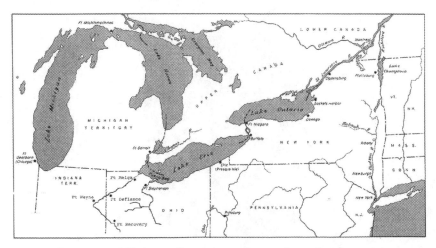

Figure 15: US Army forts along the northern border.

The only locations that had large numbers of men were Fort Stoddart in Mississippi (469 men), New York harbor (901 men), and Baton Rouge (1,244 men). Though 430 men were on the march to Fort Detroit to increase its garrison to 550 men, the majority of US Army forces were very widely spread.

Fort Niagara is not listed in the Federal fortifications listing for 1808, but it was known to be well garrisoned. One of the reasons was the fact that when the fort was in British control, it had been the supply source to ex-American Tories now living across the Niagara River in Canada. After the revolution, the British Crown gave these loyal subjects two hundred acres of land in the area near Fort Niagara; the location was selected because they could be provisioned and protected by the then British fort. Thus, the now US fort was well garrisoned to deter any aggression by the nearby "large" expatriate population.

Now, consider the subject of the arms available to the US Army. On November 1, 1811, the US Army Ordnance Department reported that there were 202,621 stands of arms (muskets) fit for service. On top of this were 4,655 pairs of pistols, 3,666 carbines, and 6,911 rifles. What is of importance, however, is the footnote at the bottom of the page: "From the number of small arms reported 'fit for service' it is presumed that a deduction of one third should be made for those which may be found to want repairs, and for British, German, and other arms, of calibers different from the standard of the United States."

Thus there were a large number of arms in Federal store that were in need of repair, or that were not the correct caliber. Taking this into account, the believed number of muskets in Federal store that were ready for service was only 135,000. More important, we now have evidence that there was an approved caliber for the US Army in 1812.

Then there is the subject of the condition of the arms that were actually in the field. Thanks to government bureaucracy, we have the inspector general reports for the Twelfth and Fourteenth Army Regiments at Niagara in 1812.

The Twelfth Regiment of Infantry, commanded
by Colonel Thomas Parker. "The muskets are good,
but some few of them out of repair. No gun slings have
been furnished; neither has there been a sufficiency of
screw-drivers, worms, picks or brushes, supplied. The
knapsacks are very bad, as are likewise the canteens.
The regiment has only about twenty-three rounds of
ball cartridge, and not two flints per man; and there
is no ammunition in store at this place. The cartridges
are many of them very bad."

The Fourteenth Regiment of Infantry, commanded
by Colonel William H. Winder. "The arms of this
regiment are in infamously bad order. They appear to
be old muskets that had probably been bought up at
reduced prices by the contractors or other public agents,
and are now placed in the hands of men who are almost
within gunshot of the enemy. The Inspector has no
hesitation in giving it as his opinion, that at least one
fifth of them are unfit for service; and that be believes,
were they to undergo a critical inspection, a much
larger proportion of them would be condemned. The
cartridge boxes, bayonet scabbards, and belts, are good;
the knapsacks are very bad. Neither gun slings, picks,
nor brushes, have been furnished; nor has a sufficient
number of screw-drivers and worms been supplied.
This regiment has a large supply of ball cartridges,
powder, and lead, but a considerable proportion of it is
very bad; some of the cartridges are said to have been
made up in 1794. There is a scarcity of flints.

The regiment is composed entirely of recruits;
they appear to be almost as ignorant of their duty as
if they had never seen a camp, and scarcely know on
what shoulder to carry the musket. They are mere

militia, and, if possible, even worse; and if taken into action in their present state, will prove more dangerous to themselves than to the enemy."

—Captain Will King, assistant inspector, US Army, October 5, 1812

In addition to the low number of troops and the issues of ordnance, the training and quality of the troops in the US Army were terrible. As General Van Rensselaer would later note in 1812, "The militia—in many cases—was more experienced than about half of the Federal Army." Army recruits in 1812 were not the best citizens, or even a true cross-section of the community. On the whole, they were poor or lower-middle-class citizens looking for employment or a means of getting started in their lives. The means for getting started was the Federal recruitment bounty of thirty-one dollars and 160 acres of land. For just five years of service, a young man could get this money, plus regular pay of five dollars a month, and have 160 acres of land to either clear and work, or sell when he left Federal service.

Furthermore, peacetime army service could be facile. Servicemen would be provided with three meals a day, shelter, clothing, and access to medical care. Of course enlisted men might end up at one of the out-of-the-way forts previously mentioned, but there was a good chance they would be sent to places like Fort Pitt, Carlisle Barracks, or one of the new defense forts at the ports of Baltimore, Charleston, New York, or Norfolk. As previously noted, New York was *the* city in the United States, and its port facilities were so important that it would eventually have a defense garrison of one thousand men.

Another group who found military life a better option as compared to that of a civilian was freed Africans. Though incapable of serving in some states due to the slavery laws, and discriminated against in other areas, freed Africans joined the army in large numbers. Many of these troops would serve with distinction during the war, though they would rarely get any credit.

Finally, the aforementioned compensations offered for service in the US Army were significantly better than that found in foreign military service. As a result, many European soldiers looked for ways to get to the United States. British army regulars stationed in Canada were particularly susceptible to the chance of higher pay. Better treatment and the chance of avoiding service in Europe fighting Napoleon were also lures. US Army recruiters were particularly interested in these men given their prior military experience.

Thus, the US Army was undermanned, and what men it had were either the dregs of society or people whose allegiance might not be as strong as the government would hope. The only good thing was they had four times as many arms as they needed—more, if one included those arms in need of repair or those of the wrong caliber.

The Militia

Figure 16: A depiction of militia, 1780.

Like the US Army, the national militia was not quite what the paperwork indicated. By government census, the nation had some 540,000 men between the age of fifteen and twenty-four years, with an additional 572,000 men between twenty-five and forty-five. Thus, according to the paperwork, the nation could conceivably field a national militia of one million men. Yet the national militia return for the year 1812 only listed 579,500 infantrymen and 188,000 muskets, or one gun for every three men. It is these militia returns that have, in recent years, been used to argue that gun ownership was not common in the early United States.[13] Yet, like the paperwork on the army, first impressions are deceiving.

Part of the problem with using the militia returns as a national firearm census (as some have tried) is that the returns are actually compliance documents showing the implementation of the 1792 Militia Act requirements. The most prominent requirement in the act was the caliber clause. Thus only muskets that were of the proper caliber were listed in the return. If the men had an arm of a different caliber (like the Federal arms not to Federal standard), they were not listed in the return.

Federal Statute 1, Chapter XXVII, May 1794, Section 5

And be it further enacted, That the President of the United States be requested to call on the executives of the several states, to take the most effectual means, that the whole of the militia, not comprised within the foregoing requisition, *be armed and equipped according to law.*

---

[13] Specifically, the argument is based on one militia return posted in March of 1803. This return, however, is actually an addendum to an earlier return in December 1802.

Where the Militia Act had specific requirements, problems arose with the returns when the states were not consistent in their posting to Washington. An example, in the 1812 return, Louisiana did not submit a return, Pennsylvania did not submit an ordnance return, and Maryland was missing altogether from the ordnance return. Thus, to get a better idea of the guns to men, one can either delete the 130,000 men from Maryland and Pennsylvania, or incorporate the ordnance report for the year 1811, where Pennsylvania and Maryland both listed arms. In 1812 Virginia is missing the nearly 3,000 rifles it listed in the 1811 return, so even when an ordnance report was submitted, it could be incomplete.

> Excerpt from the Congressional Debates on the Bill to Remove Duties on Arms Importation, January 17, 1803. Mr. VARNUM had a wish to encourage manufactures; but did gentlemen think it possible that they could supply the deficiency of arms? In Virginia, the enrolled militia amounted to 60,000, and they returned but 6,530 arms. Mr. RANDOLPH said the return was incorrect, both as to men and arms. If they have more, said Mr. V., he was glad of it. But the return ought to have been correct; it was transmitted by the Adjutant General of the State to the Secretary of War. It had been said that there was a deficiency in Massachusetts of 5,000; in that estimate the noncommissioned officers had not been included, which would make a deficiency of 9,000, and they had little short of 60,000 militia.

The militia return he is talking about is the December 1802 return, in which half the states in the union had not submitted a return by the end of the year. The addendum return, posted in 1803, doesn't mention Virginia at all but somehow finds an additional 3,000 muskets for the Massachusetts militia.

Per the 1792 Militia Act, the militia cavalry troopers were to be armed with a brace of pistols and a saber. In 1812, the United States listed 22,900 cavalry dragoons, 16,482 pairs of pistols, and 21,700 swords and sabers. The 1812 return thus indicated 72 percent compliance; when the previous return is taken into account, including the cavalry arms of Maryland and Pennsylvania, the number of pairs of pistols increases to 18,500 for nearly 81 percent coverage.

Where the cavalry was reasonably armed, as previously noted the militia returns indicated a three-to-one discrepancy of men to muskets for the infantry: 579,000 men to 188,800 muskets. But does this truly mean that there was a ratio of three men to one gun?

The answer to this comes from the returns for riflemen and rifles, in which there are only 10,556 identified riflemen to a massive 70,080 rifles. Thus, where the musketmen had three men to every musket, there was also nearly seven rifles to every rifleman.

Adding to this strange inconsistency is the fact that the return shows 42,800 fusees, which could be interpreted as either carbines or Indian trade guns.

Under the 1792 Militia Act, fusees are only for use by the officers of artillery. Yet the returns for 1811–1812 show 42,800 fusees to 13,600 officers and men of the artillery, or three guns per man. The obvious conclusion from this is that many of the men in the regular infantry were actually armed with rifles or short carbines instead of the required military-caliber, smoothbore musket.

Now, as to why these men were improperly armed, one can look to their states for the answer. Some states like Massachusetts followed the militia act requirements to the letter. Thus, they reported 55,000 infantry and 48,094 muskets (and 1,376 rifles), resulting in 90 percent coverage for the rank and file infantry.[14] Other states, like Kentucky,

---

[14] Massachusetts probably had 85,000 men who were of age for militia service, and it listed 70,500 men (officer to rank and file) on the rolls. Ignoring the sabers, Massachusetts had enough arms to equip 51,800 men, or 73 percent of the whole militia and 78 percent of noncommissioned.

were more open in their enforcement of the act. This state listed 35,483 infantry to 5,540 muskets while also reporting 2,336 riflemen to 18,175 rifles. Thus they could show they had 23,600 arms to their 37,800 men, making for 63 percent coverage.

And at least Kentucky was trying to tell the truth. Tennessee, Georgia, and North Carolina listed no riflemen in their returns but listed 30,300 rifles between the three states. Thus, these states had more rifles than there were troops in the regular United States Army, but they had no riflemen to carry them.

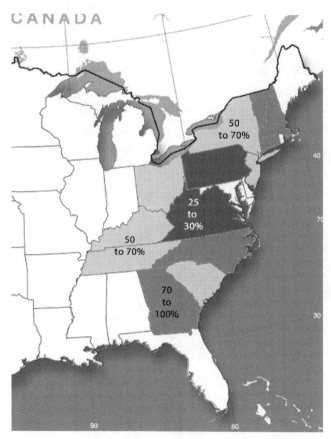

Figure 17: Arms to men enrolled in the militia.

Although the return can be read to show a nearly disarmed infantry, on further analysis one finds that the national militia had at minimum 383,000 arms for its 626,554 registered men. At that number, there were enough military-grade firearms in private hands to equip 38 percent of the total male population aged 18–45 and 61 percent of the men actually on the militia rolls. There were also some 360,000 men in the United States who were too old to be on the militia rolls but still owned their arms. Using a ratio of 38 percent to match the ratio computed for men in the militia age group, the number of arms for the retired men could be as high as 137,000 for a minimum total of 520,000 military-grade muskets, rifles, carbines, and pistols in private hands in 1812; this of course is an estimate.

Yet even this doesn't explain why only 626,554 men were enrolled in the militia out of a potential one million, and why in a nation with a heritage of firearm ownership, the militia return only listed 383,000 arms. In order to understand that, we need to learn how the militia changed under the aforementioned 1792 Militia Act and the requirements this law imposed.

The Revolutionary War Militia

Figure 18: *Stand Your Ground* by Don Troiani.

To understand how the militia that fought in the revolution had changed under the 1792 Militia Act, one needs to understand the revolutionary war militia. The primary militia in the revolution was the common militia: every able-bodied male from eighteen to forty-five years of age. In the northeastern colonies, there was also a special militia made up of the youngest, strongest, and most firearm competent men of the local community. These units were the minutemen.

Officially the Continental Congress ordered minuteman units to be created by all counties in every colony just before the war began. The reason for these units was to create a fast-reaction force that could respond to any threat in minutes. At the same time, to ensure they were large enough to do anything, one-third of all local militia was to be minuteman. Historically, only the Northern states ever fielded minuteman units. Additionally, these units did not see that much independent service during the war.

Other than the Lexington green,[15] minutemen rarely fought without the rest of the local militia. At Concord, Bunker Hill, and Bennington, for example, the minutemen units fought alongside their common militia brothers. Where the minutemen failed to shake their connection to the regular militia, however, other specialized militia groups in service during the revolution regularly fought without the supporting common militia.

Militia guerrillas (or irregulars), commanded by Thomas Sumter, Andrew Pickens, and Francis Marion, regularly attacked British troops deep behind British lines in Georgia and South Carolina. Such units attacked supply points, communications posts, and Tory militia. On October 7, 1780, an irregular force of 900 backwoodsmen (over-mountain-men) attacked 1,000 Tories at Kings Mountain in Georgia.

---

[15] In fact, the battle at Lexington almost was a common militia battle instead of a minuteman fight. The warning of the British march toward the town came too soon. The full militia gathered on the green and waited—and waited and waited. By the time the British arrived, most of the militia had returned home for breakfast, griping about another false alarm.

At a cost of only 28 killed and 64 wounded, these irregulars killed 225 Tories, wounded 116, captured 716, and killed the British commander Major Ferguson. This battle broke Tory spirit in the South, ending their military support to British General Cornwallis. After this, the militia Battle of Cowpens[16] set in motion the chain of events that ended with Cornwallis withdrawing to Yorktown, Virginia. There, colonial and French forces besieged him, forcing his surrender.

In virtually all these types of militia, the men kept arms at their homes. Contrary to modern revisionists, the Lexington militia did not form up on the village green and then march to the Concord armory to pick up their weapons before marching back to Lexington to meet the British. Neither did the Concord militia form up, march across the bridge to the arsenal, pick up their weapons, march back across the bridge to the Concord green, and then march again across the Concord bridge to engage the British troops, emptying what was left in the arsenal. The statements put forward by revisionist historians that the men of the militia were not allowed to keep arms at their homes, or own their own weapons, is impossible to support with the historical accounts of the battles that both started and ended the revolution.

The Arms of the Revolutionary Militia

And what were the arms these men kept at their homes? Whatever they could afford and use in their daily lives. Americans were primarily frugal people who owned items more for their utility than for their image. As a result, New England farmers tended to own muskets or

---

[16] The author views the Battle of Cowpens as a militia battle. The majority of the patriot troops there were militia. The commander, General Morgan, was also a militia general. Finally, the decisive victory was achieved by the return of the militia units that had left the field, as ordered by General Morgan.

Fowlers[17] (early shotguns) to protect their crops and livestock from wild animals, or to hunt for extra food.

Rifles were rare here because the forests and terrain worked against the long-range accuracy of this weapon. The opposite was true west of New York, where the terrain worked for the long rifle. In the colonies of Pennsylvania, Maryland, and Virginia, and further west and south, the rifle was more common for hunting and as the arm of the people. Only in the major cities along the coast was the primary weapon the Brown Bess musket, or a copy thereof.

The one feature all these guns had in common was the lack of a bayonet. Britain, in its own short-sighted military wisdom, had concluded that you won battles with the cold steel (the bayonet). Militia who were expected to defend and not attack did not need bayonet-capable firearms to work from behind a fort wall or a redoubt. This was true on open European battlefields, where linear tactics ruled. But in the forests of North America, where bayonet charges broke up among the trees, the riflemen ruled. During the revolution, colonial sharpshooters would pick off British officers at ranges of up to 250 yards from the safety of the surrounding woods.

Under the right terrain conditions, the high accuracy and long range of colonial rifles produced an effective combination that defeated the bayonet-equipped Brown Bess musket. Militiamen armed with rifles were faster in movements over rough terrain and forest, and they could operate with smaller amounts of lead needed for rounds and smaller amounts of powder, creating units that could operate over greater distances and for longer periods. In every way they met the description of light infantry.

For all these values, however, there were also problems. Rifles needed a higher quality of powder to operate and were prone to fouling when under continuous fire. Rifles couldn't use paper cartridges like muskets because they required an oiled patch to properly operate.

---

[17] Included in this were Indian trade guns that were the bargain basement arm of the colonies.

Thus, it took longer to load a rifle, reducing its value in the minds of many military commanders. These commanders, who primarily had their commissions due to their political connections, tended to fight in very simple ways. Long lines and massed fire followed by a bayonet charge were simple tactics. Sending riflemen forward to delay an enemy, wound or kill its officers, and generally break morale prior to the main fight was more complex.

The value of riflemen in the minds of the Continental Congress cannot be underrated. When the army was created on June 14, congress immediately called for the enlistment of "expert riflemen." By the Siege of Boston, ten companies of riflemen had been recruited for duty, becoming the first official Continentals. These riflemen would serve throughout the war at such battles as Saratoga, Trenton, and Brandywine. At Trenton, General Washington used small rifle units to delay the approach of British reinforcements while he prepared his defense. When Daniel Morgan was put in charge of this force in 1777, his first mission was to continually harass General Howe's troops as they marched from Philadelphia to New York (eventually resulting in the Battle of Monmouth). Finally, at Cowpens, riflemen were used to engage the British first and then withdraw, drawing the British straight into the regular colonial army units.

The Constitution and the Second Amendment

The war ended in 1783 with the nation governed by the Articles of Confederation. However, the articles were doomed to fail given the way the powers were divided—and the fact it was created under the pressures of the previous conflict. It took very little time before calls for reform began, and by 1785 leading members of the government were pushing for a convention to consider changes to the articles. A year later, on August 29, 1786, a mob lead by Daniel Shay stormed the courthouse in Northampton, Massachusetts, to prevent the trial and imprisonment of debtors by the Court of Common Pleas.

By 1786 Massachusetts was anything but democratic. The problem began back in the revolution when Massachusetts began paying its soldiers in bonds that would not mature for several years after the war. When the war ended, the soldiers found they needed money now to save their farms and neglected businesses from foreclosure. Into this stepped several Boston merchants, who bought up the war bonds at pennies on the dollar. Thus, by 1784 the entire war debt of the State of Massachusetts was owned by a small group of rich aristocrats.

These merchants had their own problems, as a result of the war. Though they were speculating on how much they would make in a few years on the bonds, they also had to continue to run their real businesses, which was universally shipping. Since the revolution, these merchants had been finding that their foreign creditors wanted cash payments (in coin) for trade goods. Thus, the merchants pressured the legislature to both pay off the war debt by 1787—and to pay it off in silver or gold coin. At the same time, these big merchants pressured the smaller merchants and shopkeepers they supplied with goods to also pay in coin.

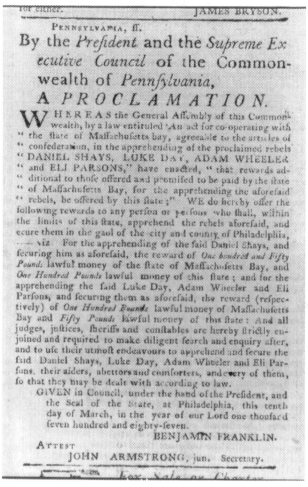

Figure 19: Proclamation calling for the arrest of Daniel Shay.

To pay off the war debt by 1787 in coin, the state levied heavy taxes with a requirement that it be paid in coin. At the same time, under pressure from the Boston shippers, the smaller shopkeepers also began demanding payment in coin. For people living in the major cities, this was no real problem, but 85 percent of the state's population was rural farmers who existed on a barter economy.

Farmers didn't pay their bills for finished goods in coin, but in flour, eggs, and vegetables. These were then to be shipped into the larger towns and cities to be either turned into finished goods or to feed the urban population. In short, the urban population, the major source of coin in the state, was trying to find every coin they could in a rural countryside devoid of it. For the farmers, this had a double irony because they who sold the bonds to the merchants to save their farms were, within a few years, now being driven to bankruptcy to pay the state taxes that were needed to pay off the bonds the farmers used to own.

To prevent reform, the merchants controlled the state legislature (called the General Court) through their relatives on the court. In order to prevent the poor from voting the politicians out of office, the state imposed poll taxes (paid in coin) and a requirement that a man had to own land in order to qualify to vote. Adding to this, to save money, some rural counties never even sent a representative to the legislature in Boston.

Thus with the legislature firmly in the hands of the merchants, the people had only one avenue for assistance or redress: the state courts. But the merchants blocked access to the high court by convincing the public lawyers to require excessive fees (in coin) to plead the cases. This left the people only the court of common pleas—a notoriously corrupt judicial body.

The seizing of the Northampton courthouse was just the beginning. Following this act of rebellion, Shay's men went on to close the courts in Great Barrington, Worchester, and Concord. The goal was to prevent the courts from sitting until after the elections of 1787 and the hopeful removal of Governor Bowdouin and others in the legislature. In response, Bowdouin called out the militia only to find that half of the force was rural farmers. Thus when General John Paterson arrived at Great Barrington with one thousand militiamen, within hours he had lost eighty percent to the rebellion.

Following the collapse of the state militia, on September 25, 1786, the Massachusetts State Supreme Court indicted Shay for sedition. In response, Shay and three hundred farmers (only two hundred armed) stormed the State Supreme Court in Springfield and prevented the court from sitting. Bowdouin responded by sending out three hundred light cavalry[18] from Boston on November 29 with warrants for the arrest of the ringleaders. They succeeded in capturing three, but the effect was hardly what Bowdouin wanted. Instead of breaking the rebellion, it added fuel to the fire.

Shay's men may have seemed to be in rebellion against the Federal government, but in truth Shay's men were actually calling for Federal help. They wanted a Federal court system to hear the pleas of citizens blocked out by corrupt state courts, the right to vote without implementation of restraints such as the poll tax, and paper money backed by gold and silver that was actually worth the same in other states. Many of these issues were actually addressed by the US Constitution and the Bill of Rights.

Figure 20: General Lincoln.

---

[18] Cavalry were volunteers who could afford the horse and equipment. As such, these cavalrymen were mostly rich men who had a vested financial interest in putting down the rebellion.

Most of the continental army had been disbanded in 1784, and so the rebellion was a shock to congress. Worse were the stories that Shay and his men were in contact with British agents in both Vermont and Canada regarding a return to British rule. It was even said that Shay's men had contacted their representatives in the General Court of Massachusetts to work toward that aim. In response to these fears, on October 20 congress called on the New England states to raise a force of 1,340 men to serve in the army for three years. The states were agreeable to this order, but the situation in Massachusetts would end well before the new Federal troops were ready for service.

While the government was trying to raise troops, Governor Bowdouin was hatching his own plan to end the revolt. With the legislature in recess, on January 4 he and several wealthy merchants raised six thousand pounds sterling (thirty thousand dollars) to fund a militia under the command of General Lincoln. With money in hand, quotas for militiamen from Eastern counties were issued, and within days a force of three thousand[19] men was raised. Made up of men who had not seen service in the revolution, it was hardly a mercenary militia or "private army," as some historians have proposed. The governor had called it out legally: he was simply creative on how it was funded. The men had been summoned by quota, as per law; they just wouldn't have come out if they had to pay their own way, as the previous summons had required.

Though Shay was informed of the approach of this force, by late January the only thing he had on his mind was sheltering his followers. It was the dead of winter, and he had over a thousand men to feed and house. Forcing local homeowners to put up his men was too much like British actions before the revolution. Thus, on January 25, 1787, Shay led 1,100 rebels to Continental Hill in Springfield— the site of the Federal Arsenal and its huge stock of arms, and the old military barracks built during the revolution.

---

[19] Most reports list 4,400 men as the size of Lincoln's force. The reality was that it was supposed to be 4,400 men, but not every county filled their quota.

Waiting for him was Army General Shepard and 1,200 local militia (lawyers, clerks, students, and scholars) and four pieces of artillery loaded with grapeshot. The only weapons fired were the cannons, twice in warning, and then two point-blank rounds into Shay's approaching column. Four men died instantly and twenty were injured. Shay's men immediately withdrew; for the first time, they had been forcibly repulsed.

When General Lincoln arrived, Shay withdrew into the neighboring towns. Lincoln then marched his men through a snowstorm in order to catch the rebels by surprise at Petersham on February 3. Governor Bowdouin then declared a general amnesty, giving the rebels a peaceful way out of the mess. A general economic improvement in 1788 (caused by the paying off the war debt and the ending the taxes) fully ended the rebellion. Two months later, congress was informed that 550 men had been raised by their previous order and required payment.

After fleeing to Vermont, Shay and the other rebel leaders were tried in absentia and sentenced to death. Soon afterward they returned to Massachusetts to be first captured and then pardoned by the new State Governor John Hancock. Only two rebels were ever executed, and these were executed for robbery not rebellion.[20]

With Shay's rebellion just barely out of the newspapers, on May 25, 1787, representatives of ten states (minus Delaware and Rhode Island) met in Philadelphia to discuss modifying the articles. In a short time this had changed to a discussion of a new document written by James Madison called the Virginia Plan.

---

[20] In the end, Shay and his men killed and injured no one; they simply intimidated people into submission. The only deaths were by General Shepard's order—an act that could have been avoided if the government had removed the weapons from the arsenal following Shepard's earlier request to do this.

Figure 21: *Scene at the Signing of the Constitution of the United States*, By Howard Chandler Christy

The Virginia plan was not the constitution, but the document that came out of all the discussions and negotiations, and the Grand Compromise over the Virginia Plan became the constitution. After two years of meetings, in 1789 the foundation was set for a new system of government and a new set of militia laws.

The constitution has two paragraphs about the militia and militia arms.

Article One, Section Eight, Clause 15

The Congress shall have power: to provide for calling forth the militia to execute the laws of the Union, suppress insurrections and repel Invasions.

Article One, Section Eight, Clause 16

The Congress shall have power: to provide for organizing, arming, and disciplining, the militia and for governing such part of them as may be employed in the service of the United States, reserving to the States respectively, the appointment of the officers, and the authority of training the militia according to the discipline prescribed by Congress.

Unlike the earlier Articles of the Confederation, under these clauses congress, not the states, determines how the militia is organized and equipped. As Rufus King is said to have responded to a question, "The word arming meant specifying the kind, size & caliber of arms and included authority to regulate the modes of furnishing, either by the Militia themselves, the State Governments, or the National Treasury." After creating this uniform and regulated militia, congress then had the power to call out the militia of a state or states, even over the objections of the state governments.

For many people in 1789, however, the new constitution gave congress too many powers. In regard to the militia clauses, people like George Mason were afraid that the central government could now restrict the militia to a weapon completely opposite that of the new national army. Put simply, the congress could have the army carrying a musket, with bayonet and firing buck and ball ammo, while restricting the militia to a hunting rifle or fowler and prohibiting the bayonet; this would be in line with hated British laws prior to the revolution. As a result of this concern, plus concerns over other sections of the document, politicians called anti-Federalists proposed a series of amendments to specify the rights of citizens and the state governments.

Both Hamilton and Madison argued against any Bill of Rights, both in letters (now called the Federalist Papers) and in statements made at the constitutional convention. On the subject of the militia clauses, however, the Federalists couldn't see what the anti-Federalists' concern was. Contrary to modern historical views, the Federalists didn't want to disband the militia; they simply wanted to make a national system that would allow for units from the various states to work together. For many Federalists, the logistical problems caused by the varying array of arms used by the militia in the early years of the revolution had to be avoided in all future conflicts. Thus the militia clause was to form a "militia of the United States" that Madison himself described as a uniform force of over half a million men in a time when the male population between eighteen and forty-five was no more than 750,000 (nearly all able-bodied men in the nation).

To the Federalists, if organizing the militia was left to the states, the individual militia units would be so different in arms and training that they never would be able to work together. But Hamilton and Madison[21] couldn't get around George Mason and Elbridge Gerry's concern that some sort of limitation was required to this and other powers now vested in congress. Thomas Jefferson and George Washington also supported the idea of a Bill of Rights. Thus late in 1791, the states ratified the first ten of these amendments. One of these is the legendary, or infamous, second amendment.

Figure 22: Eldridge Gerry, father of the Bill of Rights and by default the second amendment.

---

[21] Madison didn't write Clause 16, so there is little evidence he truly supported it. Madison's own break with the Federalists by 1800 underscores this point.

The Second Amendment

The Pennsylvania minority first proposed the idea of an amendment regarding militia, or the people's right to arms, on December 18, 1787. The proposed amendment was,

> That the people have a right to bear arms for the defense of themselves and their own state, or the United States, or for the purpose of killing game; and no law shall be passed for disarming the people or any of them, unless for crimes committed, or real danger of public injury from individuals; and as standing armies in the time of peace are dangerous to liberty, they ought not to be kept up: and that the military shall be kept under strict subordination to and be governed by the civil powers.

On April 21, 1788, this proposal was submitted, and on June 9, 1788, George Mason put forward a master draft for the Bill of Rights.

After the submittal of the master draft on June 21, 1788, New Hampshire proposed, "Congress shall never disarm any Citizen unless such as are or have been in Actual Rebellion." Six days later, on June 27, 1788, the Virginia convention proposed an amendment that was based on the 1776 Virginia Declaration of Rights.

> That the people have a right to keep and bear arms; that a well regulated Militia composed of the body of the people trained to arms is the proper, natural and safe defense of a free State. That standing armies in time of peace are dangerous to liberty, and therefore ought to be avoided, as far as the circumstances and protection of the Community will admit; and that in all cases the military should be under strict subordination to and governed by the civil power."

Then on July 26, New York weighed in with this proposal: "That the People have a right to keep and bear Arms; that a well regulated Militia, including the body of the People capable of bearing Arms, is the proper, natural and safe defense of a free State."

One year later, on June 8, 1789, Madison proposed this composite amendment. "The right of the people to keep and bear arms shall not be infringed; a well armed and well regulated militia being the best security of a free country: but no person religiously scrupulous of bearing arms shall be compelled to render military service in person." Thus, the proposals for protection to rights to hunting guns were gone, as well as the various prohibitions to keeping regular troops in time of peace. But the right of the people to keep and bear arms still remained with a new provision for conscientious religious objectors.

Madison's proposal, with all the other proposed amendments at that time, was sent to the select committee, which then submitted this amendment on July 28, 1789: "A well regulated militia, composed of the body of the people, being the best security of a free State, the right of the people to keep and bear arms shall not be infringed, but no person religiously scrupulous shall be compelled to bear arms." Now the words "composed of the body of the people" that the New York convention had originally requested were back in the amendment.

The house of representatives approved the revised amendment on August 24, 1789. It then went to the senate where it was changed again (supposedly by John Adams). Then it went back and forth between houses until September 9, when the amendment was approved with the wording we know today.

> A well regulated militia, being necessary to the security of a free State, the right of the people to keep and bear arms shall not be infringed.

By passing the second amendment, the government balanced the power of Article 1 Section 8 Clause 16. It removed the fear that the central government, in the name of a well-regulated militia, would write a law prohibiting citizens from owning suitable arms for militia duty. Granted, it did not prevent the government from declaring what was a proper militia arm and force it on the states. But it did prevent the government from regulating the militia out of existence.

In regard to the state powers, a state could still pass laws that restricted or prevented individual access to arms, but they too had restrictions. They could not ban the arm specified by the Federal government for the militia without violating clause 16. The states could not also require the militia arms to be stored at a state facility because this would violate the second amendment right to "keep." The states could write laws barring criminals and other people outside of society from possessing arms, but such people were not part of the militia or proper society anyway. They could also ban concealable weapons for the same reason, in that they were not the arms of the militia, with perhaps the exception of the cavalry pistols. As for bans on hunting weapons, any state that did this would be committing political suicide. Census data for the period shows the majority of the population was rural. To ban hunting arms would condemn a portion of its population to starvation from the inability to put meat on the table or prevent wild animal damage to their crops and livestock.

Finally, it created the third triad of this system: the people itself. By having arms at their disposal, the people could come out on the side of their choosing: the central government, or their state. Yes, they could also come out on their own as Daniel Shay did, but at the cost of standing against the US Army and those state forces that decided to stand with the state.

Given these facts, it's not surprising that within two years of passing the second amendment, the Federal government passed a law that incorporated all these requirements: a uniform militia system—standardized in kind, style, and caliber of arms—similar to that of the US Army but owned and kept by the people.

The Militia Act of 1792

Since 1789 congress had been working to pass laws to implement the powers and authorities it now had under the new constitution. One of the first such laws was the Militia Act of May 8, 1792 (see Appendix 1). Titled "An Act More Effectually to Provide for the National Defense by Establishing an Uniform Militia throughout the United States," it strove to create a uniform national militia. This law required the enrollment of all free and able-bodied males aged eighteen to forty-five in the local militia (subject to the limitations of Section 2). It also determined specific equipment and arms that the militiamen had to purchase. Failure to fulfill these requirements would result in militia fines, further personal expenses, and penalties against both the men and their states. Under section one of this law,

> Every citizen so enrolled and notified, shall, within six months thereafter, provide himself with a good musket or firelock, a sufficient bayonet and belt, two spare flints, and a knapsack, a pouch with a box therein to contain not less than twenty-four cartridges, suited to the bore of his musket or firelock, each cartridge to contain a proper quantity of powder and ball: or with a good rifle, knapsack, shot-pouch and powder-horn, twenty balls suited to the bore of his rifle, and a quarter of a pound of powder.

Once the militiaman had acquired all this gear, he had to show it to local authorities. These people then documented the fact in triplicate: one copy for the county, one for the state, and one for the federal government (Section 10 of the law).

Of course there was some opposition to the requirement that men purchase their own arms. Presented here are some excerpts from the Congressional Record of December 16, 1790.

Mr. Timothy Bloodworth observed, that as the militia was to be organized and disciplined under the authority of the United States, and to be employed for the general defense, whenever and wherever Congress should direct, it appeared but reasonable that those who were benefited by them should be at the expense of arming them.

Mr. Roger Sherman said it appeared to him, that by the Constitution, the United States were to be put to no expense about the militia, except when called into actual service. The clause is not so explicit as might have been wished; but it will be difficult to fix the construction mentioned by the gentleman from North Carolina. What relates to arming and disciplining means nothing more than a general regulation in respect to the arms and accoutrements. There are so few freemen in the United States who are not able to provide themselves with arms and accoutrements, that any provision on the part of the United States is unnecessary and improper. He had no doubt that the people, if left to themselves, would provide such arms as are necessary, without inconvenience or complaint; but if they are furnished by the United States; the public arsenals would soon be exhausted.

Mr. Thomas Fitzsimons moved to strike out the words "provide himself," and insert "shall be provided." This motion was objected to by Messrs, Elias Boudinot, Benjamin Huntington, James Jackson, George Partridge, John Vining, and *James Madison*. It was said that it would be destructive of the bill, as it would leave it optional with the States, or individuals, whether the militia should be armed or not. This motion was lost by a great majority.

In addition to the requirement that the men would provide themselves with a musket, there was a little-known caliber requirement: "and after five years from the passage of this act, all muskets for arming the militia as herein required, shall be of bores sufficient for balls of the eighteenth part of a pound." Today, the modern equivalent to this weight of shot is the term "gauge" for smoothbore shotguns. Because we don't like to describe muskets or rifles in this manner, we must determine the size of the bullet used by these guns. To do that, we use the density of lead at 6.5 oz/in^3 and the equation for the volume of a sphere from basic geometry.

We know the volume because we have the density of lead and the weight of the shot. Because we will be working in ounces, the 1/18-pound weight of the bullet becomes 16 ounces divided by 18.

$$V = \frac{W}{D} = \frac{16/18}{6.5} = 0.13468 in^3$$

The volume of a sphere in relation to its radius can be determined from the equation.

$$V = \frac{4}{3}\pi r^3$$

We already have a value for V, and so we can rearrange this equation to determine the radius.

$$r = \sqrt[3]{3V/4\pi} = \sqrt[3]{0.40404/12.5664}$$
$$= \sqrt[3]{0.03252} = 0.3196$$

Multiply the radius by two, and a bullet of the minimum weight required will be 0.64 inches in diameter. It's a little-known fact that until 1840, the ball diameter used by the US Army was 0.64 inches, which can now be assumed to be the standard mentioned in the 1811 ordnance report.

Technically, Section 1 allowed the militiamen to have either musket or, under the alternative subsection, a rifle. But after five years, all the arms had to meet this 0.64-inch bullet requirement, and no rifle fired a bullet larger than 0.60 inches in diameter (the average being between 0.45 and 0.55). Thus after 1797, all militia arms had to be muskets unless the men were specifically part of a rifle company.

Surprisingly, the law was not an aberration, but a Federal version of state acts written in the previous decade. In 1784 Massachusetts passed a law requiring every man aged from sixteen to forty to be part of the Train Band, and all other men under the age of sixty had to be part of the Alarm List. In October 1785, Virginia passed a law requiring men to arm themselves with a musket three feet eight inches long in barrel, with a firing shot of one ounce (essentially a 0.67-inch ball shooting musket.)[22] That was unless they were west of the Blue Ridge Mountains, in which they could carry rifles.

The Virginia act also had a time clause: "that two years after the commencement of this act, shall be allowed for providing the arms and accoutrements herein directed; but in the mean time, the militia shall appear at musters with, and keep by them, the best arms and accoutrements they can get." Thus the men had two years to get the required Brown Bess musket, but until then, they could appear with shotguns, trade guns, or whatever they owned or could get.

By providing these guidelines for arming the militia, congress had fulfilled its duty under Clause 16 as amended by the second amendment. Any state, county, or city could then pass laws banning or restricting firearms as long as it did not impede the arming of the militia according to federal guidelines. In the same way, the government was not prohibiting the people from owning weapons. It simply required ownership of a specific style of weapon that matched the weapons used by the Federal Army. In fact by using the same standards, the law made it possible for militiamen working with Federal troops to use Federal ammunition, or Federal troops to use militia cartridges. Yet people could also own arms more suited to farming or rural needs, or for target shooting without restriction.

---

[22] The Brown Bess is stated to be a weapon capable of firing a ball 1/29 of 2 pounds in weight. That computes out to a 0.68 diameter.

The Whiskey Rebellion

While all this was going on, a new rebellion broke loose in the western portions of Pennsylvania. Called the Whiskey Rebellion, it was actually a popular revolt against a 1791 Federal tax inspired by Alexander Hamilton. Hamilton believed such a tax was the perfect way to end the Federal debt and pay for the Indian conflict going on in Ohio. Instead, it triggered another conflict that cost the government precious tax money.

Figure 23: *To Execute the Laws of the Union, The Whiskey Rebellion;* by Donna Neary

The image depicts commander and chief Washington inspecting his troops prior to marching into western Pennsylvania,

The primary reason for the revolt was the unfair nature of the tax. Large producers were annually taxed at a rate of six cents a gallon, which meant they were taxed at the end of the year and after they had sold their product. Large producers could also get a rate reduction if they produced more than a specific amount per year, and they could pay the tax using their product.

Small producers (like George Washington or Thomas Jefferson) had a different situation. They were taxed nine cents per gallon on production, payable at the time of production—not after the sale. More important, the small producers had to pay in coin, an item most small farmers did not have (but Washington and Jefferson did). As noted in Shay's rebellion, the United States was a barter economy outside of the major cities. Given the rarity of coins, people made change among themselves by breaking coins into pieces.

By 1794 the rebellion had gone from words to full-blown civil disobedience. Not only were Federal tax collectors attacked in public, but the mail was seized by a group of protesters. This was a violation of Federal law, forcing congress and President Washington to act. With the majority of the army away with Anthony Wayne, in August of 1794 President Washington used his authority as commander and chief and requested congress summon the militia of the United States.

First Washington called for a militia force of 13,000 men from Eastern Pennsylvania, New Jersey, and Maryland. With congressional assent, the units came together at Harrisburg in October, where Washington himself reviewed them. Then they began marching, and by November they were back in Philadelphia with prisoners for trial. The major leader of the revolt had fled to Louisiana and then to Florida, where he received Spanish protection.

The Problems with the 1792 Militia Act

Though the Militia Act and Article 1 Section 8 Clause 15 functioned properly for the Whiskey Rebellion, this was only because the act didn't go into full effect until well after the rebellion was past. Once the act was in full effect, given the economics, transportation, and level of industry of the period, it became a major problem for the government. The most difficult requirement of all was the firearm requirement as is seen in this exchange during a Congressional debate on a Bill to have a detachment of militia, March 1810.

"Mr. Ely observed that the present militia law of the United States required a particular description of arms, which were not admitted to pass inspection unless they were of that description."

"Mr. Dana quoted the law to show that the arms with which citizens were required by law to furnish themselves were to be of a certain description, standard of which was fixed by law."

The caliber and bayonet requirements restricted the militiamen to only a few weapons then in production. The two most common arms in the 0.69 caliber were the French Charleville musket and Spanish military muskets. There were some 100,000 Charleville muskets scattered around the country following the revolution. The British Brown Bess musket (0.75 caliber) and German arms (0.77 caliber) may have had the bayonet, but they were too large in bore as noted in the 1811 ordnance report. As for the hunting arms of the citizens, neither the rifled muskets nor the Trade muskets (0.62 caliber) and Fowlers (0.80 caliber) were of the right bore or had a bayonet.

The French musket design was well understood by US gunsmiths and armorers. Almost half of the French arms sent during the revolution were actually assembled after delivery. Thus, even before the war ended, men were making copies of the arm for use by militiamen. Unfortunately, until the 1792 act was passed, what constituted a militia arm was up to the state legislatures. As a result, some states like Virginia selected the Brown Bess, others picked the Charleville, and some states issued no requirements at all.

Excerpts from the Congressional Debates on the Militia Bill, February 21, 1792: Mr. Kitchell moved that the clause should be struck out, which provides that the calibers of the guns be of one bore. He observed that this provision was unnecessary, and in fact impossible to be complied with. Mr. Thomas Sumpter asked what is to be done with the arms the militia now have in their hands. Are they to be thrown away? Besides he though the provision inconsistent with the actual state of the military force of the country, the laws for the regulation of which contemplate the enrolment of riflemen among the regular forces of the country. Adverting to the expense which would attend this provision, he observed it was almost totally impracticable to carry it into execution. He hoped it would not be agreed to, as it would involve an enormous and unnecessary expense. Mr. Murray offered similar remarks. He did not conceive that the excellency of the militia of the United States consisted in their being armed all with muskets of the same bore.

Excerpt from the Congressional Record, November 20, 1792 A Mr. Mercer said "He was adverted to the injustice of the requisition, which enjoins, that a man who is not worth 20 shillings should incur an expense of 20 pounds in equipping himself as a militia man."

Excerpt from the Congressional Record: Debate on the Detachment of Militia, March 19, 1810: Mr. Pitkin: "Those of the militia who had complied with the laws, and purchased their own arms at an expense of fifteen or twenty dollars each or more, might be taxed to pay for the arms of those who had not complied with the law. If any one thing could rouse the indignation of those who had furnished themselves with arms, it would be thus to tax them to purchase arms for those who had neglected their duty."

> Excerpt from the Congressional Record: Debate on the Detachment of Militia, March 20, 1810: Mr. Potter: The militia are generally composed of poor men, whose burdens are already more than they ought to be, and but few of that class get exempt from military duty by offices, and I believe that they do not own the one hundredth part of the property in the United States. Why then should they do all this duty to defend it? It now costs a poor man about fifteen dollars to equip himself, and if he has sons, it costs him as much more for them, besides all their time at trainings, which is a poor man's estate.

Congress hadn't helped matters in the years just before the Militia Act. To raise capital after the war, surplus and seized military stores were made available to US citizens at a specific cost by congress and later through the War Department. This included the auctioning off of damaged muskets and musket parts to local gunsmiths, who then fixed or assembled arms for sale to the general public. These surplus muskets put guns in many Americans' hands—just not the right type. In the end, it took money out of people's hands, making it even more difficult for them to later purchase the proper arms.

Arms Imports

Arms imports would be another source for problems in implementing the Militia Act requirements. In 1788 a British census in the Birmingham Gun Quarter found 4,000 gun makers producing 100,000 guns a year in support of the British slave trade. During the years of the Napoleonic wars, this area of England produced over one million guns, mostly the new India pattern Brown Bess musket. Add to that French, Dutch, and German makers, and Americans had many sources for high-quality guns at prices equal to or less than those of American makers. However, there was a catch.

Excerpt from the Congressional Record, June 1798: Mr. Kittera said, the State of Pennsylvania had appropriated money for twenty thousand stand of arms; one half to be purchased within the United States, and the other half to be imported. Those which were ordered to be purchased within the United States had been purchased; *but the contracts abroad, he believed, had failed*; and he believed the State Government is anxious to complete the order.

From this record, we know that that by June 1798, neither the states nor the federal government had been very successful in importing arms from Europe. The reason for this was the outbreak of war in Europe between France and Britain. So great was the British need for arms that the US minister to London, with $100,000 in hard currency, couldn't get any arms until the years 1799 and 1800, and even, then he could only purchase 3,000 muskets per year.[23]

This situation continued for a few years, but then a hiatus in the European war caused a sudden glut on the world arms market. To try to capitalize on this situation, a bill was proposed to suspend an import tariff congress had enacted several years earlier on foreign firearms. The bill was proposed immediately following the submitting of the militia return for December 1802, resulting in a very strong debate on the value of both keeping the tariff and on withdrawing it.

Excerpts from the Congressional Debates on the Bill to Remove Duties on Arms Importation,[24] January 17, 1803. Mr. Thatcher, The muskets and other arms

---

[23] Hicks, 1940, p. 14–15.

[24] In 1797, war appeared possible with France. In response congress passed a two-year embargo on arms exports, coupled with the removal of the import duties on arms. A similar embargo on exports of arms to Europe was implemented for about a year in 1793, when war began between France and England.

for sale in Europe, at the close of a war, especially those
of low price, are generally unfit for service (…) Suppose
we encourage the militia to import these arms from
different parts of Europe, what will be the consequence?
Out of the thousands we should scarcely find hundreds
fit for regular troops, or for any operation of an Army;
we should find them defective in every respect, and so
unequal in caliber that it would cause infinite trouble
to fit them with cartridges. On the contrary, those
made in this country are allowed to be superior in
every respect to any manufactured in Europe. We are
told, sir, by the petition on the table that they can be
afforded at nine dollars and fifty cents.

These European guns were sold in Rhode Island for five dollars
(one pound), and that was including the 15 percent duty. A few
months later, when the war in Europe went hot again, these low-
cost arms ceased to be available. Then in 1807 congress passed the
Embargo Act, effectively stopping all trade with Europe.

Civilian Arms Production

As Thomas Sumpter suggested in 1792, the only way for a man
to ensure that he had an arm that met the militia requirements was
to buy a new one. With European arms production tied up in the
Napoleonic wars, and given the specific requirements of the militia
act limiting the number of choices available, how did a militiaman
meet the federal requirements?

In recent years, it has been suggested that prior to the American
Civil War, firearm production in the United States was extremely
limited, leaving imports as the primary source for arms. As already
noted, however, the Napoleonic Wars made the importation of arms
difficult, and the Embargo Act of 1807 stopped all legal trade. Thus,

how does one explain the number of arms listed in either the ordnance report of 1811 or the militia returns of 1811–1812? The truth was that there were plenty of American ordnance makers, but not all of them made military grade muskets.

Before we discuss civilian arms production, we need to note Federal military production during the same period. Starting in 1795, production of Model 1795 muskets began at Springfield Armory in Massachusetts (see appendix 3). A direct copy of the French Charleville musket Model 1763, the Springfield 1795 would be the pattern for all Federal musket production for the next forty years. Initially production at Springfield was slow, but as time progressed, the rate increased eventually reaching 12,000 muskets in one year (1811), with total production by that time reaching 74,400. Six years after Springfield began operations, the Federal armory at Harpers Ferry, Virginia, was opened. By the year 1811, this facility had produced 33,000 muskets, 4,000 Model 1803 rifles, and 4,000 pistols, adding an additional 41,000 arms to the Federal production for a grand total of 115,000 arms.

In addition to the two Federal armories, starting in 1792 contracts were issued to several Pennsylvania gunsmiths[25] to manufacture military rifles based on the Pennsylvania long rifle. Called the 1792 contract rifle, these guns were a direct response to the disastrous defeat of St. Claire by Chief Little Turtle the previous year. Production of the 1792 rifle was very small, with only three thousand made between 1792 and 1794. None were ready to join Anthony Wayne or serve at Fallen Timbers; his riflemen carried Pennsylvania-style civilian hunting rifles. Service records for the weapon are limited, with one battalion of 328 rifles being formed for the Federal Army. During the Whiskey Rebellion, the 1792 rifle also armed a company of riflemen under Daniel Morgan's command. Outside of these, the five hundred rifles

---

[25] Contractors associated with the 1792 contract rifles are Jacob Welshans, Adam Angstadt, John Nicholson, Abraham Morrow, and the group of Jacob Dickert, Peter Gonter, and John Groff.

sent to Governor Claiborne of Mississippi in 1802, for sale to the men of the Territorial militia, is probably the largest known deployment.

Six years later, in 1798 contracts were issued to twenty-seven manufacturers for production of over forty-two thousand copies of the Springfield Model 1795 musket (see appendix 4). Of these contractors, seven were in Connecticut, four were in Massachusetts, three were in Pennsylvania, three were in Rhode Island, three were in Vermont, three were in Maryland, and two were in New Hampshire. In all, nineteen manufacturers were in the New England area.

Eli Whitney, inventor of the cotton gin, procured the largest of these musket contracts. He intended to fill this order by using interchangeable parts, a method developed in France by LeBlanc. The contract was only to run two and a half years, but by 1801 he had not produced one gun. When summoned to Washington to explain why in November 1801, he showed Jefferson how he had developed the tooling to create locks in which the parts were interchangeable. So convincing was his demonstration that he was given an extension to the contract, following which he delivered his first gun in 1803, completing the Federal order in 1808.

In 1807 and 1808, the government issued other contracts for the production of pistols and rifles. None of these firms were part of the earlier 1792 contract rifle group, but like the original group, they were concentrated in Pennsylvania. The rifles were to be of the Harpers Ferry 1803 type, and the pistols were what are commonly called today the Kentucky pistol.[26]

In 1808 another group of contracts were issued for the production of eighty-five thousand muskets to still another group of contractors. Some of these guns were replicas of the French 1763 musket, and others were replicas of the Model 1777. Some were like the US Army Model 1795 made at Springfield Armory, but others were similar to the improved musket built at Harpers Ferry (the Whitney

---

[26] O&E Evans was actually contracted to make a replica of the French model AN IX pistol (Hicks).

Improvement). The reason for this diversity was the fact that the government supplied different manufacturers with different example guns to use as a pattern.

Only six of the manufacturers in the 1808 group completed roughly half their order by the start of the War of 1812, for a total of 12,560 muskets. Three essentially defaulted.[27] The largest number of arms produced was by the venerable firm of W. & I. I. Henry[28] of Pennsylvania, at 4,246, however, this firm didn't make the top six because its contract called for 10,000 muskets. The total number of arms delivered by 1811 by all the 1808 contractors was 23,570.

Figure 24: Eli Whitney and his armory in New Haven, Connecticut, 1800.

---

[27] Sweet, Jenks & Sons is actually the same firm as Stephen Jenks and Sons. After receiving the first contract, they then lobbied for a second in 1809. This hardly makes them a defaulter because by 1812 they had delivered over 2,000 muskets. Also, the firm Wheeler & Morrison broke up in 1809 on Wheeler's death; Morrison completed 125 muskets and left the business.

[28] William Henry had been making guns since the French and Indian Wars, supplying arms to the British. He then made guns for the American Revolution and held numerous public offices, including being a delegate to congress. By the time of this order, however, he had been dead for over twenty years.

Taking all the Federal contracts for muskets together, we get 173,000 muskets of the right caliber delivered by 1812. Granted that this number concludes the 42,400 1798 contract muskets were completed—a big assumption given the poor quality of the records. But when you take into account a Federal dole of 16,000 muskets delivered to the states by 1808, that drops the number of arms to 157,000, which is only 23,000 over the 134,000 computed serviceable muskets reported in the 1811 ordnance report. The report also listed 21,781 proper muskets in need of repairs. Thus, it is reasonable to conclude that the serviceable arms (proper caliber) in the 1811 ordnance report can be attributed to indigenous production at the Federal armories and through civilian contractors.

In the end, we now know there was no shortage of manufacturers for arms when the government could issue multiple contracts over two decades for arms and not contract the same person twice. And these are only the Federal arms contracts; several states were acquiring arms for their own arsenals. An example of this comes from the history of Eli Whitney, who in 1812 was issued a new arms contract from the government to build a musket he had been making since 1806 for the State of New York. As for how many arms the states acquired, even the Federal government hadn't a clue, as stated in an April 2, 1806, congressional letter.

The Militia Rifle under the 1792 Act

As Sumpter noted in 1792, if the caliber clause is applied against rifles, it would effectively prohibit its use by anyone in the militia except the approved riflemen after the year 1797. According to the law (Section 4), within each militia battalion (five companies of sixty-four men each) there would be only one company of grenadiers, light infantry, or riflemen. Now, it's true that light infantry could be interpreted as riflemen, but the reality was that the majority of the light infantry units were simply the youngest and fastest members of the local militia armed with the lightest muskets that met the bore requirements (such as carbines or fusees). As noted in the beginning of this chapter, the militia returns listed far more fusees than needed for only the artillery.

Back to the point, under the 1792 act, a state could have only one company of riflemen for every three fielded militia battalions. Put another way, it was one rifleman for every fifteen musketmen. By comparison, Anthony Wayne's legion system had one company of riflemen for every two companies of musketmen. Thus, we also have an explanation as to why many western states listed large numbers of rifles but few riflemen in their militia returns.

Then there was the reorganization of the army on May 30, 1796. In this reorganization, the army returned to a post–Anthony Wayne regimental concept, where each regiment had eight musket companies supported by a corps of light artillery (four battalions) and two companies of light dragoons. Thus, where Wayne had a minimum of eight hundred riflemen at his disposal, army commanders during the War of 1812 had to depend on militia riflemen.

The act's limitation on the number of riflemen was a major side effect of the law, and the fielding of the 1803 rifle made the situation worse. The earlier 1792 contract rifle was essentially a common 0.50-caliber Pennsylvania rifle. The same could not be said of the 1803 model that was patterned after the special arms built for the Lewis and Clark expedition.[29] Secretary of War Henry Dearborn specified that the guns were to be short rifles with barrels two feet nine inches long and firing a ball 1/30 of a pound (0.54 caliber). Again, production was limited to just 4,023 examples built in four years, but in 1807 the government issued contracts to private manufacturers for an additional

---

[29] The general belief is Lewis ordered contract rifles stored at Harpers Ferry to be bored out to a larger caliber of 0.55 to limit fouling and cut down to more effective match the short Kentucky rifle in length. The short Jaeger rifle (carried by Hessian troops) and the British 1776 pattern rifle may have also influenced the design of the Model 1803.

3,000 rifles. Thus, we can conclude that the 6,900 rifles identified in the 1811 ordnance report were most likely the Model 1803.

The dimensional and caliber requirements for the 1803 rifle seem to have been taken as a firm military requirement by several states for their militia rifles; thus the older Pennsylvania and 1792 long rifles become unacceptable for militia service and were no longer listed in these state returns. As for the Kentucky rifle, only those that fired shot of 1/30 of a pound were acceptable in order to use Federally supplied ball ammunition. One piece of evidence for this is the contract report against a Joseph Henry, whose rifles were rejected because he had made them in 0.32 caliber.

Of course, some states had their own ideas on what was a suitable military rifle. All rifles made for the State of Virginia, either by the Virginia Manufactory or under contract, were 0.45 caliber. Then there is the following quote from Tennessee Governor Willie Blount to volunteers leaving to join General Jackson on December 2, 1812.

> "The Volunteers will arm and equip themselves with rifles, so far as practicable. Those having no rifles of their own—or if those they have be not immediately serviceable—will be furnished by the state to the extent of the supply on hand. But it is hoped that this reserve, scanty at best, will not be drawn upon to exhaustion. Ammunition furnished by the State. Each Volunteer, including Company officers, is entitled to a powder-horn full of the best Eagle Powder, one dozen new, sharp flints, and lead enough to mould 100 bullets that fit his rifle. Very small-bore rifles are not desirable for military service. It is recommended that none be taken along of less caliber than sixty balls to the pound.[30] It is desired to avoid smoothbore muskets as much as possible. They are heavy, clumsy, take a great deal of

---

[30] Using the method previously mentioned, the minimum ball diameter would be 0.43 inches, making for a rifle of about 0.45 caliber.

ammunition and do not carry straight. They may be good enough for regular Soldiers but not the Citizen Volunteers of Tennessee."[31]

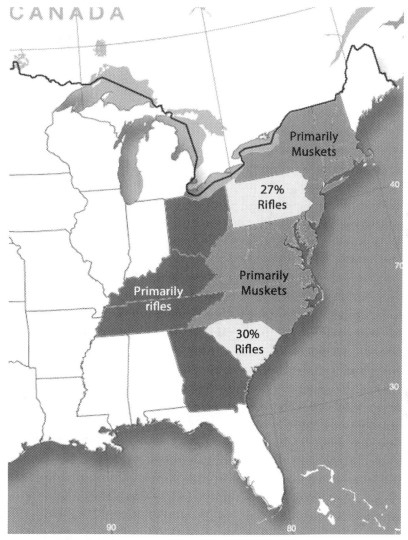

Figure 25: The Primary Arm of the Militia by Area.

[31] Bell, Augustus C. *History of Andrew Jackson: Pioneer, Soldier, Politician, President* New York, N.Y.: C. Scribner's Sons, 1904

The Haves and the Have-Nots

The point in all this is that there were arms available for sale, and there were an extensive number of US manufacturers. Unfortunately, the Militia Act requirements limited what the militiamen could purchase to a particular type of musket primarily made in northeastern states, and it was ill suited for hunting and protecting crops.

For people who lived in the major cities and did not hunt on a regular basis, to be required to own a firearm specifically for militia duty could be a financial burden. For those living in rural or wilderness areas, the law essentially required men to own two guns: one for hunting and one for militia duty. Furthermore, finding the proper arms in stock at the local purveyor of goods proved to be spotty at best, and the men of the rural communities usually didn't have the coin needed for the purchase.

The effect of these problems can be seen in the militia returns. States west of the Blue Ridge Mountains, like Kentucky, posted militia returns showing more rifles than muskets. Alternatively, states like Massachusetts, industrializing with the new textile industries and with little land to hunt on, listed large numbers of proper muskets.

Initially, the Federal government responded to this by requiring the states to levy fines for noncompliance. The fines varied with the offense and from state to state. On June 22, 1793, Massachusetts passed a law that allowed a man to be fined up to 20 shillings (five dollars) if he appeared at a muster without arms and equipment. North Carolina's July 18, 1794, law required the man to pay five shillings for appearing unarmed. New Jersey fined a man three shillings and nine pence (almost one dollar) under their June 5, 1793, act. Maryland fined the man one cent per day until he showed that he had the proper arms. Pennsylvania stated that if the man was declared unable to arm himself, he was exempted from fines.[32]

---

[32] Letter to congress from General Henry Knox, Secretary of War, December 18, 1794.

In regard to men who couldn't purchase the required arms and gear, some of the states tried to balance the scales of justice. Pennsylvania and New Jersey would exempt a man from militia duty if he were too poor to afford the required arms. Massachusetts and North Carolina went the other way and required the township of the poor man to supply the arm from town funds. The arm wasn't the man's but the community's, and if he sold the gun or deliberately destroyed it, he could be fined for the replacement cost or forced to do community service to pay the debt. These variations in the state codes explain much regarding the militia returns and the number of men and arms listed in them.

If the man wasn't determined to be destitute, under the militia laws all his goods and property could be sold at auction to pay his militia fines. If the fines exceeded the amount earned by the sale, the man could then be imprisoned for a specified period. Many poor and lower-middle-class men went to debtors' prison for nonpayment of militia fines.

Whereas the poor had to go to such lengths to stay out of prison, the rich bought their way out of militia service. Considering what some of the fines actually were, many rich men simply paid the fines, preferring to work at their businesses instead of drilling. Because some states' militia laws only enrolled property owners, other rich men convinced a landless tenant to serve in their place. All the rich man had to do was convince the landless tenant to do this; supply the man with a firearm, uniform, and powder; and then pay him for his services. Surprisingly, finding a substitute was not as difficult as it seemed.

Of course there were plenty of people who were exempted from militia duty, or who simply wouldn't do it. Under Section 2 of the act, ferrymen, stagecoach drivers, postmen, customhouse clerks, pilots, mariners, millers, doctors, and lawyers were exempted from service. The states could also add additional occupations to the exemption, and so the list continued to grow, eventually including the men of the fire wagon in Philadelphia. As for conscientious objectors such as the Quakers, they paid their fines and then petitioned to be exempted for religious reasons. Thus, we now understand why the militia rolls showed significantly fewer men than the census data would indicate.[33]

Federal Assistance: Arms Distribution

By 1798 congress realized that fining people wasn't going to solve the problem of getting proper arms (right caliber) into the hands of the militia. Thus in 1798 congress went into the firearm distribution business and into commodities trading (see Appendix 2).

The goal was straightforward: to buy proper muskets made in New England, transport them to areas of the south and west that had no indigenous musket makers, sell them to the militiamen in those areas, receive payment in some manner,[34] and hopefully not have any guns left to return to the East Coast. The debate congress had on this activity in June 1798 pointed out the problems that the government was encountering in putting the right kind of arms in militiamen's hands.

---

[33] When the first militia return was reported in December 1802, it shocked congress. In a debate over removing the duties on arms importation, several members noted that the returns were wrong in both quantity or arms and men. An addendum to the 1802 return was then posted in March 1803.

[34] Rifles and muskets sold to militiamen in the Mississippi territory by Governor Claiborne in 1802 were paid for with cotton.

Figure 26: A depiction of Dupont powder wagons in the early 1800s. Most ground transportation was by wagon over dirt roads.

Excerpts from the Congressional Record

Mr. Dayton (the Speaker) could not give his assent to the first section, and was rather in favor of striking it out, because it would be found in practice very inconvenient for the United States to become the retailers of arms to the extent therein proposed.

Mr. Shepard said the Committee who reported this bill were induced do to it from a persuasion that the Southern States are in want of arms, and have not an opportunity of purchasing them.

Mr. S. Smith felt some of the inconveniences pointed out by the gentleman from New Jersey; but when it is recollected that all the manufactories of small arms either are, or doubtless will be, engaged in public service, the necessity and propriety of

Government undertaking this business will appear evident; for, if it be desirable that the militia should be well armed and it undoubtedly is so, Government ought to aid the people in the purchase.

Mr. Harper … if this supply is withheld until the arms are wanted, the same inconvenience would not only be encountered, but the arms would come too late for the people to use them in training.

Mr. Dayton declared that he was not willing to do more than to authorize the increase of the number of armories and arsenals,

Mr. Rutledge said, as some of the States could easily supply themselves, they did not, of course, stand in need of the assistance of Government; though in other States, where arms cannot be got, it will be proper to send them … if the United States were asked to supply the militia at their own expense with arms, some objection might be made to the request; but as they were only requested to be instrumental in affording the supply, without bearing ultimately any part of the expense, he thought the proposition could not reasonably be objected to.

Mr. Varnum did not believe that the militia of any of the States are completely armed; and many of the arms which they have are of *different calibers*.

Mr. Varnum's words showed that although there was concern over whether there was complete arming of the militia, the primary concern was that the majority of the arms they had were of the wrong caliber. With the expiration of the five-year grace period in 1798, congress was now dealing with the caliber clause and the need to place guns of the same bore in the hands of all the militiamen. States could have large numbers of arms in private hands, but if these arms were not of the prescribed caliber, the system didn't recognize the arms existed. As the years went by, the standard bore requirement would become a recurring statement in the congressional record as the government fought to create a uniform militia system throughout the expanding United States.

Ten years after this congressional debate, on April 23, 1808, the government increased their involvement by appropriating two hundred thousand dollars to buy militia arms for those who could not afford them. By 1813 the amount had reached a reported one million dollars, which had been used to purchase a total of 34,447 muskets meeting the 1792 Militia Act requirements. Of these, the government distributed 26,000 muskets to the following states.

As of April 23, 1808

New Hampshire	1,000		
Vermont	2,500		
Rhode Island	1,000		
New Jersey	1,000	*Since December 24, 1812*	
Delaware	500	Connecticut	5,000
North Carolina	2,130	New York	2,000
South Carolina	2,000	Maryland	1,500
Georgia	1,000	Louisiana	1,500
Ohio	1,500		
Kentucky	1,500		
Tennessee	1,500	*Before December 24, 1812*	
Illinois territory	218	Ohio	1,500
Louisiana	250	District of Columbia	2,200

The End Result

The important point is that by the time of the War of 1812, the United States was supposed to have a huge common militia that was uniform in arms, training, and equipment per the 1792 Militia Act, as implemented under the authority of Article 1 Section 8 Clause 16 of the constitution. Instead, by 1812 the paperwork indicated that a nation of over one million men aged 18–45 had only 626,000 men on the militia rolls and less than 200,000 proper muskets. Was this a misrepresentation of the facts? Of course! But it also showed that though the nation could defend itself, actually attacking another nation and fighting in the European manner was a completely different subject.

The United States did have a decent sized army and the means and resources already on hand to enlarge it. The problem it had was in the training of the army and the quality of the commanders in it. Further, in regard to the pending conflict, the US Army was highly scattered and limited by the condition of the nation's road network. Thus, concentrating forces to either launch or repel an attack took too long to accomplish.

The problems with the US Army placed more reliance on the quality and quantity of the militia to successfully launch attacks against Canada and to repel the same. In this the nation had a large pool of manpower to call on, but not to the extent one would imagine. Religious allowances and people relieved of duty due to their occupations reduced the available pool of men. In addition, the manpower pool was concentrated in the major population zones far from the frontier, where most of the fighting would occur. The problem of moving militiamen by road was just as difficult as it was for the US Army.

In addition to the problem of finding and moving men to the areas where the fighting would occur, there was the problem of ordnance. Though the nation did have large numbers of arms in country, the number of arms of the federal standard was not as great as the war hawks in the government would have hoped. The nation did have a large manufacturing base for arms, but the musket makers were concentrated in New England. The result of this was that the majority of the musket arms were in the major population centers in the northeast, whereas the frontier, where the fighting was to start, was dominated by rifles that couldn't be used effectively in European warfare. It's not to say the rifles didn't have their uses; in fact, they would eventually play a major role in most of the US victories in the conflict. But they had to be used to their strengths, and few US Army commanders of the period seemed to understand that.

Granted that these issues only come into play when the United States was trying to defend its scattered frontier outposts or attack the major population centers of Canada across that same sparsely populated American frontier. In the same way, when the British would try to launch an attack against major American cities or ports, they would in turn always encounter a well-manned garrison of US Army troops backed up by a large militia, which in turn was further supported by every able-bodied man who either owned or could raise a musket or rifle.

CHAPTER 3
The First Year of the War

By 1812 English impressment of American sailors, trade embargoes, and support of native tribes had convinced a majority of US citizens that conflict was inevitable. Yet the British stance on these issues had been changing over time as the war in Europe continued. By 1812 the primary obstacle to a thaw in relations was Prime Minister Spencer Perceval, the author of the hated Orders of Council. That changed unexpectedly on May 11 when, en route to an inquiry on the effect of the Orders of Council, an insane man assassinated the prime minister in the lobby of the House of Commons. Unfortunately, change was not swift; it took until June 8 for the Earl of Liverpool to be seated as the new prime minister.

Seven days before the new prime minister was seated, Madison had sent congress a list of complaints against England and a demand for a declaration of war. The house took all of three days to pass the resolution, divided among party lines, but the senate took until June 18 and only passed the measure by six votes. Two days earlier, across the Atlantic and still unaware of the house vote, the British foreign minister announced that the Orders of Council and its embargo would be suspended. Full repeal would then occur on June 23, 1812—the very day the British ambassador took his leave of the United States. Thus, the war had begun just as the reason for it was repealed.

Figure 27: President James Madison (Library of Congress)
and General Brock (Library and Archives of Canada).

The British government in England would not learn they were at war with the United States until July 29, 1812. In the same manner, Madison would not learn of the repeal of the orders until August 12. But by then, any chance of stopping the conflict was gone. British General Isaac Brock, military commander of Upper Canada, had been preparing for a possible war with the United States for several years. When the British ambassador to the United States stopped at Montreal on his way to England, Brock immediately put his plans into motion. His first act was to send a message to his subordinate, Captain Charles Roberts, at Fort St. Joseph on St. Joseph Island in Lake Huron. Brock's message was simple: begin preparations for the seizing of Fort Mackinac at the linking point of Lake Huron and Michigan. That message reached Roberts on July 8, days before most US Army field commanders knew war had been declared.

Detroit

While the defenders of Canada were moving quickly, Secretary of War William Eustis also sent messages to the forces under his command. Before Madison sent his letter to congress, US Army troops were being marshaled towards their jump-off points in an ambitious, three-pronged plan to take Canada by January 1813.

One force under General Hull, governor of the Michigan territory, would march from Detroit into Upper Canada. A second force under General Smyth would cross into Canada at Niagara and march to York. The third and final force, under General Dearborn, would then march to Montreal, effectively completing the capture of Canada. The problem was that none of these commanders learned war had been declared until well after their counterparts in Canada.

Simply put, Eustis wasn't very big on the small details. When he sent General William Hull the message that war had been declared, he sent it by general mail. It wasn't until the letter reached the Ohio postmaster that the mistake was realized and an express rider was sent with the letter to Detroit.

In the meantime, Hull, who eight days before war was declared began marching his force of army regulars, Ohio militia, and Michigan volunteers to Fort Detroit, received word on June 24 that war was imminent. Hull had been taking his time moving his men, building a road and small forts along his march from Urbana to Detroit. Now he had to quicken his pace if he was to be in Detroit before war was declared. To do this, on June 30 he requisitioned the packet ship *Cayahoga* to carry thirty sick troops, the corps' musical instruments, and other supplies to Fort Detroit. These supplies also included all previous correspondence from Secretary of War Eustis to General Hull.

As the *Cayahoga* passed Fort Amherstburg (shown on the map as Fort Malden), the captain was surprised to see British troops rowing out to meet it. Just the day before, Fort Amherstburg had

Figure 28: Secretary of War William Eustis and General William Hull.

learned from Brock that war had been declared. When the *Cayahoga* was searched, the British found a treasure trove of intelligence, including Hull's entire plan for the campaign, his troop strengths, his attack route, and even his concerns over the possibility of Native American attacks. Hull wouldn't learn of the capture of the *Cayahoga* until he arrived at Detroit on July 5, three days after the express rider finally caught up with his troops. The attack was already compromised.

His plans already in the enemy hands, Hull should have either changed his plans or implemented them immediately. Instead, he first had a council with the chiefs of the locals tribes on July 7, to be followed by the sending of a regiment south to Spring Wells on July 11. The British seemed to be decoyed by this, leaving the way open on July 12, for the regiments of James Miller and Lewis Cass to cross into Canada north of Detroit at the farm of British Colonel Baubee. Very quickly the army took the village of Sandwich (now Windsor, Canada), less than twenty miles from Fort Amherstburg. Once there, Hull issued the following "bombastic" proclamation to the Canadian people.

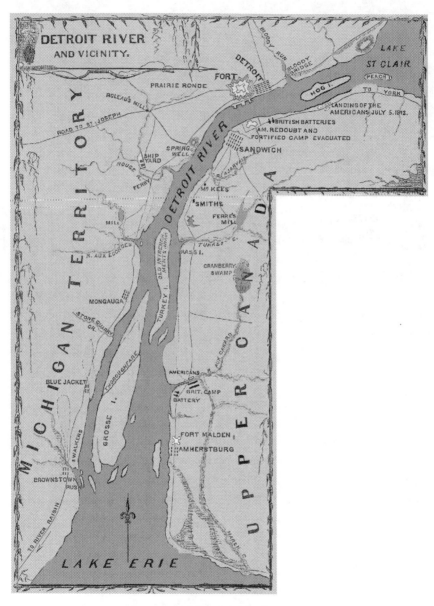

Figure 29: The Detroit frontier.

Inhabitants of Canada!

After thirty years of Peace and prosperity, the United States have been driven to Arms. The injuries and aggressions, the insults and indignities of Great Britain have once more left them no alternative but manly resistance or unconditional submission. The army under my Command has invaded your Country and the standard of the United States waves on the territory of Canada. To the peaceful, unoffending inhabitant, it brings neither danger nor difficulty. I come to find enemies not to make them. I come to protect you not to injure you.

Separated by an immense ocean and an extensive Wilderness from Great Britain you have no participation in her counsels, no interest in her conduct. You have felt her Tyranny, you have seen her injustice, but I do not ask you to avenge the one or redress the other. The United States are sufficiently powerful to afford you every security consistent with their rights and your expectations. I tender you the invaluable blessings of Civil, Political, and Religious Liberty, and their necessary result, individual and general, prosperity: That liberty which gave decision to our counsels and energy to our conduct in our struggle for INDEPENDENCE and which conducted us safely and triumphantly thro' the stormy period of the Revolution ...

In the name of my Country and by the authority of my Government I promise protection to your persons, property and rights. Remain at your homes, Pursue your peaceful and customary avocations. Raise not your hands against your brethren, many of your fathers fought for the freedom and Independence we now enjoy Being children therefore of the same family with us, and heirs to the same Heritage, the arrival of an army of Friends must be hailed by you with a cordial welcome, You will be emancipated from Tyranny and oppression and restored to the dignified status of freemen. If contrary to your own interest and the just expectation of my country, you should take part in the approaching contest, you will be considered and treated as enemies and the horrors, and calamities of War will stalk before you.

If the barbarous and Savage policy of Great Britain be pursued, and the savages are let loose to murder our Citizens and butcher our women and children, this war, will be a war of extermination.

The first stroke with the Tomahawk, the first attempt with the Scalping Knife, will be the signal for one indiscriminate scene of desolation. No white man found fighting by the Side of an Indian will be taken prisoner. Instant destruction will be his Lot.

I doubt not your courage and firmness; I will not doubt your attachment to Liberty. If you tender your services voluntarily they will be accepted readily.

The United States offers you Peace, Liberty and Security. Your choice lies between these and War, Slavery, and Destruction. Choose then, but choose wisely; and may he who knows the justice of our cause, and who holds in his hand the fate of Nations, guide you to a result the most compatible, with your rights and interests, your peace and prosperity.

After this, on July 13 Hull sent a forty-man reconnaissance force south to Fort Amherstburg. Less than nine miles outside of camp, near the Turtle Creek bridge, they found signs of a large war party. A local farmer told them that quite a few Indians were about. This news hits the US camp like a thunderclap, causing Hull to order the immediate fortification of it on all sides except the river. For the next few days, army units were chasing Indians both south and north of the army camp. It was not until July 17 that a force was sent south to take the bridge over the River Aux Canards. After taking the position, the army withdrew to Sandwich, leaving only Captain Josiah Snelling's company one mile north of the bridge at the settlement of Petit Cote.

The following day, Colonel Duncan McArthur and his soldiers were sent to relieve Captain Snelling's company. What they found when they arrived was that during the night, a British ship had sailed up river to bombard Snelling's position. Under the cover of this barrage, a British force of 60 regulars, 150 Canadian militia, 25 dragoons, and 50 Indians under Tecumseh moved in and erected a breastwork and battery at the bridge. Tecumseh then organized two attacks on the US troops, both of which were repulsed, but the attacks bled McArthur of ammunition. After calling for support, McArthur withdrew to Turkey Creek to meet Colonel Cass's unit of 150 men and a six-pound cannon. They returned to the Petit Cote settlement only to fail to take the bridge the following day. Now the road to Fort Amherstburg was closed, and Tecumseh had been seen on the field. A third attack on the bridge was mounted on July 24, but by then Hull had returned to Detroit, apparently paralyzed in fear of the Native American warriors.

Hull was now waiting for word that the other two parts of the Canadian campaign were underway. This message would never come because the governor-general of Canada, George Prevost, had implemented his own plan for defending Canada. Once war was declared, he began sending emissaries to Generals Smyth and Dearborn to negotiate an armistice with the US government. By these negotiations, Prevost succeeded in neutralizing the other two invasions, allowing Brock to concentrate on defeating Hull in the west.

What word Hull did receive was not what he wanted to hear. Within days of returning from Canada, he was informed that native forces loyal to Tecumseh were raiding the overland supply route to Detroit. Cut off from supply by Lake Erie due to Fort Amherstburg, and now having his overland routes threatened, he was becoming dependent on the long route through Lake Huron and Michigan down to the Mississippi and Ohio Rivers. Guarding this route were Forts Dearborn and Mackinac.

The commander of Mackinac was Lieutenant Porter Hanks. Out of contact with Washington for several months, Hanks was unaware that the nation was at war with Britain. All he knew was that he had sixty artillerymen and seven cannons in a well-fortified location, on an island in the middle of nowhere. He also knew the only other English-speaking people in the area were the British troops of Fort St. Joseph on St. Joseph Island, forty-five miles away. Hanks even knew the commanding officer, Captain Charles Roberts.

Figure 30: Fort Mackinac, Library and Archives of Canada

Unknown to Hanks, Roberts had gathered together three artillerymen, 47 veteran soldiers (meaning they were semiretired and regularly drunk), 150 militia (French Canadian frontiersmen) and 400 Native Americans for an attack on Fort Mackinac. For transportation, he requisitioned the armed schooner *Caledonia* and ten flat-bottom riverboats; the Indians supplied their own war canoes. On July 16 the force began sailing west for Mackinac.

After capturing a militia officer and fur trader by the name of Michael Dousman, Roberts learned that Hanks was aware of some strange activity on St. Joseph, but he was still unaware that the two nations were at war. Armed with this intelligence, Roberts secretly landed two miles from the fort on July 17. He quietly emptied out the nearby village and then hauled two six-pound cannons to the top of a nearby ridge. From there he looked directly down into the middle of the fort. After that, it took just one cannon ball to force Hanks to surrender.

Thus, within a month of declaring war, the United States had lost sixty regular troops, sixty muskets, seven cannons, and a strategic fort with only one shot fired—and a British shot at that. More important, the river route to Detroit from New Orleans was effectively blocked. General Hull would not learn this until August 4, when General Brock deliberately paroled Hanks back to Detroit. And of course, the taking of Fort Mackinac occurred twelve days before the British government even learned of the US declaration of war. Hanks's parole would occur eight days before President Madison learned of the withdrawal of the Orders of Council.

The day after Hanks arrived at Detroit, two hundred men under Major Thomas Van Horne were passing through Brownstown en route to Frenchtown on the River Raisin. Van Horne was to meet a supply column there and then escort it back to Fort Detroit. Instead, his force was ambushed at Brownstown creek by a combined force of British, Shawnee (Tecumseh), and Wyandots (Chief Walk in the Water). There is some question as to the size of the force that intercepted Van Horne, but regardless of this, Van Horne's force was put in full retreat with only half returning to Fort Detroit.

On hearing what happened, Hull dispatched a larger force of six hundred men to clear his lines of supply and communication. At the same time, on August 7 he began withdrawing from Canada. On August 9 his force, under the command of James Miller, engaged a combined Indian and British force of two hundred men at the village of Maguaga and forced their withdrawal from Michigan. But instead of continuing down to Frenchtown for the supplies, Miller waited for orders. When those orders came, it was for withdrawal back to Fort Detroit.

Hull's action was understandable in light of his situation. He had started the campaign with secure lines of supply and communications and a force of eighteen hundred men. By August he had lost all his communication and supply routes, had lost almost two hundred men in two battles to clear his supply lines, and needed to use one-third of his army to perform this last battle. Worse, his own timidity had actually inspired native tribes to revolt, increasing by the day the size of the opposition forces.

Yet he was in a strong position at Detroit with a sound fortification and thirty-five field pieces. If he could hold out until winter set in, he could then wait for reinforcements to arrive from Vincennes. In the meantime, he ordered the people at Fort Dearborn to evacuate to Fort Wayne, and the garrison transferred to Detroit. Further, he sent another force of five hundred men south to clear his supply lines.

After this force left, on August 14 General Brock crossed the Detroit River in force, setting up a strong position along Hull's supply route. He brought with him most of the forces he had at the start of the campaign, plus an additional four hundred regulars and militia dispatched from lower Canada. His total force was around twelve hundred, including six hundred native warriors.

Brock intended to wait out Hull. Eventually Hull would either have to move out against his position or surrender for lack of supplies.

However, when Brock learned of the earlier force sent out by Hull, a force that was now behind him, he had to act. He sent messages to Hull stating that if Detroit did not surrender soon, Brock would not stop his Indian allies from killing everyone. Then on August 15 batteries erected across the river from Detroit began bombarding the fort. One of the men killed was Lieutenant Hanks, who was in the stockade awaiting court-martial for cowardice.

The bombardment was too much for Hull; he surrendered the next day on Brocks terms. Days later it was learned that on August 15, the people of Fort Dearborn had been taken by Indians less than two miles from their fort. About fifty men were killed, and the rest were sold by the tribes to the British. Fort Dearborn was then burned.

Figure 31: The left is a sculpture depicting the rescue of Margaret Helm by Chief Black Partridge of the Potawatomi during the Fort Dearborn Massacre. On the right is a sketch of Fort Harrison, Indiana.

Forts Harrison and Wayne

With the loss of Forts Mackinac, Dearborn, and Detroit, the next targets of the British in this western rout were Fort Harrison and Fort Wayne. Fort Harrison was just a small stockade at a high point over the Wabash River (present-day Terre Haute, Indiana). There, future president Zachary Taylor commanded fifty soldiers, all but fifteen of them sick.

On September 3 friendly Miami Indians warned Taylor that an attack was imminent. The next morning, scouts found and buried two dead white settlers. Later that day, a multi-tribe force of six hundred warriors approached the fort and asked Taylor for a parley. Taylor agreed to speak with them the following morning. For the rest of the day, Taylor, his fifteen healthy troops, and five civilians prepared for a fight.

The attack began after dusk when a warrior set fire to the blockhouse. As women and sick men fought the fire, the remaining men fired on the attackers, using the light of the fire to see by. The next morning, Taylor had the fit men build a barricade over a twenty-foot-wide hole in the stockade caused by the fire. By this time all the ambulatory sick men were on the wall, defending the fort.

Figure 32: Depiction of the attack on Fort Harrison.

After the initial attack, the Indians made no more moves against the fort, intending to starve out the defenders. But on September 12 a relief force of one thousand men under Colonel William Russell arrived from Vincennes with food and ammunition. The siege wasn't over, however, because on the next day an Indian war party ambushed a supply column heading for the fort at a place called the Narrows. A second supply train was then ambushed at this same location on September 15, resulting in a second force from Vincennes being sent to cover future supply columns.

The same day Fort Harrison[35] was attacked, the Chief Winamac approached Fort Wayne with close to five hundred warriors. There, he informed Captain James Rhea of the situation and essentially demanded surrender of the fort and the one hundred men inside. Rhea, who was drunk at the time, had to be relieved of command by his subordinates to prevent him doing just that. While Rhea sobered up in the guardhouse, Lieutenant Philip Ostander took command of the garrison and prepared for battle.

Winamac attacked the next morning, burning the Indian village on the eastern side of the fort. At dusk Winamac tried again to get the defenders to surrender. When he was rebuffed, at 8:00 p.m. he launched a second attack—a battle that would rage until dawn the following day. The third attack then came the evening of September 6.

By this time William Henry Harrison was already en route to relieve the fort. Back on August 28, he was given command of the Kentucky militia called up earlier by the secretary of war. On that same day, he set out from Cincinnati with over five hundred men for Fort Wayne via Dayton. At the same time, he sent a scouting party to Fort Wayne to inform them that help was en route. The party, made up of sutler[36] William Oliver and Shawnee Captain Logan, succeeded

---

[35] At the same time Fort Harrison was attacked, a small stockade (Fort Madison, at what is today Bellevue, Iowa) was attacked. Essentially a follow-up to the massacre at Fort Dearborn, this small outpost survived a four-day siege.

[36] Sutler is an old term to describe a merchant who supplies provisions to the military when in the field. Usually operating out of a tent or wagon moving with the troops.

in reaching the fort and then returning to Harrison with the news the fort was still being defended.

Learning the fort still stood was one thing, but on September 4, Harrison also learned that a British force of 140 regulars and four hundred warriors was heading for Fort Wayne. As he quickened his pace, he arrived on September 8 at Girty's Town on the St. Mary's River. There he was reinforced with additional companies, bringing his force to a total of twenty-two hundred men. By September 11, the forward elements of Harrison's army were within twenty miles of Fort Wayne.

With Harrison closing in, on the evening of September 11, Winamac made his last attempt to take Fort Wayne. However, he was again repulsed with several casualties, forcing him to withdraw during the night. The next morning the defenders of the fort came out to cheer the arrival of Harrison and his men. Harrison immediately placed Rhea under arrest and put Lieutenant Ostander in charge of the fort. He then began a series of punitive raids on nearby Indian villages, clearing a safe zone around the fort equivalent to two days' march.

Within three days of the relief of Fort Wayne, US soldiers were burning the Miami villages at the forks of the Wabash. On sixteenth the buildings and fields of the Pottawattamie village known as Five Medals Town was destroyed. On the seventeenth Harrison sent three hundred recently arrived dragoons and a company of riflemen to Little Turtle's town with orders to burn everything except the buildings built by the United States.

After being relieved by General Winchester, Harrison returned to St. Mary, Ohio, to gather more troops. On the twenty-first, some of these forces are sent to Fort Defiance to reinforce that position. By the time they arrived, however, a British force under the command of Major Adam Muir (two hundred regulars, a thousand warriors, and four pieces of artillery) had taken the location. Muir's goal was the conquest of Fort Wayne.

When Winchester learned of Muir's force, he set out to meet him away from Fort Wayne. Rumors of the size of Winchester's force reached Muir, who was now marching from Fort Defiance, causing him to have second thoughts about meeting Winchester head-on. On the twenty-seventh he lost his nerve and began a retreat back to Fort Defiance. The following day 75 percent of his native troops deserted, causing his organized retreat to turn into a rout.

Now pursuing Muir, Winchester called on Harrison to reinforce him. Harrison then left St. Mary with three thousand troops on September 30, arriving at Fort Defiance on October 2. There he learned Winchester had lost Muir and begun building a new Fort Winchester, near the site of Old Fort Defiance.

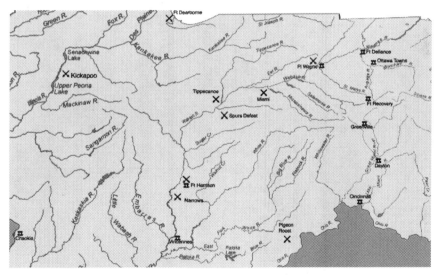

Figure 33: Battles in the northwest.

As Harrison was pursuing both Indians and British in Northern Ohio and Indiana, other commanders were planning other attacks. Back on September 3, twenty-four settlers were massacred at Pigeon Roost, Indiana, just northwest of Charlestown. This raid was so deep into Indiana that it left the entire territory in fear of Indian attacks. In

September Colonel Russell led a retaliatory raid out of Fort Harrison on the main Kickapoo village at Peoria Lake,[37] Illinois.

Though successful, he soon found himself pursued by the rest of the Kickapoo villages and was unable to link up with a Kentucky militia unit under General Hopkins, out of Vincennes. As a result, he was forced to withdraw to the Missouri River at Chaokia. Russell later learned the Kentucky militia unit was forced to withdraw back to Vincennes when the Kickapoo started a prairie grass fire against them.

After returning to Vincennes, Major General Hopkins disbanded his forces, raised three new regiments, and then set out for Fort Dearborn, following the route Harrison had followed to Prophets Town in 1811. When they arrived at Prophets Town, they burned a Kickapoo village and then began heading back to Vincennes. At Wildcat Creek, however, scouts found a Winnebago village. With three hundred men, Colonel Miller destroyed the village, only to have his scouts ambushed while looking for the inhabitants.

The following day a group of sixty rangers was ambushed, losing seventeen men in the battle now called Spurs Defeat. The next day, November 23, a snowstorm blew through the area, preventing Hopkins from engaging the Indians with his entire force. By the time the storm had left, Hopkins had lost the enemy and was forced to withdraw to Vincennes for the winter.

---

[37] Kickapoos and Winnebagos were the primary tribes that attacked Fort Harrison.

Niagara

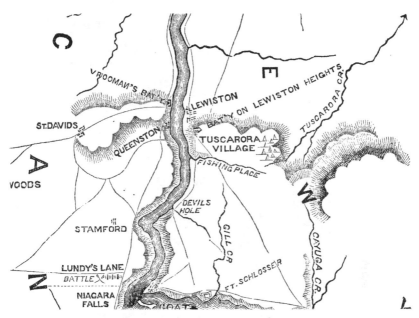

Figure 34: The Niagara frontier.

While all this was going on, the two other US invasion forces were still sitting in New York. The first invasion force consisted of the commands of Brigadier General Smyth with 1,650 regulars and 400 militiamen at Buffalo, and Militia Major General Van Rensselaer with 900 regulars and 2,300 militiamen at Lewiston. Combining these forces with the 1,300 troops at Fort Niagara made a grand total of 6,100 troops (almost 3,000 regular army) for the Niagara campaign.

To the east at Albany, New York, was General Dearborn with what is regularly described as the largest US force. Unfortunately, the size of this force is never mentioned in modern history books. He is reported to have had seven regiments of regular army troops, including artillery and dragoons. At about eight hundred men per regiment, this would represent a force of close to six thousand men. There is no information regarding the size of his militia forces, though with six thousand regular army units, the complete force had to be formidable.

Figure 35: Militia General Van Rensselaer (Library of Congress), and Brock Entering Queenston (Library and Archives of Canada).

And yet they were all just sitting there. The only action that took place was a raid by Benjamin Forsyth of the First Army Rifle Regiment, stationed at Ogdensburg, against the Canadian village of Gananoque. The village was on the supply line from Montreal to Kingston and thus was a strategic target. Forsyth with two hundred men (half regular, half militia) took the village on September 21, seized all supplies, and then burned the government depot. He then withdrew to Ogdensburg, where his regiment was stationed to get them out of the way and end the smuggling of goods out of Ogdensberg into Canada. Forsyth would still be sitting there waiting for new orders when the British took Ogdensburg on February 22, 1813.

Part of the reason they were waiting was they expected a peace treaty or armistice to be signed. Governor General Prevost had been in contact with Generals Smyth and Dearborn from the beginning, supposedly trying to reach a peaceful solution. To Dearborn and

Smyth, the concept of an armistice was possible because the British had withdrawn the Order of Council. There was also the pending presidential election, in which many though the Federalists might win both the presidency and congress and withdraw the declaration of war. The Federalist candidate, DeWitt Clinton, was in fact in New York campaigning against the war as Dearborn and Smyth were preparing for invasion.[38]

Of course Clinton wasn't the only Federalist politician in New York. Van Rensselaer was also the leading Federalist candidate for the New York governorship. The incumbent governor, Daniel Tompkins (Democratic Republican), had arranged Rensselaer's command just to get him out of the race. As long as he was in service, he couldn't run for the office, and if he did poorly as a general it would hurt his reputation. Of course if he was successful, it would be to his benefit, but he would have to be able to leave service prior to election day in April 1813 or it would be for nothing. Thus where Smyth and Dearborn were willing to wait out the election and a possible change in government policy, Rensselaer wanted a quick victory.

In the end, by early October Militia General Van Rensselaer had had enough and ordered Smyth to bring up his troops for an attack on Queenston. To Van Rensselaer, his and Smyth's forces would have no trouble sweeping aside the three hundred troops at Queenston guarding a fortified battery. Smyth, an army general and not a militia general, never recognized Van Rensselaer as his superior. Initial orders for him to join Van Rensselaer were ignored until October 10, when he finally began moving his troops to Lewiston.

---

[38] In the New England states Clinton was anti-war and pro-war in the south and west.

Figure 36: Queenston Heights as seen from the town.

Unfortunately for Van Rensselaer, the next day an early winter storm came through the area, forcing Smyth to stop his march because of muddy roads. When told that Van Rensselaer had postponed the attack because of the weather, Smyth then turned around and headed back to buffalo. Thus on October 13 Van Rensselaer launched his attack alone with his 3,200 men.

On the opposite side of the Niagara River was General Brock. After his victories in the west, he had moved the bulk of his forces east to counter the invasion of General Van Rensselaer. Though he disagreed with Governor General Prevost on the armistice, he used the month of September to prepare his defenses. In October he had even begun gathering intelligence regarding the strength of US forces by having his aide, Lieutenant Colonel John McDonell, escort Van Rensselaer's aide, Colonel Solomon Van Rensselaer, through the British lines to meetings with Governor Prevost. Colonel Solomon Van Rensselaer had been a go-between for Governor General Prevost and the US generals regarding an armistice. Brock used the trips to gather intelligence on the US forces: Of course Van Rensselaer was doing the same thing, gathering information on the territory on the Canadian side of the river.

The surprising event then occurred on October 12. Brock sent Major Thomas Evans to see Colonel Van Rensselaer to gain the release of British seamen taken during a raid on October 9. When Evans asked for the colonel, he was informed that the colonel was ill with fever and could not meet the officer. A representative of the general then met Major Evans to inform him that nothing could be done until the day after tomorrow. The phrase was repeated several times in the course of the meeting, which only heightened the major's concern. Then on his way back, he spotted hidden boats along the shoreline.

The report by Major Evans only confirmed information the British had received two days earlier from a deserter, a Lieutenant Sims, who was the chief boatman of the invasion force. Sims had in fact prevented the invasion from occurring on October 10 by taking all the boat oars with him as he fled across the river to Canada. The irony of this is that on that same day, Lieutenant Colonel Chrystie had arrived at Four-Mile Creek with an additional 30 boats and 350 men. Thus Sims' sabotage of the invasion could have resulted in Van Rensselaer launching his attack with more boats. But Van Rensselaer wouldn't wait and ordered the attack to commence once the oars had been replaced. Thus, in his first wave, Van Rensselaer would only be able to land 520 of his 3,200 men.

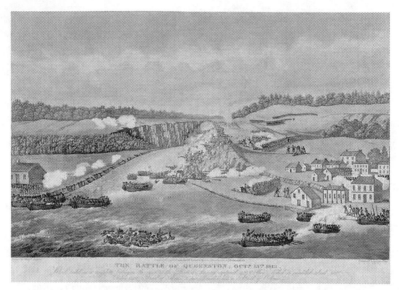

Figure 37: Depiction of the American landings at Queenston.

The American forces began moving across the river just after 3:00 a.m. on October 13. General Van Rensselaer had only twelve 30-man boats and two 80-man boats. Thus, he could not send over more than 520 men at a time. It took less than ten minutes for the boats to reach the opposite shore, but this speed didn't prevent them from being spotted by a British sentry, who immediately rushed to inform his commander. Before the still ill Colonel Solomon Van Rensselaer could organize his troops, they came under fire from a company of British grenadiers. Van Rensselaer was wounded several times, forcing Captain John Wool to take command.

The battle quickly degenerated into urban fighting that was as difficult then as it is now. British Captain James Dennis's men, after meeting the US troops at the river, withdrew into the houses of Queenstown, where they then fired on the advancing troops. While this was going on, the fortified British eighteen-pounder on the heights opened fire on the US forces. In response, an American eighteen-pounder at Lewiston (with additional guns on the river bank) began shelling the British side of the river. Further downriver at

Vrooman's Point, a huge British twenty-four-pound carronade began firing on Lewiston, aiming at the flashes of the US Army cannons.

As the boats returned to get the next wave of troops, a company of York militia and a light infantry group lead by Captain Williams reinforced British Captain Dennis. His renewed attack was repulsed, but it also stalled the US advance on the Heights and injured Captain John Wool. Then, as the sun rose, the gunners on the heights could now see the second wave of US troops approaching in the boats. Now the fire from the Heights became deadly accurate, sinking one boat, forcing another to land at Hamilton Cove (were the men surrendered), prompting a third to surrender at Vrooman's Point, and forcing a fourth to withdraw back to Lewiston. Wool had to take the Heights—and take it with the troops he had—or the landing would fail.

Figure 38: *Push on, Brave York Volunteers,* by John David Kelly.

By this time Brock, awaken by the sound of battle at his base at Fort George, had arrived to take stock of the situation. After riding through American cannon fire, he had just dismounted at the battery

when Captain Wool and his men over ran the Heights. Now forced
to withdraw to the village, Brock sent a message to Fort George to
bring reinforcements, and then he prepared to retake the battery.
Twice he tried to retake the position, the last time resulting in him
being mortally wounded.[39]

The battle could have gone any way at this point. The invasion
was now five hours old, and the British general and his top aide
were dead. The British had withdrawn outside of the village, and
the Americans had succeeded in landing a field piece and unspiking
the British eighteen-pounder on the heights. Though the gun at
Vrooman's Point was still shelling the Americans, additional troops
had landed, bringing American forces up to 1,300 men. Included in
these reinforcements were General Van Rensselaer, Brigadier General
Wadsworth, and a young Colonel Winfield Scott, taking the first of
what would be many army commands.

It was at this point, between one and two in the afternoon, that
Chief John Brant (son of Chief Joseph Brant) launched an attack on
the American position with three hundred Mohawk warriors. Brant
led an assault on the Heights, only to be repulsed by the Americans.
For the next hour, his warriors harassed the US troops until Scott led
a force down the heights to drive Brant off. By then British General
Sheaffe's column of troops could be seen moving from Vrooman's
Point. With Colonel Christy now arrived, General Van Rensselaer
immediately returned to the US shore to push the remaining troops
across the river. Returning with him was Captain Wool, who was only
then being evacuated due to his injuries.[40]

---

[39] Common history says a sharpshooter with a rifle felled him. But it was common
practice to blame US riflemen for the death of British officers, particularly officers
standing in the rear. However, Brock was in the front of battle, making him
vulnerable to standard musket fire.

[40] It is said the boat was so overloaded with the wounded and refugees that it
almost capsized.

Figure 39: Chief John Brant of the Mohawks and Lt. Col. Winfield Scott (Library and Archives of Canada).

Van Rensselaer's return almost cost him his life. Before Shaeffle left Vrooman's Point, he left two additional guns to shell the town and prevent any more American reinforcements from landing. These guns were set up in the courtyard of a Queenston militia officer's home—a location that gave them full range of fire against the US boats. As the smaller guns engaged any approaching boats, the larger gun concentrated on the staging points on the US shore. By the time Van Rensselaer arrived back in Lewiston, he had lost two more boats and a scow, reducing the number to seven boats. In short, he could only ferry 260 men at a time across the river.

General Van Rensselaer now tried to get the militia to board these remaining boats and cross the river. It was then that the militia, under fire for hours from the gun at Vrooman's Point, said no. They had seen the wounded men being removed from the boats returning from the British side, as well as their own wounded from the British shelling. They had also heard the Mohawk war cries during the attack on Scott's position. With the added British batteries in Queenston, even the boatmen revolted, making it impossible for Van Rensselaer to evacuate the troops already deployed. With the US forces in Canada now cut off, at 4:00 p.m. General Shaeffle moved against Scott with eight hundred men and three hundred Mohawks. Scott now only had about three hundred regulars and some five hundred militiamen.

The assault began with Lt. McIntyre leading a light company of the Forty-first plus militia and Indians against the New York riflemen Scott had stationed on his right flank. The riflemen fired a volley, but without bayonets and being unable to reload quickly, they were quickly dispersed. With the right flank already fallen, General Sheaffle then threw his entire force against Scott's front line. Scott's forces broke, retreating down the Heights to the river. Wadsworth and three hundred militiamen surrendered on the top of the Heights to the British. In turn, Scott, already down the Heights at the riverbank, was being subjected to a merciless barrage of musket fire by Indians on the Heights. As men tried to swim to safety, Scott, while under fire, approached the British general and offered the surrender of the whole force. With that, the Battle of Queenston Heights finally ended.

As Scott and Wadsworth were led away, the total scope of the misadventure came to them. The United States had 90 dead, another 100 wounded. and nearly 900 prisoners for a total loss of 1,100 men (900 militia). These totals stunned Scott and Wadsworth, who had over 400 men on the Heights at the final battle. Their British captors then informed them that some 200 militiamen had been captured when the current swept their disabled boats to Vrooman's Point. Another 400 militiamen, having lost their officers, had been found hiding in the homes and along the bank of the river.

The defeat at Queenston was just the beginning of the disaster that would be Niagara. General Van Rensselaer resigned[41] to be replaced by Smyth, who with a combined force of 5,000 men continued to sit.

---

[41] Following resignation, Rensselaer then entered the New York Gubernatorial race, only to loose to Tompkins 43,324 votes to 39,718.

For the remainder of the month, he issued windy proclamations and marched his men back and forth to the river. This morale-breaking activity was intensified by the complete breakdown of the payroll system. The Twelfth Army Regiment had not been paid since August 31, and the Fourteenth was last paid in July. General Smyth would later report in early November that the Fifth and Twenty-third Army Regiments had mutinied on a march for lack of pay. Two other volunteer units also mutinied on account of late pay and lack of winter clothing. One volunteer commander stated his men would not enter Canada until they were paid and properly clothed. Thus, in November the militia was sent home, and the regular troops went into winter quarters at Fort Niagara and Buffalo.

Lake Champlain

As noted previously, General Dearborn sat at Albany. By the time he began moving north to take Montreal, winter was beginning. After reaching Plattsburg, his advanced guard (approximately three hundred men) moved across the Canadian border to a place called Lacolle Mills, just north of the village of Champlain. There, on November 20, they engaged a blockhouse defended by British regulars, Canadian militia, and a few Mohawks.

The outnumbered defenders were very quickly forced from the blockhouse, leaving the advanced guard to move in and make themselves at home. Unfortunately, after dark a New York militia unit following the advanced guard arrived and mistook the blockhouse occupants for British. A short battle then occurred that completely demoralized the two units when they learned what had happened. Soon after this, a British force of 530 men arrived to take back the blockhouse. The now completely confused US forces had no choice but to withdraw to Champlain.

It is said that at this time, the militia stated they would not cross the border into Canada on constitutional grounds. The reality was they had already crossed into Canada at Champlain. The real reason was lack of pay, no winter clothing, and poor food—all problems caused by the government (which is why it is never mentioned). With winter setting in, the troops knew that they needed to head for home, increasing the morale problem and the desertion rate. Furthermore, finding Mohawks at the blockhouse probably had the same effect on the militia as the war cries had at Queenston.

Thus by the end of the first year of the war, the United States had lost three strategic forts, over three thousand men, as many muskets, and at least thirty-five cannons—and they had nothing to show for it. The one good thing that did happen was that on December 3, 1812, Secretary of War William Eustis, the man who prepared the nation for this conflict since 1809, resigned. His replacement would be General John Armstrong on February 5, 1813

The Little Ice Age

Figure 40: *Washington Crossing the Delaware in 1777,* by Emanuel Leutze.

A final note regarding the year 1812 before we finish. This was the year Napoleon would suffer his greatest strategic defeat. On June 23, Napoleon crossed the Niemen River into Russia with the Grande Armée of France, 650,000 men and arms. To put it into perspective, Great Britain had only 100,000 men in its entire army in 1812, and the Grande Armée was only *a part* of the entire French army.

After marching across Russia, on September 14 Napoleon arrived in Moscow expecting an immediate Russian surrender. Instead he found a burning city as the Russians torched their own capital and retreated. Even though it was September, the Russian winter was already setting in. Now deprived of shelter and supplies, Napoleon had no choice but to retreat back to Poland. Troops died by the thousands from the cold, lack of food, and attacks by Russian Cossack cavalry. By the time the Armée reached the border of Poland, they were down to only twenty-two thousand men. Napoleon then had to hastily return to France to prevent a coup, and the Russian campaign ended in defeat.

Many historians view a weather phenomenon called the little ice age as a major factor in this French defeat. This cold weather period had been affecting the earth from the early 1300s to the early mid-1800s, bringing harsh early winters to both Europe and North America. Extreme though these winters were, at intervals the weather would warm for a decade or more, creating the feeling that this period was over—only to have that belief broken by a new round of cold harsh winters.

An example of this can be found in the famous painting of Washington crossing the Delaware by the painter Emanuel Leutze. This painting, done in 1851, was for decades viewed by historians as an embellishment of the story based on the fact that the Delaware had been ice-free during winter for several decades. Few who saw the painting for the first time, other than the painter, had experienced a harsh little ice age winter.

In truth, neither had Napoleon. Born in 1769 on the Mediterranean island of Corsica, he had never experienced the depths of the little ice age in Northern Europe. By 1789 Northern Europe and North America were in a warm spell, though in France the failure to adapt agriculture to the potato and an eruption of an Iceland volcano caused a major famine that triggered the French revolution. For the next two decades, Europe, the United States, and Canada experienced mild winters, resulting in clothing styles progressing towards lighter garments.

All this changed from 1811 to 1817, with the worst being the "year without a summer" in 1816. Documents show that winter set in early in Canada in 1812, ruining the late harvest. Other documents show that one year later, on October 12, 1813, two feet of lake-effect snow occurred in western Pennsylvania and western New York. A decade earlier, to have snow that early was almost unthinkable.

Documents show that the sudden change in the weather caught the US Army by surprise in 1812. On October 5, the US inspector general noted that neither the Twelfth nor the Fourteenth Regiment under General Smyth's command had been issued winter clothes, and some of the men in the Fourteenth were without shoes. The inspector general also noted that for the previous week, cold and stormy weather had been the norm. Again, General Van Rensselaer didn't begin his attack at Niagara until October 13, 1812, immediately after another strong storm had swept through the area.

Thus, an early winter, a lack of winter clothing, rotten tents, bad food, no commissary, no pay, and finally a measles epidemic added to the primary problem of poor leadership within the US Army. Thus ended the first year of the War of 1812.

CHAPTER 4
The Year 1813

As we left the US Army (and the United States government) in December 1812, the people in charge were trying very hard to put their war machine back together. Though the western states and territories had suffered a tremendous defeat at Detroit, the combined victories at Fort Wayne and Fort Harrison had given hope back to the American people. Leading this fight was William Henry Harrison, who was now leading a force of over six thousand men back toward Fort Detroit.

The Great Northwest

An experienced Indian fighter, Harrison was no fool when it came to fighting in the great northwest. Regardless of the 1792 Militia Act's prohibition against rifles, he had a large force of riflemen drawn from Kentucky (where there were three rifles for every musket). These men were dead shots, practically the best marksmen in North America.

Figure 41: *Remember the River Raisin*, By Ken Riley.

A depiction of mounted riflemen at the Battle of Thames River, 1813.

One such unit of riflemen was the Indiana ranger unit of mounted riflemen used to attack the Kickapoo city near Peoria, Illinois, in late 1812. Richard Mentor Johnson, commanding the Kentucky militia that had relieved Fort Wayne, saw this group in action. After returning to congress in late 1812, he proposed a plan to create mounted rifle units specifically to fight the Indians.

The reason for this new type of military unit was simple. When regular infantry moved toward an Indian village, all they would find were abandoned buildings. The natives always had enough time to evacuate with provisions into the forest. The same occurred when regular troops contacted warriors in the field: the Indians simply disappeared into the woods. The mounted riflemen would have the advantage of speed, allowing them to rapidly move on the villages before the evacuation could be completed. When the riflemen encountered warriors, they were to dismount, take cover, and pin down the enemy. Any other mounted units within earshot of the fight were to ride to it, dismount, and then surround the warriors.

President Madison supported Johnson's idea, but William Henry Harrison had reservations about trying it in the dead of winter. The best evidence Harrison had for this was the late 1812 Battle of the Mississinewa. As noted in the previous chapter, after relieving Fort Wayne, General Harrison had been launching punitive strikes throughout the Indiana Territory. By December this wave of destruction was directed on the Miami Indians along the Mississinewa River. On December 14 a force of six hundred mounted troops rode out from Fort Greenville. Three days later the force razed a village, destroying all food and shelter there and taking seventy-six people prisoner. By this time, however, a significant portion of the force was suffering from frostbite, forcing a withdrawal back to Greenville. By the time the unit returned to Greenville on December 28, half of the force had frostbite to some degree.

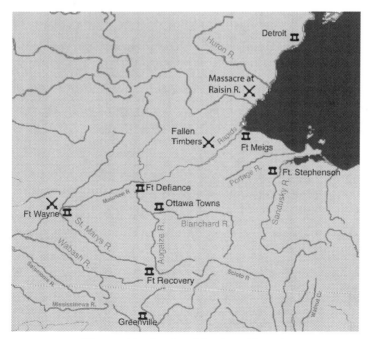

Figure 42: the Road back to Detroit

The cold weather would now play a pivotal role in one of the worst massacres of the war: the Massacre at the River Raisin. General Winchester, encamped with 1,500 Kentucky militia at Old Fort Defiance in Ohio, had been trying to move out toward Detroit for months. Back in early October, Harrison had ordered General Edward Tupper to move his eight hundred mounted men down the Maumee River past the rapids (present-day Grand Rapids). But between Tupper's slow response and his own men's complete dislike for him, instead of moving north he ended up in Urbana, discharging his troops. His move to the rapids doesn't begin until November 10. On November 14, while trying to cross the smaller Portage River, he lost many of his men and arms in the swift current. Only after all this did he reach the rapids, at which time his scouts found a hostile Indian unit just across the river.

When General Winchester's learned of Tupper's various calamities, he sent reinforcements under the command of Col. Lewis. But the reinforcements arrived at an abandoned camp; Tupper was across the river engaging the Indians. Thinking the Indians had defeated Tupper, Lewis returned to inform Winchester at Fort Defiance. Winchester didn't learn the truth for some time and only began moving to join Tupper on December 29, fighting heavy snow and freezing rain all the way to the rapids on January 10. By this time, Harrison had actually sent orders to Winchester to fall back to Fort Jennings (near Fort Recovery).

After arriving at the rapids, Winchester learned of British threats to burn Frenchtown. Immediately he sent a message to Harrison, telling him he had arrived and asking for support. This message, however, is delayed by snowstorms, preventing its arrival to Harrison until January 16. While Harrison was trying to send up additional troops, on January 18 Winchester sent a force of 500 men to Frenchtown. The following day they dispersed a British-led force of 100 regulars and 400 Indians. By this time, Winchester himself began marching to the River Raisin with an additional 250 men. On the twentieth he arrived and set up his camp, secure in the belief that the British would need several days to mount a counterattack.

Figure 43: *Tecumseh Saving Prisoners*, By Virtue, Emmins & Co. 1860 (Library of Congress.

Harrison, still at the Rapids, was concerned that Winchester had moved too far ahead, and he sent an aide forward to determine the situation. It was a wise move because Winchester hadn't counted on the skill and inventiveness of Canadian Colonel Procter. Using sleds to move six cannons and other supplies, on the evening of January 21 he crossed the frozen Detroit River with five hundred troops and eight hundred native warriors under the command of Chief Walk in the Water. By the dawn of January 22, Winchester's force had been completely surrounded.

The regulars on Winchester's right wing were the first to crumble under a hail of artillery fire. Flanked by the Indians, they withdrew only to be cut down as they fled. On the left flank, however the Kentucky militia was actually doing well and had to be ordered by the now captured General Winchester to surrender. In all, the United States had lost another 800 men and arms (220 killed, 80 wounded, and 500 prisoners). Procter had lost 24 men with 161 wounded, not counting the casualties among the Indians.

Procter may have won the battle, but he wasn't staying. His Indian scouts had told him that a US force of nine hundred men was heading for Frenchtown. Thus, he packed up his wounded and prisoners and headed back across the river to Fort Amherstburg. He left the eighty wounded US troops in the care of Chief Walk in the Water. The next day warriors killed the majority of the wounded men. When Tecumseh learned of this, he openly criticized Procter for allowing this to happen.

When Harrison heard what happened, there wasn't much he could do. To arrive at the Rapids by the twentieth, Harrison had traveled by sled instead of by foot. Thus, he had actually outrun his own troops and was essentially defenseless. On the twenty-second, he ordered a retreat from the north side of the rapids, burning the blockhouse Winchester had built earlier. He then met up with Pennsylvania troops at the Portage River and moved them to a location on the south side of the Maumee, across from the old British Fort Miami. There his troops built Fort Meigs, and almost three thousand men went into winter quarters there.

As for the rest of his force, Harrison sent these troops further east to establish Fort Stephenson on the Lower Sandusky. By March 1813, Harrison had less than 1,500 men (mostly Pennsylvania and Kentucky militia); the rest, having reached their required service time, had been discharged and left for their homes.

While General Harrison was trying to raise new troops, on May 1 British Colonel Procter attacked Fort Meigs with 2,000 regulars and 1,000 warriors under the command of Tecumseh. When the initial attack failed, Procter began a siege, shelling the fort with twelve- and twenty-four-pound cannons. Then on May 5, Colonel Clay arrived with 1,600 men to reinforce the fort. Several hundreds of Clay's men were captured, but Procter began to realize the siege was useless, and on May 9 he withdrew into Ohio. Harrison then spent the next few months chasing Procter or Tecumseh throughout the western half of Ohio.

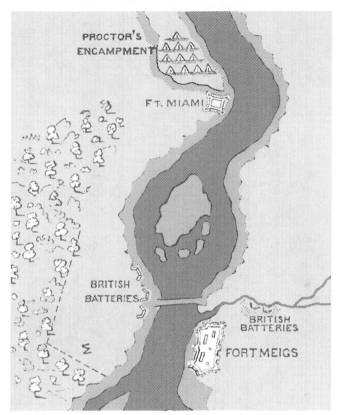

Figure 44: Fort Meigs, Ohio.

The Spring Campaign (Niagara)

While Harrison was trying to keep his troops together, Dearborn's troops were marching from Albany to Sackets's Harbor on Lake Ontario. On orders from the secretary of war, Dearborn had been ordered to abandon his march to Montreal and instead take command of the Niagara operation. Smyth had retired during the winter, leaving his remaining troops at Buffalo without a commander.

Figure 45: From upper left corner, clockwise: General Henry Dearborn, General Zebulon Pike, and the Death of Pike at York, Canada, 1813.

Further, Commodore Isaac Chauncey had been assembling a fleet at Sackets's Harbor, with which he intended to take control of Lake Ontario. An early April combined army and navy action against Kingston, the Canadian harbor on the lake, would break British control of Lake Ontario and all the surrounding areas. Immediately following this victory, Dearborn could then take York and Fort George with little resistance.

The problems were that Dearborn was ill and thus couldn't command. Further, both Dearborn and Chauncey had received intelligence that Governor General Prevost had reinforced Kingston with several thousand troops (false intelligence; Prevost had only six hundred troops). Thus they changed the plan into a straight attack against York, the army to be led by Brigadier General Zebulon Pike.

Pike landed four miles west of the town with 1,700 men on April 27. Immediately he engaged a strong point defended by a garrison of 600 men. In Pike's force were elements of the United States Army's one rifle regiment, the First. The fighting was fierce but short, and Pike's superior numbers quickly drove off the garrison. Then it happened. By order of the British commander, the strongpoint's powder magazine was detonated. General Pike was killed in the explosion, as were over 100 US and British troops. The battle had cost Dearborn 20 percent of his landing force and his field commander.

Figure 46: Upper image: Location of Fort George to Fort Niagara. Lower image: Capture of Fort George By Alonzo Chappel.

Though Dearborn was at the battlefield, he was too sick to leave his command ship, the corvette USS *Madison*. With Pike now dead, this left the troops on shore essentially without a commander. In their rage over the magazine detonation, they went on a rampage through the city. From April 29 to April 30, they looted York's public buildings and burned the parliament. By the time the troops left York on May 2, there was little left to support the British military. The effect was thus the same as the Russian's burning of Moscow had had on Napoleon's forces the previous year. This is not to justify the action, only to note that in this war, denying one's enemy supplies and shelter was a standard procedure.

Dearborn would not go on the offensive again until May 25, when Fort Niagara began shelling Fort George across the Niagara River. With the British commander's attention focused on this bombardment, Colonel Winfield Scott and Benjamin Forsyth were landed on the opposite shore. After fighting a pitched battle on the landing beach, Scott's forces repelled the British forces sent against him and quickly moved on the fort.

Sensing defeat, the British commander then ordered a retreat from the fort, as well as the spiking of all cannons and the detonation of the magazines. Scott and Forsyth were so close on the heels of the British troops that these last orders were not completed. As a result the fort, Newark, and the village of Queenston fell into US hands.

While all this was going on, Prevost had decided that the best defense was a good offense. Knowing that Dearborn had probably stripped all available troops and ships from Sackett's Harbor for his offensive against Fort Niagara, on May 26 Prevost struck with 800 regulars against the Sackett's Harbor defense force of just 400 regulars and 750 militiamen. Unfortunately for Prevost, General Jacob Brown of the New York militia was in charge of the defenses.

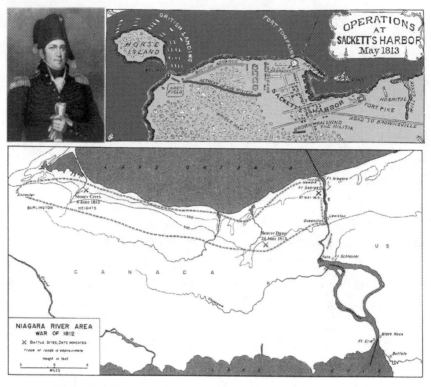

Figure 47: Upper Left- General Jacob Brown. Upper Right-
The Battle of Sacketts Harbor. Lower Niagara Pennisula

Brown performed a textbook defense involving two forward
lines of militia in front of a fortified battery of regulars. The first
line of riflemen fired and withdrew in what looked like a rout. The
second line then fired and withdrew to the fortified position with
the regulars. There the combined force threw back two assaults by
Prevost's troops. By that time, General Brown had rallied the first line
and launched it against Prevost's right flank.[42] Prevost's men, sensing
that they were about to be flanked and cut off from their boats,
withdrew from the battle in a panic. Suddenly the United States had
another major victory.

---

[42] This tactic is nearly identical to that used by General Morgan at Cowpens
during the revolution.

Unaware of Prevost's defeat at Sackett's Harbor, Dearborn now had total victory in his grasp. All he had to do was quickly pursue the British who had abandoned Fort George, and he would have control of all of Ontario, Canada. Unfortunately, his illness was preventing him from being the commander he once was. In the end, he waited several days and then sent two thousand men after the retreating British. These troops finally caught up with the British at a place called Stoney Creek on June 6. There, in a daring night action, the British routed this force with a group of only seven hundred troops.[43]

Dearborn then learned that Chauncey's squadron had withdrawn for no reason. Now unsupported by the sea and fearing a British naval landing behind his lines, he withdrew to Fort George. Two weeks later, he sent out a 500-man detachment to check the surrounding area. After spending the night at Queenston, the unit headed west for several miles until, at a place called Beaver Dams, they were attacked by about 450 British and native troops. The US troops promptly surrendered. Dearborn, stating he was incapacitated by his illness,[44] resigned his commission in early July,[45] thus ending what could have been the decisive campaign of the war.

---

[43] The commanding general, William Winder, was captured when, in the dark, he mistook the British as his own troops.

[44] This illness is never identified, but it may have been malaria. Lake fever was reported in Commodore Perry's command on Lake Erie, and "disease" was reported have taken a serious toll on both British and American troops in the Niagara area.

[45] His resignation was denied, and he was instead given an administrative position in New York City. He would later serve as the commanding officer for the court-martial of General Hull.

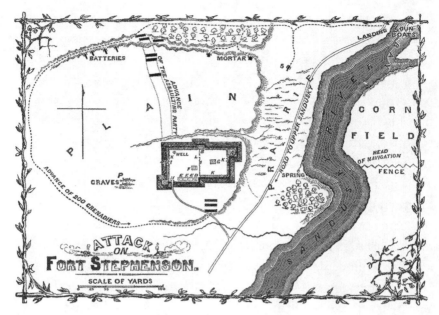

Figure 48: Attack on Fort Stephenson.

In July, Procter, having avoided Harrison's forces and being pushed by Tecumseh, tried to take Fort Meigs again. This time he tried to draw the small 100-man garrison out of the fort with a ruse that a reinforcement force was approaching. When this failed, he turned his attentions to Fort Stephenson, which he began shelling on August 2. The 160-man garrison at Stephenson again held off the attacks. Finally, Procter had no choice but to withdraw back to Canada. Now Harrison could begin plans for taking back Fort Detroit.

Assisting Harrison was Commodore Perry, who had just received from Dearborn twenty 24-pound carronades that Dearborn's troops had seized at York. Perry would use these guns to build a naval squadron and take control of Lake Erie from the British. If this was accomplished, the seizing of Fort Amherstburg and Detroit would be easy. The problem was actually building the fleet given the resources available at Presque Isle, Pennsylvania (present-day Erie).

Perry began by insuring that Presque Isle was well defended with two thousand troops and fortifications. A natural barrier Perry had going for him was a large sand bar at the mouth of the harbor. This barrier prevented the British from sailing into the harbor fully loaded—but it also prevented Perry from leaving harbor in the same way. Thus, for quite a while the British squadron of six ships was able to keep up a blockade of the harbor, but this had to be abandoned on August 1 due to lack of supplies.

While the British were sitting off the harbor, Perry built his fleet using shipwrights and boat builders recruited from as far away as Philadelphia. By late July he had completed several vessels, including two large brigs: the *Lawrence* and the *Niagara*. When the British returned on August 2, they found that in their absence Perry had moved the bulk of his fleet, including his largest ships, across the sandbar and then prepared them for action. Now outnumbered, the British commander withdrew to Amherstburg.

Figure 49: *Battle of Lake Erie,* by William H. Powell.

Perry, with ten ships at sea, was now the commander of Lake Erie. He could either wait for the British commander to come out to fight, which was inevitable, or he could support the movements of General Harrison against Detroit and Fort Amherstburg. Either way, the British would have to come out and fight. Since the failure at Sackett's Harbor and the lost of Forts George and Erie, supplies for Fort Amherstburg now had to come overland from Montreal. This time it was the British who were running out of supplies.

On September 9 the British came out to try to unblock the sea route to Montreal. Leading the force was their new ship, the *Detroit*, which had just been completed at Amherstburg. The following day the two forces clashed at Put-in-Bay. A four-hour battle ensued, costing Perry one hundred men and his flagship. But the day was his with the capture of all seven British ships. After a few days' worth of repairs, Commodore Perry was now the commander of at least fourteen ships. His next action was to ferry 2,500 infantry to Fort Detroit to link up with General Harrison and his one thousand mounted Kentucky militia. Procter—now seriously short of supplies, outnumbered on land, and subject to naval bombardment—abandoned both his forts and headed east for Montreal.

Figure 50: The Battle of the Thames and the death of Tecumseh.

Harrison pursued and, on October 5, caught Procter 85 miles east of Fort Amherstburg at the River Thames. There he ordered his Kentucky cavalry to charge the British ranks instead of using standard linear formations. The maneuver worked, and the 900 British troops and 1,000 warriors under Tecumseh were routed.[46] Of the 900 British regulars, only around 250 escaped. As for Tecumseh and his warriors, after giving a far better account for themselves than the British, he and several of his warriors were killed. The remaining warriors vanished into the forest.

The Battle of the Thames was the decisive victory Harrison wanted. With it he had secured the Michigan territory, Forts Detroit and Amherstburg (now renamed Fort Malden), and Lake Erie. He had also cut off supplies to Fort Mackinac and St. Joseph Island. With this accomplished, he dismissed his Kentucky militia and then took ship to Fort Erie to join the forces controlling Niagara.

Alabama

From this point forward, we have to switch to another battlefront in the war—a very unexpected battlefront. First, even with the previously noted defeats in 1812, the Southern War Hawks (not to be confused with House Speaker Henry Clay and John C. Calhoun) were supporting a move against Spanish Florida. Leading the charge was Andrew Jackson, who had raised his own militia of five thousand men and was ready to invade western Florida at Mobile. Congress, however, didn't want Jackson to be responsible for this and instead tasked General James Wilkinson, the governor general of Louisiana, to do this. This is the same General James Wilkinson who was a spy for the Spanish Crown.

---

[46] An example of how men knew total victory was near and how much they wanted to be there. Riding in the front line of the Kentucky militia was a very non-frontiersman, twenty-eight-year-old Commodore Oliver Hazard Perry. He wouldn't be left behind on the lake.

Figure 51: General Andrew Jackson By James Barton
Longacre 1820 and General James Wilkinson, By Charles
Willson Peale

On April 13, Wilkinson's men marched unopposed into Mobile.
By taking this port, US goods and produce from Alabama and western
Georgia could now travel down the Alabama River to the Gulf of
Mexico. Taking this port also greatly reduced revenue to the Spanish
forces operating out of Pensacola.

Though Wilkinson was given the authority to take Mobile, Andrew
Jackson didn't find out until he and his militia had traveled down the
Mississippi to Natchez. There he was ordered to disband his unit and
send his men home. Given that the men were not paid to cover the costs
of rations and other supplies, and that the trip down had been through
ice-choked sections of the upper Mississippi and Ohio Rivers, Jackson
wouldn't abandon his men. He trekked back to Tennessee with them,
earning his most famous moniker "Old Hickory."

The Summer of Missed Opportunities

As Old Hickory was making news, back in February a band of Creek Indians (previously under Tecumseh's command at Detroit) were heading back to the Creek nation in Alabama. Along the Ohio River, they massacred two families of settlers before entering the Tennessee River for home. Following their arrival in the Creek nation, the chiefs who were supporting the treaties with the United States had the warriors executed for murder. This was the spark that ignited a Creek civil war.

The warriors were what are now called Red Sticks, a band of upper-town Creeks who were radicalized by Tecumseh as pro-British and definitely anti-American. For months after the executions, the Red Sticks terrorized Creek villages that were, in the minds of the Red Sticks, assimilating into white culture. The United States didn't get caught up in it until July 21, 1813, when a group of soldiers stopped a group of Red Sticks returning from Florida with guns and ammunition.[47] The Battle of Burnt Corn, as it became known, is viewed as the Red Sticks' declaration of war against the United States.

By this time Dearborn had asked to be relieved of his command. This action made Wilkinson the senior military officer in the United States. Thus Secretary of War Armstrong gave him Dearborn's command coupled with a plan for a new invasion of lower Canada. Replacing Wilkinson in the South at Armstrong's insistence was Andrew Jackson, now promoted to major general. Wilkinson immediately went to Washington, leaving the Southwest in Jackson's control.

While Wilkinson was heading for Washington, another general was heading north to Burlington, Vermont. A few months earlier, General Hampton had been given General Dearborn's old Lake Champlain command. Soon after he arrived on July 3, the British took control of the lake using captured US Navy boats. For the next

---

[47] The leader of the Creeks had a letter of introduction to the Spanish governor from a "British" officer at Fort Amherstburg and four hundred dollars in cash.

two months, Hampton drilled and trained both his troops and his officers while a fleet was built to take back control of the lake.

While Hampton drilled his troops, Wilkinson arrived in Washington in late July. After consulting with Secretary of War Armstrong, on August 11 he headed north to take command of the US troops around Lake Ontario. He arrived at Sackett's Harbor on August 20 and then held a meeting with the general officers present on August 26 to take formal command. A few days later, he took to sea for Fort George and Fort Niagara to gather the troops for the campaign that was to start on September 15.

Going by the sea route might sound leisurely, but it wasn't. Lake Ontario was a war zone with the US and British fleets jockeying for position against the other since the lake unfroze in early April. By not attacking Kingston in April, the Americans lost a chance to take control of this important transportation route. By not following up the British failure at Sackett's Harbor, they lost a second chance at neutralizing the British fleet. Then in August, two US Navy schooners were lost in a lake storm followed by two more captured by the British. Thus, there was a distinct chance Wilkinson could have been captured en route to Fort George.

The risk of capture was far less concerning to Wilkinson than seeing Secretary of War Armstrong, who was due to arrive on September 5. Armstrong was going to take personal command of the invasion and had set up his command post in Sackett's Harbor. In fact he ordered that all correspondence between General Wilkinson and General Hampton at Albany was to go through him. This was because these two generals despised each other. Soon after arriving, however, he took ill with fever, leaving the preparations for the offensive in Wilkinson's hands.

While at Fort George, Wilkinson seemed to wait. What he was waiting for has been a matter of theory for over a century and a half, but it could have been troops: a reinforcing group of New York militia would not arrive until September 30. At this time Wilkinson gave Winfield Scott orders to move the majority of the regular troops to Sackett's Harbor. He then took a fast boat to Sackett's harbor, covering the distance in two days to arrive on October 4. He was so seasick when he arrived that he had to be carried ashore.

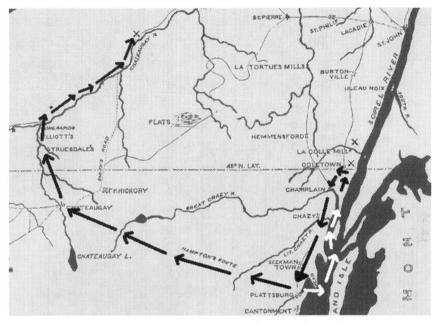

Figure 52: General Hampton's Line of March.

Of course, in Vermont Hampton was already moving north. On September 19 he sailed up Lake Champlain with four thousand men to the town of Champlain, seizing two outposts at Odelltown during a night landing. The next day he surveyed the situation. He was on the main road to Montreal with only a nine-hundred-man British force in front of him. But the summer weather was hot and dry, leaving him with a shortage of fresh water. At this point he decided to shift his offensive forty miles west to Four Corners, New York, on the Chateauguay River.

Though Hampton didn't intend for this to happen, his move westward caught the British completely by surprise. To make matters worse, the British spies in New York (disgruntled Federalists) were informing Prevost that Hampton was improving the road from Four Corners back to Plattsburg to allow him to quickly move back and forth.

Unable to determine from which direction Hampton was planning to move against Montreal, Prevost decided to push and sent Lt. Col. De Salaberry to raid Hampton's base at Four Corners. The raid was unsuccessful in either damaging Hampton or goading him into moving. It did, however, push Hampton to add to Governor General Prevost's problems by ordering Colonel Isaac Clark (Old Rifle) of the Burlington militia to raid British outposts on the north end of Lake Champlain. On October 11–12, Clark successfully raided Philipsburg, capturing a detachment of Canadian militia, as well as seizing contraband supplies being sold to Canada by New England war profiteers. Before long, the north end of Champlain was on fire as small British and US units raided across the border.

By this time, Wilkinson had recovered from his sea voyage and was getting ready to begin his movement up the Saint Lawrence River. He had ordered all available troops from Fort George to Sackett's Harbor to piece together an army of six thousand men. But to do it, he had essentially left undefended every place in western New York except Sackett's Harbor. This would come back to haunt the US Army before the year ended.

After having gathered as many troops as he could, on October 17 Wilkinson set out for Grenadier Island. The next day a three-day storm blew in, wreaking havoc on Wilkinson's flotilla. Fifteen large boats were lost, as were large amounts of rations, medical supplies,[48] and half of the force's gunpowder. On the twentieth the storm abated, allowing brigades that weathered at Henderson Harbor to reach Grenadier Island. Rains then began again, though not as strong, and

---

[48] It is said that following the storm, hundreds of Wilkinson's men were drunk. The reason? Two schooners carrying medical supplied had floundered in the gale. The surviving crewmen and troops salvaged some of the medical supplies, particularly the medicinal rum. The rest is history.

continued off and on through the twenty-four. While this storm raged, on October 21, Hampton began his march up the Chateauguay River. At this point the plan truly began to fall apart.

Hampton's earlier move west may have seemed correct, but when he began moving north, he was moving through heavy forest (ten to twelve miles in extent) that limited his movement to the road. De Salaberry added to Hampton's troubles by blocking the road with obstacles and then scattering Indian and French Canadian riflemen in the forest along the road. After two days of slow going, Hampton stopped to rest his troops and improve the twenty-five miles of road he had made behind him. He didn't begin the march again for two days, and when he did, he didn't get more than six miles before he encountered a British militia force of five hundred to eight hundred men blocking his path in a well-fortified position.[49]

The Battle of Chateauguay River would be famous in Canada as the battle that saved Canada. In reality it was an example of how a well-laid military plan can be destroyed by a single ill-sent message. The night before the battle, Hampton had sent one thousand men around to flank the British position with a second one thousand men to attack from the front. This left a strong reserve to follow up the eventual breakthrough.

Unfortunately, after the flanking force had departed, Hampton received a message from Armstrong that he misinterpreted as saying that the invasion was off and he should begin building winter quarters for his troops. Thus when the attack began, he withheld his reserves. This was a serious military error because he was basically leaving his committed troops to their fate. The flanking unit was repulsed, and after demonstrating perfect parade ground military maneuvers, the forward unit was intimidated into withdrawing without even scratching the Canadian defense. Hampton's whole force then marched the 30 miles back to New York with only 150

---

[49] De Salaberry had been building his defense at this point on the river road since Hampton had arrived at Four Corners in late September.

dead, wounded, or missing out of the 4,000 men he'd started with. By the thirtieth they were back in Four Corners.

Figure 53: *Bataille de la Chateauguay*, By Henri Julien. Depiction of Canadian Troops at Chateaugary, and Lt. Col. De Salaberry (Library and Archives of Canada).

On returning to Four Corners, Hampton sent a letter to Wilkinson, via Armstrong, informing him of the events. Armstrong was no longer at Sackett's Harbor, having abandoned his headquarters and returned to Washington, completely fed up with the situation. The reason he was fed up was Wilkinson, who had been coming back and forth from Grenadier Island to Sackett's Harbor with nothing but tales of disaster.

Letter, To Secretary of War Armstrong from General Wilkinson, October 24, 1813. "The extent of injury to our craft, clothing, arms, and provisions greatly exceed our apprehensions, and has subjected us to the necessity of furnishing clothing, and of making repairs and equipments to the flotilla generally. In fact, all our hopes have been nearly blasted; but, thanks to the same providence that placed us in jeopardy, we are surmounting our difficulties, and, god willing, I shall pass Prescott on the night of the 1st or 2d proximo."

Wilkinson tried to fulfill this promise, having actually sent troops to French Creek on the twenty-ninth. But the weather never seemed to relent, and ten inches of snow had fallen before the flotilla left

Grenadier Island. The British were also out in force, having eluded Chauncey's blockade of Kingston.

On November 1 they found Wilkinson's advanced force under the command of General Brown at Alexandria Bay. Before the day was out, two brigs, two schooners, and eight gunboats with troops attacked. The British withdrew after two days of fighting, giving the United States a victory.

Wilkinson arrived at French Creek the following day, still unaware that Hampton had already returned to Four Corners. It was here that he informed his men that their target was Montreal and not Kingston, and on the fifth his flotilla of three hundred boats set sail. The British immediately followed with as many men and boats as they could gather.

By evening US forces had reached Morristown, where they waited until morning. The next day they moved to just three miles from Ogdensburg, where Wilkinson disembarked most of his troops. He was going to march his troops around the town to Red Mill while having the now lightened boats run past the guns of Fort Prescott (across the river from Ogdensburg). It was at Ogdensburg that Wilkinson finally learned of Hampton's defeat.

Wilkinson immediately sent orders to Hampton to renew his march and meet his force at St. Regis. That evening General Brown succeeded in moving the flotilla past the British batteries with only minor damage, and on the seventh the force again was moving down river. That was all but 1,200 men under Col. Macomb, who were landed on the Canadian shore. These troops were to engage small British posts along the river before the flotilla arrived.

Among the troops landed were Lt. Col. Forsyth and the First Rifle Regiment. Forsyth had enlarged his unit by arming New York militiamen with federal rifles. These forces would be very effective in the days to come as the flotilla continued to move downriver.

On the eighth Wilkinson, now too ill to stand, held a council of officers to determine whether they should proceed to Montreal. After receiving an affirmative, he then began landing his dragoons on the Canadian shore to march with Macomb along the river road. This took all day, and after nightfall on the ninth Wilkinson learned that behind him was a large British force with ships and gunboats. Furthermore, he soon learned there was a blockhouse at the base of the Longue Saut Rapids.

Wilkinson sent General Brown forward to take the blockhouse while the rest of his army kept the British flotilla at bay. The British boats were beaten back, but the defense took the majority of the day, and the boat pilots would not brave the rapids at night. Thus Wilkinson was forced to moor his boats near the farm of a Mr. John Crysler a few miles from Williamsburg.

The next day Wilkinson was informed that the blockhouse was taken and the route was clear, but in taking the blockhouse, Colonel Forsyth had been wounded and was no longer fit for service. On hearing this, Wilkinson ordered the march resumed down the river. Within the hour, Wilkinson received the news that the British were advancing on his rear, having disembarked their troops from their boats the previous evening.

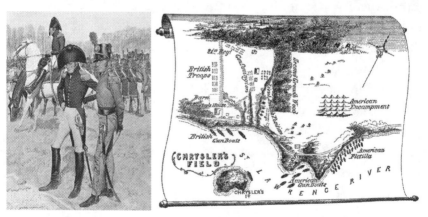

Figure 54: First Rifle Regiment and the battle map of Crysler's farm.

Wilkinson ordered General Boyd to engage the enemy with his forces. Boyd, a soldier of fortune, was hardly the best choice for this mission. Yet there was no one else available. Brown, Macomb, and

Scott were on the other side of the rapids. Boyd throws his units at the British with little regard to position, terrain, and artillery support. His units slammed straight into British units in well-selected positions. For a time there was a chance the United States would turn the British left flank, but poor leadership and low ammunition (problems the British didn't have) forced the US troops to withdraw.

On the right flank, the US commander, Col. Covington, mistook the grey uniforms of the Forty-ninth Regiment (the Grey Tigers) as being the uniforms of militia. It was an unfortunate mistake because he sent his lesser regular troops against these experienced troops. Soon he was mortally wounded, as was his second in command. With no commanders on the field, the US units began disintegrating.

US artillery finally arrived at this point, only to find itself the target of the British advance. The Forty-ninth advanced through grapeshot against the cannons—only to suddenly find itself the target of the US Second Dragoons. After repeated attacks, the Forty-ninth forced the dragoons to withdraw, but by then most of the US guns had also been withdrawn. Finally the American Twenty-first Regiment under Macomb arrived to check the US retreat and defend the cannons. At this point the British ended the assault and withdrew back to more defensible positions.

The United States had lost 102 killed, 237 wounded, and 14 missing; the British had 22 killed, 150 wounded, and 13 missing. In percentages the United States had lost less than 6 percent of all its troops, whereas the pursuing British had lost 23 percent of its unit. But the reality was that the British won because Wilkinson could only commit two thousand men to the attack and had lost 17.5 percent while not gaining any ground. The next morning Wilkinson went down the rapids to Cornwall. There, he learned Hampton would not be meeting him at St. Regis. At this point Wilkinson, with the blessings of his junior officers, crossed back into the United States.

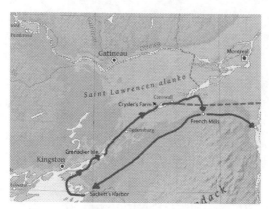

Figure 55: Wilkinson's line of march.

The flotilla then traveled up the Salmon River toward French Mills (now Covington, New York). There in this little outpost, almost six thousand US regulars waited until late January for orders while trying to keep from freezing or being killed in British raids. Eventually they were ordered to abandon the post. Half under General Brown marched to Sackett's Harbor, and the rest under Wilkinson marched to Plattsburg.

Regarding Rifles and Riflemen

Some points to be noted at this time. At Chateauguay General Hampton seems to have only had riflemen among his militia and this appears to be by accident. The fact Burlington Militia Colonel Isaac "old Rifle" Clark used riflemen in his raid on Philipsburg was simply his preference. Hampton doesn't seem to have had any use for them even as French Canadian riflemen harassed his troops up the road to Chateaugary.

As for General Wilkinson, the distribution of spare federal rifles to New York Militia by Col Forsyth indicates that in at least his mind there were not enough riflemen in the invasion force (even among the New York Militia). The use of the riflemen in the land force, to clear hardpoints along the banks of the St Lawrence river, showed that Wilkinson was at least willing to use them. The battle at Crysler's farm however points to the difficulty of trying to be in two places at the same time: having all the riflemen clearing the blockhouse at the Long Saut meant there were none at Crysler's farm to engage the British before the US artillery arrived.

Finally, it should be noted where the riflemen went after the invasion was abandoned. From the records the New York militiamen returned home with their new guns while Forsyth's 1st Rifle companies went to Plattsburg. No Riflemen followed General Jacob Brown to Sackett's Harbor, though he would eventually get one company of riflemen.

The End of 1813

Now that this tale of stupidity is over, let's finish this wonderfully dumb year in US history. As previously noted, in order to build his army, Wilkinson virtually stripped the Niagara zone of any regular troops, leaving only militia to secure the forts taken that year. Armstrong had ordered William Henry Harrison to Niagara after the battle of the Thames, but that was in mid-October. Harrison only arrived at Sackett's Harbor with 1,300 men on November 16, four days after Crysler's Farm and the final end of the second Canadian invasion. His orders had not required him to leave any troops at Fort George or Fort Niagara on his way up to Sackett's.

Back at Fort George, Militia General McClure was beginning to feel the cold. He had only 60 regulars and some 140 Canadian and US volunteers, most at Fort George. His militiamen, who arrived in September, were reaching the end of their required militia service. This militia was also filled with New York Federalists who were anti-war and wouldn't cross the border; thus, they were posted at Fort Niagara.

Figure 56: *A Soldiers Wife at Fort Niagara*, By T. Walker, 1860.

A depiction of the South Redoubt at Fort Niagara where a six-pound cannon was fired at the British. What is open to question is whether a fort officer's wife was actually loading (Source: Library of Congress).

Feeling his situation impossible, on December 10 McClure withdrew from Fort George and consolidated his regulars in Fort Niagara. While leaving, he burned the towns of Newark and Queenston but left Fort George intact. He then withdrew his troops and the majority of the militia units to Buffalo. It set the stage for a disaster.

The British were so enraged by the burning of these towns that they launched military actions across the Niagara River into the United States. On December 19 in a daring night attack, the British took Fort Niagara from its 320-odd regular army defenders.

Using a stolen password and other tricks, the attacking force was able to get through the gates before the defenders could raise the alarm. Only the south redoubt and a barracks used to house sick personnel gave the attackers a fight. At the end of the battle, the

United States had 64 dead, 360 captured, and 4,000 stands of arms seized. The fort commander was then taken prisoner at his home a few miles away.

Then Riall launched a series of cross-river attacks directly against US towns and villages, all to be burned. Lewiston, Manchester, and Fort Schlosser were lost. Buffalo was only saved by the action of the Canadian volunteers at Tonawanda Creek. The British came back days later with 1,000 militia and 400 Indians, and they burned Black Rock and a portion of Buffalo. As for McClure, after arriving at Buffalo, he was told the militia wouldn't follow his orders. The defense was actually handled by the 1,200 militia of General Amos Hall, who gave the British commander Riall considerable trouble before withdrawing.

The Creek Civil War

With western New York in flames, a civil war had broken out in Mississippi. You may remember that when Wilkinson was sent to Sackett's Harbor, Andrew Jackson was placed in command of all Southern troops. You may also remember that a Creek civil war had broken out, which for the moment the United States was watching from the sidelines. That changed on August 30 when eight hundred Red Sticks massacred almost five hundred mixed-blood Creek settlers, whites, and Africans at Fort Mims, Alabama.

Jackson immediately began rebuilding his earlier force of Tennessee militia (two thousand men). Five days later, however, Jackson was nearly killed in a personal fight in a hotel in Nashville. It would not be until mid-September that he was fit enough to command his troops. On September 27 his units assembled at Fayetteville and moved south to Huntsville, where they linked up with Brigadier General Coffee. From there they marched to the Coosa River and built Fort Strother on the western bank, where the Coosa links with Canoe Creek. Nearby was the first of the Red Stick villages, Tallushatchee.

Figure 57: Massacre at Fort Mims.

On November 3, when Wilkinson was working his way north to Montreal, Jackson's forces surrounded this village and annihilated it (200 dead of a population of around 284). From there he moved to Talladega, where he killed almost 300 more Red Sticks who had been besieging the village: the Talladega Creeks were pro-United States. After relieving the town, he returned to Fort Strother to await supplies.

The war in the South almost ended at this point because many Creek warriors began leaving the Red Stick movement; the destruction of Tallushatchee and their defeat at Talladega made many reconsider their situation. But fate intervened on November 18 when forces under General Cocke, without orders from Jackson, attacked a Hillabee Indian village that had sent a peace party to Jackson.

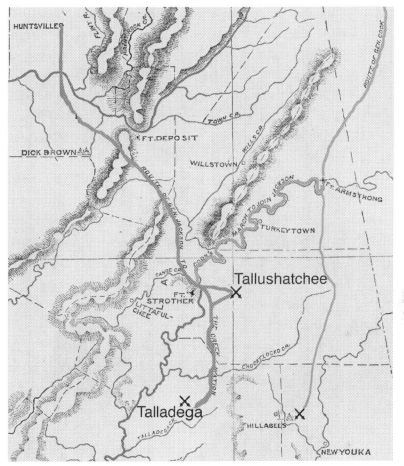

Figure 58: Jackson's line of March 1813.

Cocke had stopped at a point on the Coosa River, some seventy miles from Fort Strother. There he awaited supplies and built his own Fort Armstrong in honor of the secretary of war. But the supplies never came; the water level on the Tennessee River was too low for boats. Not wanting to have to share his meager supplies with Jackson, who he believed was equally low on supplies, he decided to stay at Fort Armstrong. In the meantime he sent a detachment of mounted troops and Cherokee Indians to attack villages to the south that he believed harbored Red Stick leaders.

The detachment under General White cut a path of destruction through Creek territory. When they arrived at the chief village of the Hillabees on November 18, they attacked without provocation and without mercy. Sixty warriors were killed, and 250 widows and orphans were forced to march back to Fort Armstrong as prisoners. The remaining Hillabee villages, not knowing Jackson wasn't involved, blamed him for the crime and entered the conflict on the side of the Red Sticks.

The attack on the Hillabees was just the beginning. To the south Brigadier General John Floyd commanded 950 Georgia militiamen and a force of friendly Creek Indians under the command of William McIntosh. Floyd planned to attack Auttose, which was a holy ground to the Red Stick movement. On November 28 he attacked killing 200 Creeks and destroyed 400 homes. Now short of supplies but burdened with other items, he withdrew back to Fort Mitchell on the Chattahouchee.

Major military action for the year then came to an end in early December, when Jackson's militia, like McClure's, reached their required service time. Jackson had no choice but to let them leave and go into winter camp at Fort Strother. General Cocke joined him there on December 12, bringing with him a large amount of supplies finally shipped up the Tennessee River, as well as anything that wasn't nailed down along his path of march.

Military action in the South officially ended on December 23 when General Clairborne attacked the Indian village called Econochaea with 1,000 men and 150 Choctaws. The village was a hotbed of Red Stick activity and was reported to have been executing both whites and half-breeds in large numbers. The attack killed 30 warriors and resulted in the destruction of 200 Indian homes. Clairborne then withdrew to a supply cache called Fort Deposit on the Alabama River. There, his volunteers and militia reached the end of their terms of service, leaving him with only 60 men by January 23, 1814.

In Closing

By the end of 1813, the United States could only claim the successful taking of Lake Erie and Fort Detroit. They also had close to 6,000 regular army units (freezing) at the New York–Canadian border. The size of the Federal Army had almost reached 30,000 men, and the militia system had succeeded in deploying close to 104,000 militiamen throughout the country. But the United States had lost control of Lake Ontario, had lost Fort Niagara and Fort George, and had had most of the towns and villages along the Niagara frontier burned. British ships were blockading the major US harbors, and British forces had started raiding and burning coastal towns and villages from Maine to Virginia. Finally, in the South, there was an Indian civil war that was threatening the security of Tennessee, Louisiana, and Georgia.

Of course the real problem was in Europe. Following Napoleon's failure in Russian, 1813 had been another bad year for the emperor: he had lost Spain and then much of Eastern Europe. As a result Britain could now redirect large military units to the North American campaign. By the time Wilkinson actually reached Cornwall, Prevost was massing close to fifteen thousand militia and regulars to stop him. The chance to take Montreal had long been lost. Now the problem would be not losing the United States.

CHAPTER 5

The Spring and Summer of 1814

We have reached the third year of the war. As we have seen, the previous two years had not been good for the United States: poor generals, lack of proper supplies, bad roads and a limited transportation system, poorly trained regular troops, and a militia wondering whose side they actually were on. The war had shown the problems with the US military system to the *n*th degree. Yet it also showed that the United States was resilient enough to survive these calamities, and a part of that was the government's allowance of debate and criticism.

But the government did have a problem with prima donnas. In our modern system, the president is the primary prima donna followed by the VP and then the speaker of the house. In 1812 they also had the secretary of war, the secretary of state, and the individual army generals. All acted as if this conflict was to be their means of achieving the kind of power in North America that Napoleon had achieved in Europe.

Henry Clay, the speaker of the house and the head of the war hawks, saw the war as a means of elevating the stature of both himself and the country. Armstrong, by trying to lead the troops to Canada, was trying on the mantel of George Washington and commander in chief. Monroe was also looking for an excuse to resurrect his military career and gain the power that would bring. The only one who wanted out of the war seems to have been President James Madison, who as a congressman had constantly pushed for a law giving men the right to abstain from forced military service on religious grounds. Now he was required to force every male in the United States into military service to save the nation.

Too Late a Change in Policy

The problem of who was in command was just one of the hard lessons the United States was learning at this point in the war. Another was the problem caused by the caliber clause in the militia act. As noted, there was a major lack of riflemen in the regular army. At the start of the war, there was one rifle regiment in the entire army compared to the force Anthony Wayne had at Fallen Timbers. French Canadian riflemen were a serious threat in the mind of General Hull at Detroit. Wilkinson ran ragged his one battalion of riflemen in driving off Canadian riflemen during his advance up the St. Laurence River. In numerous other events, either the presence of US riflemen saved the day, or the lack of them proved to be a liability.

This didn't mean there were no riflemen, as noted by the militia returns. There were plenty of riflemen in the militia, particularly in the militia in the western and southern states. But east of the Blue Ridge Mountains and north of Pennsylvania, riflemen became a rare item. Of course there was little support for such men by the Federal government with the exception of the Ranger Corp in the far west. That all changed on February 10, 1814, when congress passed Statute II, Chapter XI, an act to raise three regiments of riflemen. This law called for three units to be raised immediately, and the men would serve for five years or the duration of the war. Each regiment would have 10 companies of 106 men each (16 officers and noncoms and 90 privates), making for over 4,000 army riflemen when the First Rifle Regiment was included.

The problem was when the war began, there was only 6,911 rifles in Federal ordnance, and many of these guns had been lost, broken, or otherwise distributed by this point in the war. As an example, during Wilkinson's march up the St. Lawrence, Major Forsythe had distributed to New York militiamen several hundred Model 1803 rifles. When the men's service time was up, they were allowed to keep the arms, though some of the men may have purchased the weapon. Another example of losses of rifles can be seen in such events as the Battle of Ogdensburg were the First Regiment was effectively run out of town by the British, leaving any spare arms to be seized. Add to this simple breakage while in service—in the three years of war, Harpers Ferry had repaired over 750 rifles—and one can begin to wonder how the government was going to arm these new units.

Documents from the period indicate they did have a problem. Springfield Armory didn't make rifles, only muskets. Although Harpers Ferry did make rifles, in the war it was busy making over thirty thousand muskets and repairing another three thousand. To support this action would require a complete change in production activity at the two Federal armories, plus new civilian contracts. On January 19, Callender Irvine of the Commissary Generals Office began this transition with a letter to the US inspector of arms, M. T. Wickham at Harpers Ferry. In this letter Wickham was informed of the new regiments and the need to begin production of new Model 1803 style rifles in the "shortest possible time." Further, Wickham was to have two rifles made immediately: one to be sent to a New England facility for contract production, the other to Virginia.[50] The rest were to be built as quickly as possible using rifle parts, or even damaged rifles, already in Federal store.

Three months later in late April, Callender had succeeded in getting the Philadelphia arms firm of Deringer and Tyron to begin making the rifles without a Federal contract. But getting rifles into production wasn't the same as fielding them, and in June Callender Irvine reported that there were no rifles in store near the city of Philadelphia that were fit for service (i.e., that met Federal standard).

---

[50] This facility in Virginia may have been the Virginia Manufactory, where rifles were built for the State of Virginia.

A request for three hundred Federal model rifles could not be filled unless the arms were made at Harpers Ferry. Callender then suggested that the rifles distributed by Forsythe be collected even if the men had paid for them.

Ramping up production would continue, and on October 3 the secretary of war ordered three experienced armorers at Harpers Ferry to be sent to Springfield with a pattern rifle. This would result in the production of some three thousand rifle parts that would later be assembled at Harpers Ferry as the Model 1817 Army rifle. The next month Robert Johnson of Connecticut began production of two thousand rifles of the later 1817 pattern. Of course none would be delivered before the war ended.

In the South

When we finished 1813, Jackson was without supplies and almost out of men. With the arrival at Fort Strother of nine hundred mounted Tennessee riflemen (sixty-day volunteers) in early January, however he was again able to take the offensive. On the fifteenth he led seven hundred of these men to Talladega, where two hundred Cherokee and Creek Indians joined him. From here he began marching to the Tallapoosa River to perform an "excursion."

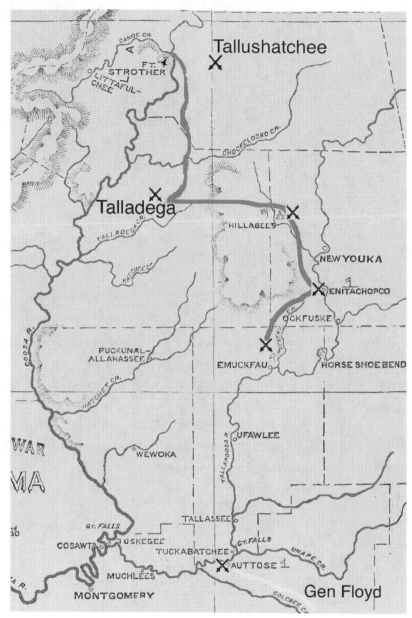

Figure 59: Jackson's second offensive.

First, he went east to the Hillabee Creek and the site of the attack the previous year. Then he followed the river south to Enitochopco on the Tallapoosa River. After camping outside the Creek town, he headed for Emucfau Creek and the town by the same name at the bend in the Tallapoosa River. He barely was within sight of Emucfau when several hundred Creek warriors attacked on January 2. Jackson's men repulsed them, but the number of injured in his force, and the determination of the Creek warriors, forced him to abandon his plan to attack Emucfau.

As he withdrew, the Creeks pursued, catching him as his force was preparing to cross the Enitochopco Creek on January 24. Whereas at Emucfau the recruits had performed perfectly, here after an initial attempt to stand and fight, many fled toward the creek. Only twenty-five Tennessee riflemen held their ground, standing off more than a hundred Creek warriors.

As the riflemen fought, Jackson's artillery unit, which was halfway across the river, turned around and dragged the six-pounder into position on the creek bank. There they succeeded in firing two charges of grapeshot at the Creeks while under fire. A company of musketmen also returned to shore to join the Tennessee riflemen, followed soon by Jackson and the rest of the force. Very quickly thereafter, the Creek warriors were driven off.

In just three days of battle, Jackson had lost 20 men and had 75 wounded. Considering the size of his force to begin with, he had suffered 13 percent casualties. For the Creeks, out of an estimated 500 warriors, the number of dead from both battles is estimated at 189, with 26 at Enitochopco Creek. On a whole, Jackson could claim victory by the numbers, but Jackson was extremely lucky.

The reason Jackson survived was because the majority of the Red Stick force was either at Horseshoe Bend or assembled to ambush General Floyd. The Georgian militia that had burned Auttose the previous year had been resupplied and reinforced to 1,227 men and 400 Indians. General Floyd was now heading for Tuckabatcha to continue the conflict. While encamped on Calebee Creek, however, on the night of January 26 the Red Sticks attacked his force. In the darkness the Creeks had Floyd at a disadvantage, but as dawn broke, Floyd could see what was happening and thus concentrated his forces against the warriors. These forces included riflemen under Captains William E. Adams, Merriweather, and Ford, who finally broke the Creek forces. These riflemen then chased the Creeks back into the swamp from which they had emerged the previous night.

In all, Floyd had 17 dead and 132 wounded, not including the deaths of five friendly Indians and the wounding of 15 more. It is uncertain how many Creek warriors were involved in the battle, though 37 were reported dead. Though essentially the victor, the battle forced Floyd to withdraw, returning to Fort Mitchell by early February.

The withdrawal of Floyd left Jackson's small force as the only Federal force in Alabama. On returning to Fort Strother, he set his men to building flatboats. These were to be used to move supplies down the Coosa River from Fort Armstrong to Fort Strother. He then ordered his sixty-day volunteers to march to Huntsville for honorable discharge. This obedience to the enlistment terms produced a strong enthusiasm in Tennessee to serve under him, and by February two thousand fresh troops were in the shadow of Lookout Mountain heading for the Coosa River while an equal number were arriving at Huntsville.

Jackson's joy at the news of these reinforcements was added to on February 6 with the arrival of the six-hundred-strong Thirty-ninth Regiment of the US Army. Soon after this, General Coffee's brigade of mounted men arrived followed by the news that the entire Choctaw nation had joined the war against the Red Sticks. Suddenly Jackson was at the head of a three-thousand-man force whose only limitation was supplies.

The Creeks were of course aware of these developments and had decided to concentrate themselves at Horseshoe Bend. The defenders included the entire populations of the Creek towns of Hillabee, Ockfuske, Eufaulahache, New Youka, Oakchoie, Hickory Ground, and Fish Pond. This situation prompted still other chiefs to look toward Jackson. They informed him of the gathering—information Jackson then used to put his army in motion.

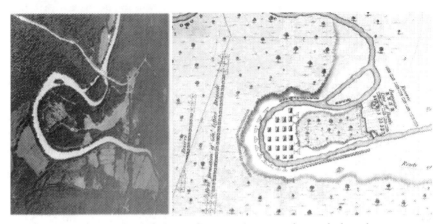

Figure 60: Aerial shot of Horseshoe Bend coupled with a map of the Creek Indian defenses.

After assigning four hundred men to the defense of Fort Strother, Jackson ordered the Thirty-ninth Regiment south by way of the Coosa River with all the flat boats and stores they could handle. While this force was moving downstream, he marched directly south to the Cedar River, where they met the flat boats on March 21. There he built Fort Williams, to store the supplies and provide a safe haven if the attack against the Creeks wasn't victorious. Finally, on March 24 he marched with two thousand men to Horseshoe Bend, or Choloco Litabixee as the Creeks called it. He arrived there on March 27 after cutting a new trail across the ridge that separated the Coosa River from the Tallaposa.

Where the Creeks saw the Horseshoe as a highly defensible position, Jackson saw a barrel to shoot into. The Creek plan had been to build a defensive wall across the peninsula—one that they could shoot from with immunity.[51] Behind this they placed obstacles to slow the movement of anyone who succeed in penetrating the wall. In case escape was necessary, enough canoes were positioned along the riverside of the peninsula to be used to evacuate the encampment. The problem was, what would they do if the canoes suddenly ended up in the enemy's hands?

Figure 61: The Battle of Horseshoe Bend.

---

[51] There is some information that Spanish agents from Pensacola helped in planning the wall for the Creeks.

Jackson started his siege by launching an artillery attack against the wall (or Breastwork) at 10:00 a.m. in the morning of March 28. As the cannonballs from his two guns bounced or embedded in the wood timbers of the wall, General Coffee and a group of Cherokees swam across the river and removed the canoes. While the Creeks watched Jackson seeming to bang his head against their wall, Coffee paddled back across the river, loaded two hundred men, returned to the Horseshoe, and then began burning the cabins and huts of the town.

The smoke was Jackson's signal to launch his true attack. While the Creeks were now busy fighting the fires and the members of Coffee's attack force, at noon the Thirty-ninth and a brigade of East Tennessee volunteers moved against the wall.[52] The battle became intense as the Creeks used both gun and arrows in an attempt to prevent the breaching of the wall. One arrow struck a young ensign named Samuel Houston,[53] later to become famous in Texas.

Once the wall was crossed, the battle was essentially lost for the Red Sticks. They could do nothing but try to flee by swimming the river. About 250 were killed trying this by the Tennessee riflemen of General James Doherty. Others tried to hide in the brush and thickets of the obstacle zone, only to be discovered and killed. None surrendered, forcing Jackson to clear the entire Horseshoe with fire, gun, and sword.

It took well into the evening for the battle to truly end, at which point Jackson had killed close to 800 of the 1,000 Creek warriors that defended the Horseshoe. He had also taken prisoner over 300 women and children. As to his own losses, Jackson had 32 dead and 99 wounded among his soldiers, along with 18 dead and 36 wounded

---

[52] In taking the wall, Major Lemuel Purnell Montgomery lost his life. His Grandfather Hugh Montgomery died in the assault on Quebec during the revolution. The city of Montgomery, Alabama, is named for Hugh, and the county is named for Lemuel.

[53] Houston continued in the battle only to be shot twice in the shoulder later.

among the Cherokees and five dead and 11 wounded among the friendly Creeks who went in with Coffee.

After defeating the Red Sticks at Horseshoe Bend, Jackson returned to Fort Williams on April 2. After determining that spring rains had made the river too swollen for the boats to carry his supplies, on April 4 Jackson marched his men with as much as they could carry toward the Hickory grounds at the confluence of the Coosa and Tallapoosa Rivers. From there he went up the Tallapoosa to Fushatchie, where he hoped to make contact with the eastern army, which he hoped would have supplies. All he found were a few prisoners.

After this, Jackson withdrew back to the Coosa and the site of the old French fort of Toulouse. Here he erected Fort Jackson, and while awaiting resupply he received Chief William Weatherford,[54] the leader of the Red Sticks. Chief Weatherford had survived the Battle of Horseshoe Bend, but instead of fleeing to Florida as others had, he now voluntarily surrendered to Jackson. Jackson was so impressed that he spared Weatherford's life and used him to bring the remaining upper Creeks to the peace table. On April 20 General Pinckney arrived with troops from the Carolinas, relieving Jackson and his command. It is said when Jackson's men heard they were free to go home, in two hours the whole force was moving up the Coosa River. Jackson returned home with his men to the Hermitage near Nashville, Tennessee.

Though the Creek war was over, the war in the South wasn't, and Jackson's rest would be short-lived.

---

[54] Weatherford was only thirty-four years old when he became the leader of the Red Sticks. Following the war, he settled down on a farm in Monroe County, Alabama. Ten years later, he died from excessive fatigue following a bear hunt.

Figure 62: *Interview Between General Jackson & Weatherford*. By John Reuben Chapin 1859

Lake Champlain, 1814

When we last left General Wilkinson, he was at French Mills suffering from frostbite, typhus, and anything else one could think of. In January Armstrong ordered him to move his unit to Plattsburg, while General Brown returned to Sackett's Harbor with two thousand men. It was the beginning of Armstrong's plan to get rid of the dead wood in the army general staff.

Armstrong had in his mind those he wanted in high command positions, and the defeats of the previous year had given him his chance. The war had shown him the men he wanted: Andrew Jackson, Jacob Brown, and Winfield Scott. William Henry Harrison was not on the list because Armstrong despised him so much he effectively stripped him of his command. Eventually Harrison couldn't take anymore, and on May 11, 1814, he submitted his resignation. Officially, the president should have accepted or denied the resignation, but the letter reached Armstrong first, who accepted in the president's name. That left only Wilkinson, and Armstrong had placed him in a location where he couldn't do anything since he had not done the honorable thing and resigned as Dearborn, Smyth, Hampton, and Harrison, had done.

When the spring came, however, Wilkinson saw a chance to regain his reputation. In late March he believed he could take Lacolle Mills, the site of the earlier battle in 1812. On March 30 he moved out with a force of four thousand men, including Forsyth's riflemen. Also in the advance was General Macomb, who was in charge of Wilkinson's artillery units. It was these units that Wilkinson was betting on because he had a huge eighteen-pound cannon among the other artillery pieces. Wilkinson wasn't going to storm the blockhouse—he was going to blast it completely out of existence.

The defenders at Lacolle numbered less than one hundred men, though mostly regulars with a smattering of Canadian militia with rifles. Whereas before they were in the wooden blockhouse on the north bank of the Lacolle River, now men were also placed in a large stone structure (a mill) on the south side of the river. In addition to the stone mill, around the blockhouse were entrenchments to assist in repelling an attack.

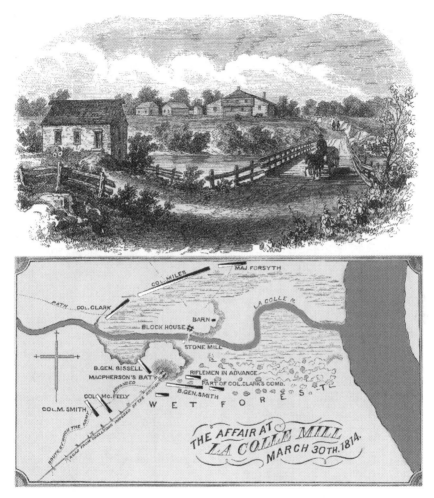

Figure 63: Engraving showing the stone mill and the blockhouse.

Wilkinson should have sent in Forsyth and his riflemen to quickly storm the position and take both the blockhouse and the stone mill. Instead, he sent Forsyth and his riflemen across the river to get behind the blockhouse and prevent a British retreat. Of course, this meant Forsyth and his men were effectively out of the battle unless the British tried to retreat or reinforcements came to help.

The British noticed the movement of troops behind them, and following the sending of runners for help, they waited for the attack. They waited and they waited, but Wilkinson's massive artillery bombardment never began. A sudden, unexpected thaw in the ground south of the stone mill made the soil too soft to emplace the huge eighteen-pound cannon. Thus, Macomb tried to make do with three smaller twelve-pound cannons and a 5.5-inch mortar.

The smaller weapons had to be emplaced closer to the mill (approximately 250 yards), placing the crews within range of the few rifles in the stone mill. As the bombardment began, Macomb then realized that the thick stonewalls of the mill were practically impervious to the shells of his smaller cannons. The British troops at the blockhouse now fired Congreave rockets over the mill and into the forces commanded by US General Bissell, who were visible on the left flank of the battery. Several men were injured, including the main artillery officer, Captain McPherson, who was wounded under the chin. He continued to command the battery until he was shot in the thigh by a British rifleman. A further rifle shot killed the second in command, Lieutenant Larrabee, leaving only Lieutenant Sheldon in command of the cannons.

While the bombardment was underway, two British companies arrived at the blockhouse from the river. Now reinforced to nearly five hundred men, the British commander, Major Handcock, decided to assault the cannons. Under normal circumstances, it would be a foolhardy venture given the differences in strength of the forces, but Handcock didn't know the size of Wilkinson's army because several units were hidden in the woods on the right flank of the cannons. When the British charged, they would encounter these units under the command of General Smith, as well as a few of Forsyth's riflemen left behind with the main force.

Several attempts were made to seize the US cannons, to no avail. Then two additional British companies, one Voltiguers and one Fencible Grenadier, pushed their way past Colonel Clark's men and reached the blockhouse. Now having close to nine hundred men, Handcock again tried to take the guns only to again be repulsed.

It was at this point Wilkinson realized his chances of achieving a victory had passed. With the British forces now increased in size by a factor of nine, plus the addition of small cannons that the British navy had delivered by gunboats, the defensive forces were now too strong. Furthermore, the strongest cannon Wilkinson could deploy against the stone mill couldn't make a dent in its strong walls. Thus, as dusk began to fall, Wilkinson began withdrawing his troops. He had 13 men dead, 128 wounded, and 13 missing. Handcock had 11 dead, 44 wounded, and 4 missing.

As Wilkinson marched back to Plattsburg in defeat, the combined forces of Europe marched into Paris and forced Napoleon to abdicate. Within the month, the emperor was on Elba, and the British turned their full attention toward the United States. Sixteen veteran regiments were to be transferred to Canada while an additional six regiments were to be used to raid the eastern coast of the United States. The War of 1812 had entered a new phase where the British were no longer on the defensive.

The Great Northwest

After General Harrison defeated the British at Thames River, there was only one action left to take: retaking Fort Mackinac. For over a year and a half, the fort had been unreachable by US forces. Now with Detroit back in US hands, the retaking of this strategic point should have been easy, particularly because the fort had been without supplies for the entire winter of 1813–1814.

Unfortunately for the United States, the British were not going to make it easy. In February a force was sent from York to establish a new supply line. In with this force were sailors and carpenters to complete the schooner *Nancy* being built at St. Joseph Island. The men and supplied finally arrived at the fort on May 18, much to the cheers of the starving defenders. Once there, the commanding officer, Colonel McDouall, began enlarging the fortifications to include a stockade on the hilltop, which in 1812 had proven the Achilles heel of the then US fort.

While McDouall was building on Mackinac, at St. Louis, Missouri, Governor William Clark (of Louis and Clark fame) had concluded that a fort was needed at Praire Du Chien in what today is Wisconsin. This old French trading post was at the confluence of the Mississippi and the Wisconsin Rivers, which in turn led to the Fox River and then to the Great Lakes.

There were two reasons to build this fort. First, back in September 1813, local tribes had besieged Fort Madison, Iowa, forcing its defenders to burn the fort.[55] This left no military outpost between this British trading post and St. Louis, Missouri. The second reason was to cut off Britain from some of the richest areas in the fur trade. This meant a major loss of revenue to the British, and it weakened Britain's support with the tribes.

On May 1, Clark and a force of some two hundred men[56] began moving upriver to Praire Du Chien. Clark arrived on June 2, and construction of Fort Shelby began on June 6. Clark then returned to St. Louis on the seventh with the fort's barracks being completed on June 19. At the end of the month, the fort was nearly completed, at which time the 140 volunteer militia in the force completed their 60-day service requirement. Most returned home, leaving only about 61 men in fort and 40 volunteers on the river gunboat Governor Clark moored nearby.

When McDouall heard of this, he quickly assembled a force of some 650 regulars, militia, and Indians under Lt. Col. William

---

[55] To escape the siege, the American defenders had to tunnel to the river, where they then took a boat to St. Louis.

[56] Zachary Taylor of Fort Harrison fame was supposed to be with this force but was replaced by Lieutenant Joseph Perkins for personal reasons.

McKay to take the location. They arrived on July 17 and immediately ordered Lieutenant Perkins to surrender. When Perkins refused, the battle commenced, with the British attacking the gunboat. Whether McKay knew this ahead of time, or whether it was dumb luck, Governor Clark held most of the fort's supplies of ammunition, food, and all of the US cannons. After several hits, the volunteers withdrew downriver, leaving the fort with only 60 men, no cannons, and limited supplies.

After driving off the gunboat, McKay then concentrated on the stockade. This proved ineffective, but on the third day, McKay began preparations to fire red-hot cannonballs into the fort. Perkins, now low on ammunition and having had the fort's well run dry, asked for terms. On July 20 the fort was surrendered with no loss of life, and all the men were allowed to return to St. Louis. McKay then took the fort, renamed it Fort McKay in his honor, and headed back to Mackinac, leaving the fort under the command of Captain Thomas G. Anderson.

In the meantime, a second battle was occurring down the Mississippi River. Learning that Fort Shelby was under threat, a force of 120 rangers in six keelboats headed upriver to reinforce the garrison. When they reached the Rock Island Rapids, they encountered Chief Black Hawk and four hundred Sauk and Fox Warriors. Casualties were mounting until the timely appearance of Governor Clark escaping the siege at Fort Shelby. The Americans then withdrew with sixteen dead and twenty-one wounded.

As the far west fell to the British, McDouall turned his attention to Detroit. While McKay was away, the Americans had built a new fort at the Detroit River entrance to Lake Huron. Named Fort Gratiot, this was to be a staging base for a major expedition of five brigs and gunboats and seven hundred troops to reclaim Mackinac. The force sailed on July 3 with the plan of first taking the supply post in Matchedash Bay, then St. Joseph Island, then the trading post at Sault Sainte Marie, and finally Mackinac. But in doing all this, the force didn't arrive until July 26, leaving McDouall time to finish his defenses.

The US ships shelled the fort for two days before realizing they were doing nothing to the defenses. The shells fired at Mackinac did practically no damage, and the new stockade (Fort Holmes) built on the ridge behind the fort was too high to be engaged by the US guns. Dense fog then blanketed the area for a week, preventing any further action until August 4 when US troops landed at essentially the site where the British landed in 1812. But this time the defenders knew of the landing and were ready, manning a breastwork along the only line of advance the Americans could take to the fort. The battle was short and confused, and the US troops finally withdrew with thirteen dead and fifty-one wounded. Thus ended the second Battle of Mackinac.

As the Americans withdrew, they returned to Matchedash Bay and finally found the supply post at Nottawasaga. There they also found the schooner *Nancy* and destroyed it. The American gunboats *Tigress* and *Scorpion* were then detached to patrol the lake and prevent any supplies from reaching Mackinac. This was in mid-August, with the two gunboats to remain in the lake until October, when bad weather would make it impossible for small boats to supply Mackinac. The only problem was the British decided to take the gunboats (which occurred in September) and then used them to deliver six months' worth of supplies to the garrison at Mackinac.

To add to this tale of defeat, on August 23 some 330 troops under Zackary Taylor left Cap Au Gris in eight fortified keel boats to take back Fort Shelby. Sent to stop them was Lieutenant Graham of the British Indian department, thirty British regulars and a cannon, and 1,200 Sauk, Sioux, Winnebago, and Kickapoo Indians. On September 5 the US force was ambushed while anchored in the Rock River and was forced to withdraw back downriver to St. Louis. There would be no further attempts to reclaim the upper Mississippi River.

The Last Niagara Campaign

One would think that with battles occurring from Wisconsin, Alabama, and even Montreal, the secretary of war of the United States would have more to be concerned about than the fact that he now had to clear all new military campaigns through the president. Yet in 1814, with seasoned British troops sailing for North America, what commanded Armstrong's attention was that Madison had finally stood up and required that he be kept in the loop regarding the planning of any new offensives. This of course meant that his chief adviser, James Monroe, was also to be kept informed about any new campaigns. Though Madison had no real military ambitions, Monroe clearly wanted to be in military command, even if by proxy. In the end it added another person that shouldn't have been meddling in the fighting of the war.

If anything good was happening, it was that the men Armstrong had moved up into command positions had some idea of what they were doing. Unlike the previous commanders, these men brought with them a certain amount of military discipline and basic intelligence that had been lacking in the previous commanders. The best example was Winfield Scott, who took command of the units at Buffalo following the late December raid by Riall.

To restore the units to some semblance of a military regiment, he started with proper military hygiene and commissary. Once the men were being fed properly and regularly, and once the filth of the camps had been cleaned out, the sick rate dropped—and so did the desertion rate. Then through the proper use of drill, he developed both their opinion of themselves (now dressed well and looking sharp) and their ability to work with each other. The only thing Scott didn't have to do was dull them to the shock of battle; after two years, most of the regulars had already seen several battles.

The problem was what to do with this army. Armstrong wanted an attack on Kingston. The secretary of the navy wanted to take back Fort Mackinac. Madison and Monroe didn't know which idea to take, and all

General Brown cared about was where he was supposed to go. Eventually, the decision was made for Brown to take the offensive in Niagara with his 3,000-plus troops. He would be facing two British commanders: Riall with 2,300 men at Fort George and Fort Niagara, and Drummond with close to 4,000 troops on the Burlington Heights defending York.

On July 1 Brown was ordered to cross the river, take Fort Erie, take the fortifications on Chippewa Creek, threaten Fort George, and (if supported by the Ontario fleet) seize the Burlington Heights. Brown showed skill, determination, and energy—something extremely lacking in previous US generals. Within forty-eight hours, in the dead of night he sent General Scott across the river just north of Fort Erie. That same evening he sent a second force under General Ripley[57] just south of the fort. Then, to confuse the British commanders, Brown sent a strong militia detachment with a band marching to Lewiston to make it look like an attack on Queenston was planned.

Scott landed his division just before sunup on July 3, 1814. Two hours passed, and he was still undetected by the British, even though he now had his entire force assembled. By this time, a small boat had arrived to carry General Brown and his staff. Ripley had yet to move his men across the river, much to Brown's dismay. Brown crossed and ordered Scott to send a battalion forward to observe the movements of the fort's garrison. Scott did so, though instead of observing, his unit actually overran the British pickets on the west side of the fort. So successful was this that Brown began considering taking the fort without Ripley's forces.

When Ripley did arrive, the only person he met on the beach was his own commander's adjutant general. The landing of the ordnance was completed as quickly as possible, and an eighteen-pounder was quickly emplaced on Snake Hill. Brown then issued the British his surrender terms, with two hours to consider. The British surrendered

---

[57] Ripley actually tended his resignation the night before, on the grounds that he didn't have enough men to perform the mission. His resignation was denied, and he stayed in command.

in an hour, and by 6:00 p.m. the garrison was marching out to become prisoners of war. The total cost of the attack for the United States was four killed and two wounded from cannon fire when the pickets were overwhelmed. The British lost one man during the same engagement.

With the fort in his hands, Brown immediately began preparations to face the forces under Riall. Riall had learned of the pending attack on July 2 and had sent reinforcements to Fort Erie the next morning. Their march was interrupted by the news of the fort's surrender, prompting a withdrawal to Chippewa for additional forces. The next day, July 4, Winfield Scott moved out to confront Riall's forces.

What was to be a march was in truth a running skirmish as units of the British One Hundredth Regiment under the Marquis of Tweedale harassed Scott's every step. Every bridge over every creek on the way to Chippewa was ripped up. Every time Scott began rebuilding the bridges, the Marquis riflemen would snipe at them. For twelve hours this went on all the way to Street Creek, on the road to Chippewa. It was behind this creek that Scott camped his forces for the night.

Early the next morning, General Brown arrived with the main US Army. At roughly the same time, British militia and Indians crossed the Chippewa River and began attacking Scott's pickets from the woods on Scott's left. The situation finally reached a boiling point at around noon, when a fifty-man picket unit was forced to withdraw.

General Porter, who had only just arrived with a force of three hundred Pennsylvania militia and four hundred Iroquois Indians, was given the task of pushing back the British. Initially Porter was successful in this, but as he approached the Chippewa River, he discovered that Riall's full force had crossed and were assembling for an attack. As the vanguard of Riall's forces passed Porter's troops in the woods, his men opened fire on its right flank with rifles and Indian trade muskets. The British vanguard, made up of light companies of the royal Scots, Lincoln militia, and three hundred Iroquois Indians (Canadian), fired two volleys into the woods and then charged with bayonets. The militia, again using rifles without bayonets, fell back while the Indians (armed also with traditional weapons), began hand-to-hand combat with the troops as they entered the woods. This event has been marked as the first time since the Iroquois nations came together that they had fought one another. It was at this point that Porter ordered a withdrawal back to Street Creek.

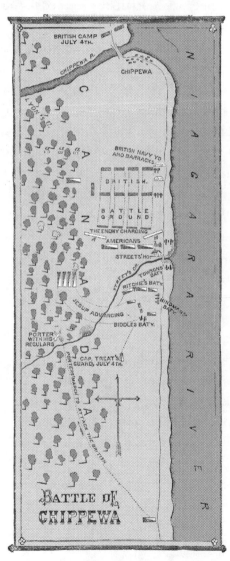

Figure 64: Battle Map of Chippewa.

While all this was going on, General Brown had been giving orders. He had been observing Porter's troops driving off Riall's scouts when he saw a large dust cloud coming from Chippewa. He immediately sent orders to Ripley to bring up his unit and cannons while also escorting Captain Ritchie and his battery to the field in front of the Street Creek Bridge. Then he turned and rode back to Scott's headquarters to get him in motion. On crossing the bridge he found Scott ready to hold a parade drill on the plain where Brown had just left Ritchie and his battery.

Figure 65: *Battle of Chippewa*. By H. Charles McBarron Jr.

A depiction of Scott Greys at the battle of Chippewa.

Having forced Porter to leave the field, General Riall now spotted a force of grey-clad troops preparing to cross Street Creek Bridge. "It is nothing but a body of Buffalo militia!" said Riall, who detested militia (even his own). He immediately concluded that a few cannon shots would disperse them and ordered his field guns to engage. Riall had nine pieces of artillery, including two massive twenty-four-pounders. These began dropping solid shot into the grey line of men that was crossing the bridge. It took a moment, but as the men took up a proper formation while under fire, Riall suddenly realized the truth and exclaimed "Why, those are regulars, by God."

Riall had been deceived by fate. Like the Grey Tigers at Crysler's Farm, these troops were not what their uniforms made them out to be. When Winfield Scott took command, one of the issues he had to solve was getting his men decent uniforms. He ordered regulation blue uniforms from the government quartermaster, but the demand from all the army units then in the field had produced a serious shortage of blue cloth. Knowing that wearing all the same uniforms would improve the morale of his men. Scott thus decided to have the uniforms made from grey militia cloth. Thus came into existence Scott's Greys, one of the first legendary US Army brigades.

Though Scott had taken Riall by surprise, the battle wasn't over yet. What he needed now was a few miracles. The first was Towson actually hitting the ammunition wagon of one of Riall's batteries. The next was Riall, who for some reason chose to advance his troops in line instead of column; this made his advance extremely slow and thus vulnerable to the fire from both Ritchie and Towson. If Riall had chosen to advance, halt, fire, and then advance again alternately, using the line formation would have maximized his firepower against Scott. Instead, he ordered that his men fire only one volley and then charge with the bayonet. Thus they held back firing until they were ready for the charge.

Scott didn't fight that way. He advanced, halted, fired, reloaded, and again fired, always allowing Riall to close the distance between the two forces. By the time the front lines were within one hundred yards of each other, Scott had done some serious damage with just his muskets. But now the fight truly became fierce as Scott's men loaded their muskets with buck and ball (where one had three small buckshot loaded with a single large ball).[58] Scott had also positioned two regiments at oblique angles to the advancing British line; this allowed

---

[58] Buck and ball was a favorite of American commanders from the revolution to the Mexican American War. A paper distributed in the 1840s bemoaned the fielding of a standard army rifle in place of the musket because the rifles couldn't use buck and ball.

these regiments to fire not just at the British front but also against the British flank for maximum effect. In addition, Towson switched from solid shot to canister shot, producing murderous results along the British left flank and center. Then came the US bayonet charge, at which point the British center and left flank broke completely.

There has always been some confusion regarding what happened on the British right flank. Riall had his Vanguard unit on his right moving through the forest. After this unit had repulsed Porter, they could have moved against Scott's left flank and turned the tide of the battle. But Major Jesup of the Twenty-fifth Regiment had forded Street Creek and, after being joined by Porter and some of his men, moved to check the British right. The fighting is reported to have been fierce, but Jesup succeeded in driving them off, completing the British defeat.

The cost was decent for the United States with 65 dead, 255 wounded, and 19 missing. The British got the worst of it with 148 dead and close to 400 wounded or captured. In all, 1,700 British troops were defeated by 1,500 US Army troops. General Brown and General Ripley ended up missing the entire battle because Brown tried to lead Ripley's unit behind the British right flank in a wide, sweeping movement. By the time this was done, Scott had defeated Riall and was pursuing him back to the river.

At this point, a new stalemate ensued as Brown looked for a way of crossing the Chippewa without excessive casualties. What he discovered was an abandoned lumber road that could be seen from the street house near the Street Creek Bridge. This road ended at the point where Lyon's Creek entered the Chippewa River. On July 7 Brown explored this road and determined he could use it to get around Riall's defenses. A detail was sent to make the road passable by artillery, and by the morning of the eighth the road was ready. Unfortunately, General Ripley wasn't.

It didn't matter, because Riall was aware of what Brown was doing and had resolved to abandon his position and withdraw to Queenston. Brown followed as quickly as he could, and by the tenth he was encamped at Queenston. Riall had in turn moved his men to the Burlington Heights. There he was reinforced and promptly moved back to a position at Fifteen Mile Creek.

Now began a waiting game as Brown looked for the appearance of the US fleet off Fort George. Without the fleet, he could not be reinforced or supplied. Furthermore, he felt he needed the reinforcements before he could retake the fort or move on to Burlington Heights. As Brown waited, Riall was also awaiting reinforcements before he would again tangle with US forces. In the meantime, small scouting and raiding parties mixed it up around the various camps. Around July 14, General Swift[59] was killed as part of a unit of 120 men that was sent to capture some British pickets outside of Fort George. A few days later on the nineteenth, on a foraging mission Colonel Stone burned the village of St. David's, which lay less than three miles from the US camp.[60]

Finally, on July 23 General Brown learned that the US fleet would not be arriving. The following day, Brown withdrew to the Chippewa in the hope of gaining supplies from Fort Schlosser on the opposite bank. As the Americans withdrew, the British followed. But now there were two commanders: Riall with his forces, and Drummond, who commanded reinforcements from Kingston.

Brown wanted Riall to follow him all the way back to Chippewa, where he would beat him again on the same battlefield. On July 25, however, Brown received information that the British had instead moved across the river to take Lewiston. Now believing that most of the British army was across the river, Brown sent Scott back down the road to Queenston to draw out Riall's remaining forces. It would set the stage for the worst battle of the war.

When Scott arrived at Niagara, a Mrs. Wilson told him that he had just missed General Riall and his staff at her home. Further, she

---

[59] General Swift was a Revolutionary War hero who had volunteered to return to service following the declaration of war. A British soldier who had already surrendered and was being led back to the American camp shot him.

[60] Stone was immediately dismissed from service following court-martial.

said just beyond was a force of over 1,200 men plus artillery. Scott didn't believe it, deciding instead that the British were likely across the river. Thus, he had his men rush forward directly into the British guns. Suddenly Scott was in a position where he couldn't stand or retreat. The Battle of Lundy Lane was on.

Figure 66: *Lundy's Lane* By Alonzo Chappel, 1859

The situation was not quite a series of US mistakes. The British force Jacob Brown believed was attacking Lewiston did exist. General Drummond had sent Colonel Tucker and five hundred men across the river to threaten Lewiston in the hope of getting Brown to cross the river to protect it. What Drummond didn't think would happen was that Brown would believe this small force was the entire British army, and in an attempt to get the British back onto the west side, they would send Scott out to threaten Fort George. When Riall discovered that Scott was moving toward his position on Lundy Lane, he ordered a withdrawal back to Queenston. Drummond, who was advancing on the lane with his own troops, quickly countermanded this order. Thus the battle was to begin with the 1,200 men of Scott's division against the 1,800 troops under Riall.[61] But Riall not only had more troops,

---

[61] Riall had 1,200 men directly under his command. At the time the battle began, an additional 600 men had arrived from General Drummond's force.

he held the high ground and had placed his guns at the highest point (the cemetery of the Methodist church). Scott's only advantage was it was forty minutes until sunset.

As Scott marched forward into the fire from Riall's guns, Major Jesup moved his unit through the woods on the east side of the road. While Riall was occupied with Scott's main force, Jesup moved against the British left flank. By 9:00 p.m. Scott had forced the British right flank to withdraw while Jesup had both driven off the left flank and kept Drummond's reinforcements from arriving. In the course of events, Riall had been shot in the arm and then captured by Jesup's men while trying to leave the field. This success hardly made up for the fact that Scott's division had been nearly decimated.

It was at this point that General Brown finally arrived with Ripley's unit and moved to take the guns on Lundy Lane. The task was eventually assigned to the Twenty-first Infantry under the command of Colonel Miller.[62] Miller approached in stealth, in the dark, until his unit reached an old fence line approximately ten yards from the gunners. From there they opened fire, killing the gunners. The attack alerted a nearby British force, which returned fire on the US troops and then charged with the bayonet. The Twenty-first fired back and succeeded in driving off the British. Drummond now arrived with his reinforcements and tried to retake the guns and the heights. Ripley's division met them, and the battle continued until half past ten at night. In the end it was a battle of attrition as men and commanders on all sides began falling.

By 10:00 both sides had lost over eight hundred men and officers, including General Scott and General Brown. Scott had first been injured in the leg by a rebounding cannon ball; two hours later, he was shot in the shoulder. Brown had been shot in his right thigh and then a few minutes later hit in the side by something. Now the commander was Ripley, who withdrew to Chippewa to regroup the

---

[62] Miller is reported to have said, "I'll try, sir," when given the orders to take the guns. Today it is the motto of the Twenty-first US Infantry.

now shattered forces. He was supposed to return at dawn to recover the cannons taken by Miller, but he was slow in returning the next day and found the heights occupied by Drummond. Thus ended the Battle of Lundy Lane.

Figure 67: The Twenty-first takes the British guns.

The losses in Scott's division (560 of the 800-plus men lost), as well as the loss of both Scott and Brown in command positions, were major blows to the American force. The United States had entered Canada with 3,500 troops, and in just two battles they had lost 1,100 men or one-third of their force. Once Brown, Scott, and Jesup (also wounded) had been placed in boats and sent across the river, Ripley abandoned the Chippewa area and moved the entire army to the Black Rock ferry. If it hadn't been because of a near mutiny of the remaining officers, his plan was to ferry the entire force to Black Rock and abandon the campaign. When he tried to get General Brown's orders to do this, Brown nearly relieved him of command. Ripley then returned to the army and led it to a position just above Fort Erie. He built at Fort Erie in preparations for a siege.

The attack on Fort Erie began on August 7 with the start of a cannon bombardment. The siege then continued until the thirteenth, when Drummond brought to bear his heavy guns for a two-day bombardment, to be immediately followed by a direct attack against the fort. This initial attack was repulsed, but the siege continued. On August 28 General Gaines, then in command, was severely wounded and forced to turn over command to Ripley. Brown, still recovering in Batavia, heard of this and returned to Fort Erie on September 2 to take command. After he arrived, he prepared for a counterstrike against Drummond. By September 17 he was ready, and he launched an attack on Drummond's siege battery on the western edge of his line.

Porter and his militia would attack from the forest and take Drummonds Third and Fourth Batteries. Then General Miller would hit the center of the line with the remains of Scott's old regiments. The attack was a success in that the batteries were taken and Drummond was forced to end the siege. The long-running battle had cost the British nearly 1,500 dead, wounded, or missing, whereas the United States had lost only 630, of which 80 were killed and 400 were wounded in Brown's attack.

With the siege lifted, Drummond retired to Chippewa River to await the enemy. Brown wasn't in a position to follow and waited the arrival of General Izard, who had been previously ordered to leave Plattsburg with several thousand men and move west. Izard arrived on October 11 and then moved out with close to eight thousand men to Drummond's position. There, they tried to feel each other out until late October, when Drummond withdrew to Fort George. Izard, himself noting the lateness of the season, withdrew back to Black Rock with the American forces. As for Fort Erie, US Army engineers destroyed it on November 5.

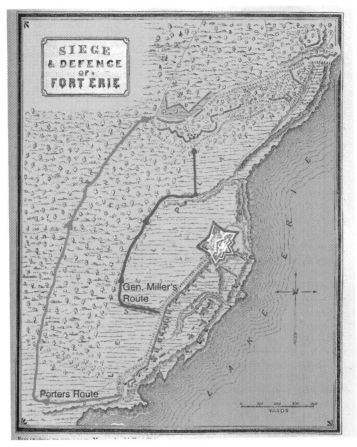

Figure 68: Battle of Fort Erie.

Lessons Learned

As the spring battles of 1814 showed, there was both a lack of riflemen in many areas of the country, and even when they were present, the generals had to both know how to use them and be willing to use them. Jackson was probably the only commander capable of both. For him, even undisciplined militia riflemen were an integral part of his force, and he used them to their strengths. Riflemen were effective from heavily forested regions and were usually faster in movement over difficult terrain. Mounted riflemen were in fact more flexible than dragoons, as shown both at the Thames River and in the fights in Alabama.

Where Jackson had faith in militia riflemen, Wilkinson didn't even have a use for a regular army unit of riflemen. Instead of using them to countersnipe against the British troops in the stone mill and cover the approach of his infantry, he chose to place them out of the way. If he had decided to use his riflemen as the British were already using their own riflemen—to pin down enemy artillery or keep enemy troops in hardened positions from using their weapons—he would have taken the stone mill within an hour. Once this was done, his artillery could have been trained on the blockhouse, whose wooden walls would not have been a defense.

Of course all this would have been irrelevant if Wilkinson had been able to bring his big gun to bear on the mill. But if Wilkinson had taken the mill intact, it would have become an effective defense point along his line of supply and communication. Instead, his holding to his initial plan of attack ensured his defeat.

Then there is Winfield Scott and his grey-clad soldiers. Scott had done the impossible: create a US Army unit that was as drilled as any British unit. For US Army historians, this is an important event in showing the US Army was now a true European army. Yet where the Battle of Chippewa is an example of US Army discipline and training, Lundy Lane is an example of the limitations of the old European form of battle.

If Scott had had any riflemen in his unit at Chippewa, they could potentially have been a liability. The slowness of Riall's approach, however, would have given the riflemen more than enough time to engage in multiple reloads before Riall's men could have charged. That plus the canister shot would have produced more deaths among Riall's men than the less accurate, shorter range musket fire. Only when the subject of buck and ball comes in can one see any liability of having riflemen scattered in Scott's force.

The complete lack of riflemen at Lundy Lane helped produce the disaster that occurred. If Jesup had had riflemen instead of musketmen, he could have begun attacking the British left flank before he broke from the woods. His riflemen could have also engaged the artillery at distance, opening the door for Scott's regular infantry to close for the attack. Instead, Scott's men took the full force of the artillery unit while they tried to engage the British right. The result may have been a victory, but the cost was pyrrhic to the United States campaign in Niagara.

In closing, the brave and stealthy approach of the Twenty-first Infantry to the British guns during the night could have also been avoided if rifles were present. Instead, they had to close to within twenty yards to unleash their musket barrage on the gunners. If they had been detected while approaching, they would have suffered the same fate as Scott's units earlier that evening.

The effect of the lack of rifles and riflemen in 1814 was yet to reach its zenith, for three battles were yet to be waged. In one battle, riflemen were issued muskets while men with rifles were placed in a position where they could not defend themselves. The result was one of the worst events the United States could ever imagine. In another battle, two riflemen changed the very course of the fight. And finally, riflemen and musketmen, working together, helped prevent one of the most dangerous British assaults of the conflict.

CHAPTER 6
Washington, Baltimore, and Plattsburg

Invasion United States

Since the War of 1812 began, it was Americans invading Canada that produced all the confrontations. With Napoleon cooling his heels on Elba, Britain now had the troops and ships to launch a concerted invasion of US territory. The question was where to send them.

Quite a number of troops had been already sent to Canada to protect Montreal—so many that the country was having difficulty supplying them. Canada had for years been buying food from the United States, and even through the war, there was illegal trade in food. Now with so many troops in country, Canada had to import large amounts of basic staples directly from Britain.

To make matters worse, moving large amounts of supplies meant it had to go by water. To supply a decent size force to take Fort Detroit required shipping up the St. Lawrence, then across Lake Ontario, then along the Niagara River, and then finally up Lake Erie to Detroit. Doing that required first seizing of Fort Erie, which in August was in US hands, and then building a fleet to defeat the US fleet on Lake Erie.

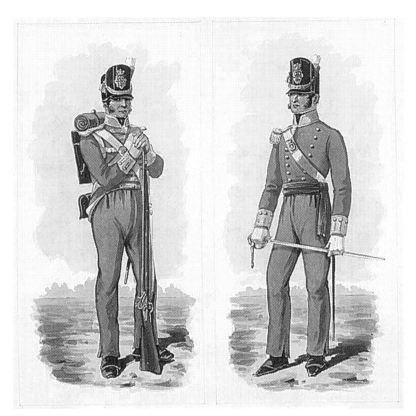

Figure 69: British infantry (Library and Archives of Canada).

As noted earlier, with the US Army in Niagara checked by General Drummond, additional troops were not needed to defend that front. Until Drummond retook Fort Erie, any move against Detroit was impossible. Thus the British commanders looked for targets that could be immediately threatened—targets selected to show the United States that they were still a small people compared to the great British Empire. After defeating Napoleon, it was the British military that had an ego to pamper.

Thus came the three-phased invasion plan. One phase would be a force to invade the middle colonies along the Chesapeake Bay. This force would draw away troops from both the southwest and New

York State. Once this was done, phase two would begin with the newly arrived British units in Canada marching down from Montreal to take Albany, New York. This force would split off the Federalist, anti-war northeastern states from the rest of the nation. Considering that in these states a cession movement was already underway, it could have shattered the nation permanently.

Finally, the third phase would invade the Louisiana territory and seize the Mississippi River all the way up to Canada. If this action had been completed, the Northwest Territories would have fallen to Britain, as well as the states west of the Appalachia Mountains.

Unlike the US attacks in 1812 and 1813, none of these forces had to attack at the same time. These forces were large and well equipped, capable of taking their targets by themselves. They also were operating under loose orders of battle that allowed them to attack targets as they saw fit, avoiding targets that were too strong, or attacking only when they could assure themselves of victory.

The British Attack, Phase One

For some time, a British fleet under the command of Admiral Cockburn had been blockading the Chesapeake Bay. On June 2 a flotilla of small armed boats under the command of Joshua Barney came into the bay to challenge Cockburn. For a few days, Barney chased Cockburn's lesser ships until, on June 7, Barney came up against Cockburn's two 74-gun ships, the HMS *Dragon* and HMS *Albion*. Now the hunted, Barney was chased all the way up the Patuxent River to St. Leonard's Creek. The larger British ships couldn't pursue due to shallow water.

Figure 70: On the left: Admiral Cockburn, the city of
Washington burning behind him. By John. J. Halls Esqr
On the right: Major General Robert Ross.

Though Cockburn had Barney bottled up in the creek, Barney's
presence prevented Cockburn from going further upriver with his
smaller ships. Thus, from June 8–10, Cockburn sent several small boat
groups up the creek in an attempt to defeat Barney's unit. Following
this, he then sent troops upriver to burn the towns and villages of
Calverton, Prince Frederick, and lower Marlboro in order to force
Barney to come out. Then in late June, land forces arrived to assist
Barney in a breakout. This was successful, allowing Barney to flee
further upriver to Benedict Maryland and then later to Nottingham.
Cockburn landed troops at St. Leonard's Creek and burned the town
of the same name.

On July 17 Cockburn again landed troops on the Patuxent River
at Hunting Creek and destroyed private property in the community
of Huntingtown. By the time General Winder had moved three

companies of militia to the Woodyard, as well as units of the Thirty-sixth and Thirty-eighth Army Regiments to Upper Marlborough, Cockburn had pulled out and gone back downriver with large quantities of tobacco.

Cockburn then began threatening communities along the Maryland side of the Potomac River. This left Winder perplexed as to what Cockburn's real target was, Washington or Annapolis. By July 26 Winder was convinced an attack on Annapolis was near, and he tried to position a detachment from Virginia and a cavalry unit from Carlisle to counter it. Within another week, the situation had changed, and on August 4 Winder was moving units of the Thirty-six and Thirty-eighth Infantries to Piscataway to help defend the people in Charles County from Cockburn's depredations.

In reality, Cockburn's attacks were simply covering his examination of the Patuxent River to determine the optimum location to land a much bigger naval force. These examinations showed that the best location was the town of Benedict, some fifty miles from Washington D.C. With Barney's flotilla trapped a few miles upriver at Nottingham and no US land forces nearby, he simply waited for the arrival of Admiral Cochrane's fleet on August 17. Traveling with Cochrane's force was Major General Robert Ross and four thousand veterans of the Spanish Peninsula War.

Ross's initial problem after landing his troops on August 18 was the condition of his troops. After weeks at sea, these troops (the Fourth, Twenty-first, Forty-fourth, and Eighty-fifth Foot and the Second Battalion Royal Marines) could not march or function for two days as they stretched their legs. If the American government could have sent a group of light infantry or cavalry against these units, the British invasion could have been routed within a day of its landing.

Of all the places to attack, Maryland could have been called the soft underbelly of the nation. Maryland's militia return listed 28,000 infantry but less than 4,000 muskets,[63] no riflemen but 530 rifles, 1,100 dragoons but only 462 pairs of pistols, and 478 sabers. The militia was disorganized, and the regular army was being reorganized.

On July 2 the government created the Tenth Military District under the command of General Winder.[64] This district encompassed all of Maryland, Washington D.C., and that part of Virginia lying between the Rappahannock and Potomac Rivers. Up until then, D.C. had been part of the Fifth Military District that encompassed all of Maryland and Virginia down to the North Carolina border. Under the new district, the 873 men of the Twentieth, Thirty-fifth, and Thirty-eighth Army Regiments at Norfolk were not included. Thus, Winder had under his control only the 300 troops of the Thirty-eighth Regiment at Baltimore, and 320 troops of the Thirty-sixth Regiment at St Mary's.

As for militiamen, he had 1,700 under his direct command in Washington, another 1,400 troops under the direct command of General Smith, and a smaller group of 250 men at Bladensburg, making for a total force of 3,970 men. This would confront General Ross and his 4,000 veteran troops.

The Volunteer Militia Requisition of July 4, 1812

Two days after the president created the Tenth Military District, Secretary of War Armstrong issued a request to all the state governors that they summon and hold in readiness 93,500 militiamen.[65] In making this request, Armstrong stated that volunteer units were preferred over the regular militia in the states.

---

[63] Maryland also only listed 2,000 flints. Most states had either two flints to each musket, or more. The only state worse then Maryland was New Jersey, with 14,500 muskets and only 844 flints.

[64] Son of the governor of the State of Maryland.

[65] This represented 15 percent of the men on the militia rolls.

Figure 71: *Battle of North Point* by Don Troiani.
The depiction is of a volunteer rifle unit and not of Federal troops.

Under the 1792 Militia Act, the states were allowed to create special militias. Under section four, every militia division was to have one company of artillery and one troop of horse made up of volunteers from the common militia. There is also mention of other "Sundry Corps" of artillery, cavalry, and infantry that then existed in several of the states, which by the laws, customs, or usages thereof have not been incorporated with or subject to the general regulations of the militia. All of these units classified as special militia under the Militia Act.

These volunteer militia units were not the minutemen of the revolution, in that the men were not above average with a musket, extremely strong, or even young. The volunteer militias were made up of rich or upper-middle-class gentlemen uninterested in having a military career but with a military leaning. Another description for these men was rich men's sons who had lots of money and very little to do. Unlike normal militiamen who despised militia duty, these men liked to come together to drill, shoot, and do other military style activities (another form of men's club).

In the beginning, the volunteer militias were few and far between. Prior to 1790, they were mostly in the northeastern area, where there were lots of wealthy men with little to do. As the nation began industrializing and more men began making their fortunes, more of these gentlemen's clubs began forming in the middle and southern states.

The different types of units in the volunteer militias made involvement more appealing for these men. Men with an interest in riding or the owning of horses would join a militia dragoon or cavalry unit. The cavalry loved to put on their uniforms (selected by their brigadier) and ride about the muster on their personnel horses (all paid for by them). Of course the cavalrymen also carried two pistols that unfortunately were used for duels between these wealthy men. As this problem grew, the horse pistols were replaced with dueling pistols that were lighter, smaller, and less robust weapons. The 1792 act held no specific requirements for the pistols other than the volunteer had to own two, and so in the War of 1812, many a volunteer cavalryman would find out the hard way the difference between a dueling pistol and a horse pistol.

Unlike the cavalry that tended toward the more athletic types, the artillery groups also had their following. Men interested in this activity tended to come from the more scientific or craftsmen groups, to whom working the guns required some skill in math. At the musters, they liked to show their skill at handling the big guns, riding them in, setting them up, and firing for the crowd.

Along with these two types of units, section four also required each battalion of militia have a company either of light infantry, grenadiers, or riflemen. In Europe these units were specialist or elite troops with special uniforms to distinguish themselves from regular troops. Grenadiers were assault troops with an emphasis on physical strength and size. Thus, they were the foot soldier version of the cavalry units, populated by athletic rich men who didn't like horses. Light infantry was the polar opposite: lightweight and nimble young men used to make fast scouting and skirmishing attacks against enemy troops. As for the riflemen, they were the men who tended to hunt for sport or recreational purposes. Thus, the militia duty was in many ways an extension of other activities (hobbies) these men already did.

But the Federal problem with these units was that they were too specialized. The government wanted volunteer infantry units that were as uniform as the special units already mentioned. Unfortunately, at an expense of seventy-two dollars for a uniform, arms, and field gear, creating a significant number of basic infantry units was nearly impossible. That all changed in 1807, when "An Act authorizing the President of the United States to accept the service of volunteer companies, not exceeding thirty thousand men" was passed.

Unlike earlier acts in the 1790s, where eighty thousand men were selected from their state militia for a year's service, the government accepted men who volunteered for a two-year service. The men still had to perform their regular militia duty, but now they would be armed and equipped by the Federal government. If they decided to arm themselves, the government would then reimburse them for any damage sustained when in active federal service. One more difference was if the man was activated at the end of his service time, he still was committed to twelve months of service, whereas under the older acts, the men were required to serve only three months.

The Statute of 1807 started the trend of arming men for volunteer federal militia, but the program intensified in 1812 when a new statute was proposed for accepting fifty thousand volunteers. This new law not only allowed for the men to be provided arms by the government, but on honorable discharge (service longer than one month) they would receive the gun, the bayonet, and other items as public testimonial to their service to the country. All of this drew a number of "volunteers" who either couldn't afford the basic militia gear required by the Federal law of 1792 or didn't want to pay the cost of a musket and uniform.

February 14, 1814: Mr. Troup of Georgia

> By a law passed in 1812, the President was authorized to accept the service of fifty thousand volunteers. Under this law, as many men as made up about six regiments, had been called into actual service, viz: one regiment in new Hampshire and Maine, two in New York, one regiment partly organized in Virginia, two in the state of Louisiana and the Mississippi territory.

The problem with the volunteers was that although they looked like professional soldiers, they were anything but uniform in training or operation. Many volunteer units operated under the Von Steuben drill code, whereas others followed the system devised by Hamilton in the 1790s. Still others used an English translation of the French military drill manual of Napoleon.

The volunteers in the Lake Champlain or Niagara campaigns tended to be this type of good looking volunteer militia. They had nice uniforms, the same type of musket and could follow their manual perfectly. They also ran as fast as anyone else when bullets began flying past their ears. In the end, regardless of how they were trained or how they looked, only men who had been under fire before, whether militia or regular, could be counted on to stand their ground at the first whiff of powder.

Of course, there were also volunteer militia who were not rich or financially set for life. The volunteer Kentucky mounted militia that Harrison used at Thames River was mostly made up of frontiersmen who lived by the gun and with their horses. The same can be said for most of the volunteer units from Tennessee under Andrew Jackson, or the companies of rangers formed by legislation at the start of the war. Being able to ride and shoot wasn't a hobby, but the way these men made their livelihood. After almost two decades of Indian wars driven by the British or Spain, these men had no fear of native warriors.

The late British General Brock understood the issue of experience in battle at the start of the war. To reduce the possibility of whole lines collapsing in battle, he mixed his experienced units in with newly formed troops. The experienced men would hold the line and give the raw recruits someone to look at and follow the lead of. They would be the anchors to these units, which is why so many Canadian militia units proved to be more consistent alongside their British regulars than federal militia with US Army units. Following Brock's death, the Canadian government wisely continued this system throughout the first two years of the war.

In addition to the lack of experience, the more affluent nature of the East Coast volunteers made them far less supportive of the war. Units from the northeastern states, whose members had suffered under the Embargo Act, were either anti-French or pro–Federalist Party. Such militia units were more inclined to find excuses not to fight—excuses such as lack of pay, lack of required clothing, or the presence of the Canadian border. On the other hand, the less affluent yet equally political Kentucky and Tennessee militia (volunteer or otherwise) tended to be very willing to go anywhere if it meant fighting Indians or the British. It was these less affluent volunteer units that Armstrong was primarily requesting. Yet he was asking for them from an affluent area of the country.

Run-up to Bladensburg

Whereas Armstrong was requesting that the state governors get all their volunteer units ready for combat, Winder had other ideas. On July 18 he received approval from Armstrong for the summoning of the following quotas of militiamen.

State	Men
Maryland	6,000
Virginia	2,000
Pennsylvania	5,000
District of Columbia	2,000
Total	15,000

Winder started trying to build his forces on July 20 with a request to the governor of Maryland for three thousand men to be sent to Bladensburg. On August 5 the governor responded that only one brigade could be sent; the other two could not be moved without threatening the defense of Baltimore. Thus, Maryland would not be sending much to defend Washington.

Even before Winder received the Maryland governor's response, he'd sent a letter to the governor of Pennsylvania, formally making his request for that state's quota of five thousand troops. Two days later, he sent a second letter requesting that as many of the troops as possible be riflemen. Three days later, Pennsylvania State Secretary Boileau, under the direction of the governor of Pennsylvania, informed Winder that on August 1, the state's 1807 Militia Law expired. As a result, the state militia was in chaos with all commissions voided. Further, under state law, a new act could not be enforced until the fourth Monday in October. Eventually five thousand men would be mustered at York for service with the Tenth District; they mustered on September 5.

The only reinforcements were coming from Virginia. On July 14 the governor of Virginia informed the secretary of war that the state had already activated fifteen thousand militiamen to repel any invasion. Unfortunately, they were not "organized upon the military establishment of the United States, nor for a longer term than three months; which, with other considerations, prevented the acceptance of any part of those State troops, as a compliance with the requisition of the General Government." Virginia would send other troops to fill the two-thousand-man quota.

Regardless of the manpower situation, within twenty-four hours of the British landing, US troops began moving. Unfortunately, it was Captain Thornton's troop of cavalry, which had been appropriated by Secretary of State James Monroe to go with him as he reconnoitered the enemy positions. Thus a unit of cavalry, which could have been used to harass the enemy, was playing bodyguard for a member of the cabinet. Adding insult to injury, fifty-six-year-old Monroe forgot to bring his telescope and was thus trying to determine the size of the enemy force without it. After seeing all he wanted to see, Monroe then broke contact with the British and rode back to Washington with the entire troop of cavalry in tow.

Earlier that day, two other units of cavalry under Colonel Tilghman and Captain Caldwell were dispatched from Washington to harass the enemy forces, but there is little recorded as to what effect this had.

While Monroe was acting like an army colonel, back in Washington General Smith and Winder tried to assemble the city militia. Due to a massive lack of essential equipment (like flints for the muskets), the force was dismissed until the next morning. A reason for this trouble was recently disclosed by Washington D.C. during the 2008 Heller Supreme Court case. Its turns out in 1801, the District (then called Georgetown) prohibited the firing of guns within the city limits. This action included the city militia during the musters, effectively preventing the firing demonstration required by a separate Federal Act passed in 1803. The city's law was not amended until March 1813 (under Federal pressure) but didn't go into effect until after January 1 1814. The first muster to occur after the law was changed was on July 4, 1814, a month before the British arrived. It was hardly enough time to correct twelve years of City legislated neglect.[66]

---

[66] The 1812 militia return showed only 628 muskets to 2,088 men. But in 1812, the government gave the city 2,200 muskets. The city should have had a surplus of 800 muskets when the British attacked.

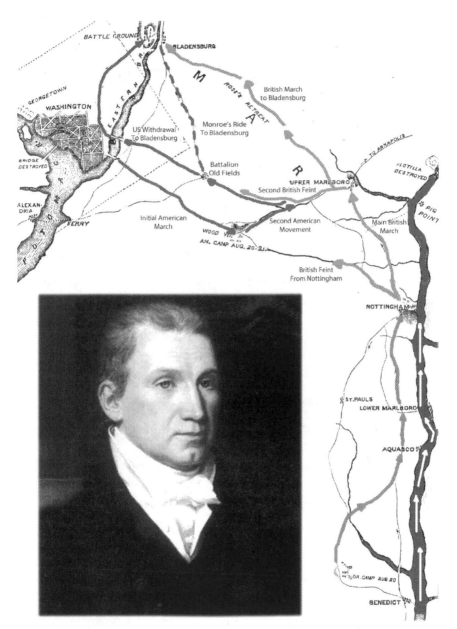

Figure 72: The British line of march from Benedict to Bladensberg. The picture is of Secretary of State James Monroe by John Vanderlyn 1816

The next morning was spent trying to get things in order, preventing the militia from marching out until 3:00 p.m. By leaving so late in the day for Nottingham[67] (a small town on the Patuxent River), the force barely got further than four miles past the eastern branch of the Potomac before stopping for the night. There they continued to get organized, and by the morning of the twenty-first they had assembled a force of around 1,070 troops: two companies of artillery and 12 six-pounder field guns (210 men), one company of Grenadiers (40 men), five companies of light infantry (250 men), 670 militia, and two companies of musket-armed riflemen (170 men) under the command of a Captain Stull. You read that right—no rifles! The secretary of war only furnished muskets.[68]

As the militia was marching to Nottingham, on August 20 Ross moved his troops out of Benedict to a location roughly at the present town of Patuxent (about six miles). The troops still were unlimbering themselves, and the force did not have horses or wagons to carry supplies. The British had three cannons, two three-pounders and a six-pounder. The next day the British troops again marched toward Nottingham along Aquasco Road, changing to Croom Road to stay hugging the Patuxent River.

Following in the river was Cockburn with a force of marines on small ships to give support and a quick exit to the land units if required. Cockburn's river force also carried a marine Congreve rocket artillery unit.

While the British were marching to Nottingham, on the twenty-first the articles of war were being read to the Washington militia. Following the noon arrival of marines under Captain Miller, the force again began marching to Nottingham, stopping at the Woodyard,

---

[67] Nottingham no longer exists today. The only remaining vestige is Nottingham Road, which takes you to a segment of Patuxent River Park. The town essentially was on the river directly east of Naylor, Maryland, in Prince George's County.

[68] A letter from General Winder on July 20 also indicates the rifle company, under the command of a Captain Dougherty, had rifles that were very defective. Later, these riflemen were reported to have been armed with muskets for the Battle of Bladensburg.

seven miles farther from Washington. There the Thirty-sixth Army Regiment (350 men) under Lt. Col. Scott and the cavalry unit under Colonel Tilghman joined the force. Following this, Colonel Monroe arrived to personally report the strength of the British force.

Monroe's view of the situation was clearly worse than that of militia Colonel Beall, who had also just arrived. Monroe put forth that the enemy had 6,000 men, whereas Beall stated he had counted some 4,000 troops entering Nottingham. Since Winder had still only assembled about 1,500 men, the difference between a three-to-one enemy advantage and a two-to-one was academic. However, as Winder's forces grew, this overcount by Monroe would have serious implications. After giving his report, Monroe retired to bed. Beall was given orders to meet a detachment coming from Annapolis under the command of a Colonel Hood and take command. Thus, Colonel Beall was now effectively out of the picture and was unable to remind General Winder of what he had seen.

At dawn on the twenty-second, General Winder, Monroe, and the general staff rode toward Nottingham to spot the enemy. Behind them was the army, broken up into two parts. The advanced group consisted of Lavall's cavalry, a light detachment of troops, and the regulars under Lieutenant Colonel Scott. This advanced group was to engage the British head-on as they marched from Nottingham to Washington. In theory, the two armies were now on a collision course.

After effectively leaving his troops in his dust, Winder stopped at a Mr. Oden's, about a half mile from a road junction that connected the road to Nottingham to the road to Upper Marlboro. There he sent Lavell to a place called Page Chapel, which was along the road from the Woodyard to Nottingham. Lavell was to contact the enemy and maintain contact until additional US forces arrived. Today we know the location as St. Thomas Episcopal Church in Croom, Maryland, which sits at the end of St. Thomas Church Road.

Lavell didn't have to wait long before the British were seen approaching the chapel. On hearing this, Winder and Monroe came forward to observe the approach until the British were within two miles of the structure. At this point Winder concluded that the advanced guard of his troops would not reach the Marlboro-Woodyard road junction behind him in time to intercept the British force. Thus he sent orders for his men to stop at an advantageous location and set up a defense. Winder then rode back to this location to assist Colonels Scott and Peters. At some point during this trip, Commodore Joshua Barney arrived with four hundred marines and sailors; the day before, he had abandoned his barges and come over land from Marlboro to join Winder's troops.

With additional troops now in hand, Winder rode back to the road junction—only to realize the British were not heading to Washington but had marched to Upper Marlboro. Now Winder's unit was out of position to intercept the enemy if they took the road from Marlboro to Bladensburg. Thus he ordered General Smith to retire his force to the point where the Washington and Woodyard roads linked with the road to Marlboro. Unfortunately, the order was misunderstood, and the army advanced from the Woodyard to the old Marlboro pike. Not planning to defend at that location, Winder ordered the force to retire to the Battalion Old Fields (now Forestville, Maryland) on the Marlboro road. Here Barney's men heard the explosions of his barges, destroyed by volunteers left behind to prevent the British under Cockburn from capturing the boats.

Though the British stopped in Marlboro at 2:00 p.m., they were in no hurry to leave. Units were rested, and contact was established with the flotilla under Cockburn in the Patuxent. In the meantime, Tilghman's cavalry caught some British stragglers that convinced Winder that the British didn't intend to leave Marlboro until morning. Winder then left to rejoin his units at Battalion Old Fields. On arriving, he became aware that his troop strength had reached almost three thousand men. Later that evening, however, he was told that President Madison, the secretary of war, the secretary of the navy, and the attorney general had arrived. With Colonel Monroe still present, the majority of the executive branch of government was now in camp.

That evening a spooked sentry awakened the entire camp at about three in the morning. Before it was realized that it was a false alarm, the entire force had been mustered and drawn up in battle lines. Within three hours, they were again awake taking down their tents, and by 8:00 a.m. the troops were being reviewed by President Madison. By 10:00 a.m. an advanced force under Major Peters was moving toward Marlboro with a troop of dragoons to make contact with the British.

Within a short time, firing was heard toward Marlboro, and reports came in that the British were marching up the Marlboro road toward their position. Captain Stull's corps of musket-armed riflemen had engaged the British less than six miles from the main body of United States troops. By the time Stull's unit withdrew, they had fired between four and five volleys at the advancing British troops. By 3:00 p.m. the whole force was arranged to repel the British: three thousand men, four hundred horses, and twelve cannons against four thousand troops and three cannon. At that point President Madison left the field with the secretaries of war and navy, returning to Washington. At the same time, Secretary Monroe took the attorney general with him to Bladensburg to meet General Stansbury, who had arrived at that location the night before.

With the dignitaries gone, Winder was finally in command of his own troops and was ready to do battle. All that was needed was the appearance of the British army, which he expected within the hour. When the British failed to appear by 5:00 p.m., however, General Winder realized they had stopped their pursuit of his advanced force. Now instead of having an afternoon battle in daylight, he was becoming concerned that the British were planning a night action. In such an event, the militia would be prone to flee, and his advantage in artillery would be nullified.[69] Thus after holding his troops at the ready all afternoon, he now ordered his troops to march back over the Eastern Branch Bridge into Washington.

---

[69] Winder may have also been concerned over his own ability to see at night. He had been captured the year prior when, in the dark, he had mistaken British troops as his own.

After arriving in the city, Winder now had to ensure that the British didn't seize the two bridges over the Eastern Potomac River (now called the Anacostia River) that led into the city. He placed units at both bridges to prepare them for destruction and to defend them against a surprise attack. These plans included barges full of kegs of black powder that would be floated down from the Washington navy yard to demolish the bridges. While arranging these measures, however Winder injured his arm and ankle when he fell into a ditch while en route to the navy yard.

Like his men, Winder was at the point of exhaustion. He had not slept well the previous night, and now he was out until almost 4:00 a.m. planning the defense of the bridges. He was also injured, which added to the mental distractions he had. His men were equally in distress, not sleeping well the previous night, being awake all day expecting a British attack, and then marching back to Washington in the evening. They were also unfed, having only been issued two rations in the previous four days. This lack of food was caused by Federal officials who had been requisitioning the quartermaster's wagons to carry important Federal documents out of the city.

Supplies for the force had always been a problem. Before the army left Washington, a request for one thousand musket flints had been made. Without these items, a major portion of the force could not function. Yet by the time the force had left, only an additional two hundred flints had been acquired. When the army returned to Washington, General Winder learned that five hundred Virginia militia and one hundred cavalry had arrived the day before under the command of Colonel Minor. The force was unarmed, and the officer authorized to distribute arms from the city arsenal, Colonel Carbery, could not be found for an entire day. After hearing this, Winder issued an order for the arms, and Minor marched his entire force to the arsenal to confront an immovable object: the young man guarding the arsenal.

Excerpt from the testimony of Colonel George Minor, October 30, 1814. "On my arrival at the armory, found that department in the care of a very young man, who dealt out the stores cautiously, which went greatly to consume time; as, for instance, when flints were once counted by my officers, who showed every disposition to expedite the furnishing the men, the young man had to count them over again, before they could be obtained, and at which place I met with Colonel Carbery; who introduced himself to me, and apologized for not being found when I was in search of him, stating he had left town the evening before, and had gone to his seat in the country. After getting the men equipped; I ordered them on to the capitol, and waited myself to sign the receipts for the munitions furnished; and, on my arrival, was informed by Major Hunter, who commanded in my absence, orders had been given to march to Bladensburg."

While all this was going on, Monroe had arrived at Bladensburg, aware that the British were moving but unaware whether a battle had occurred. On arrival at midnight, he met General Stansbury, who had taken up a position on the Marlboro road just south of the village. Stansbury had also heard of the British movements but also had no idea if any battle had occurred. Further, there was a rumor that Winder had been taken prisoner and the forces of the United States were now under the command of General Smith. Monroe, having not seen Winder return to the Battalion Old Fields before he left, could not deny this rumor. Instead, Monroe ordered Stansbury to move south and attack the enemy flank. Stansbury responded that he had been ordered to defend Bladensburg and that leaving could be viewed as deserting his post. He also told Monroe that many of his men had just arrived from Baltimore and were too fatigued to move. On hearing this, Monroe departed for Washington.

That night at 2:00 a.m., a sentry fired his gun, rousing the entire force at Bladensburg. A half hour later, the force was allowed to again return to their tents, though the damage had already been done. About the same time, a message was received from General Winder stating he had returned to Washington and that Stansbury was to resist the enemy for as long as possible if the British arrived at Bladensburg. On hearing this, after consulting his junior officers, Stansbury decided to move his unit across the Bladensburg Bridge toward Washington. There they again set up camp and tried to rest.

At about 10:00 a.m. on the twenty-fourth, General Winder learned that the British were heading toward Bladensburg. After ordering General Smith to follow with the bulk of the army, he rode out to take command. Already en route was James Monroe, who couldn't have had any more sleep than Winder. Monroe arrived at Bladensburg just after 11:00 a.m. and immediately began giving commands.

Stansbury had begun laying out his troops for about an hour before Monroe arrived. He had placed his units on the left side of the road from the bridge with three field guns under Captain Burch[70] positioned about four hundred yards from the bridge. To the right of the guns was a unit of riflemen under a Major Pinkney (of which not all had rifles). To the left was placed a unit of musketmen, and directly behind the cannons was the Fifth Baltimore Regiment. Stationed behind these units under the cover of an orchard were the regiments under Colonels Ragen and Schutz. These units were resting, having not fully recovered from their march from Baltimore. Adding to this force, a militia unit from Baltimore under the command of Colonel Beall crossed the Bladensburg Bridge around 11:00 a.m. and rushed past Stansbury's units to take up a position one and a half miles away at Brick Kilm where Stansbury had spent the previous night. Thirty minutes later, British troops could be seen cresting the top of Lowndes Hill behind Bladensburg.

Monroe wasn't in command at Bladensburg, and neither was he a trained military officer. Yet his position and name immediately caused the junior officers under Stansbury to follow his orders without question. First he positioned Burch's cannons in the redoubt near the

---

[70] This was what was left of one of the six-gun units Winder had at Battalion Old Fields. One of the guns had been left in Washington to cover another bridge to the city. Two more guns were left on the main road over a mile from the bridge. Winder's own after-action report shows he was completely unaware of this even though he ordered the guns left at these locations.

bridge while Burch was trying to find General Stansbury. He then advised Colonel Lavelle to place the cavalry in a ravine on the other side of the Georgetown road. Then he moved the Fifth Baltimore Regiment from directly behind the three cannons to the left side of the battle line. Finally, the two regiments under Ragen and Schutz were ordered out from under the cover of the orchard and placed on a hill behind the orchard.

Some facts need to be noted at this time. A field gun of that time had a maximum range of about fifteen hundred yards. Rifles, in the hands of a man who had some skill with it, could pick off a soldier at three hundred yards; in the hands of a novice a range of a hundred and fifty yards was expected. A musketman had an effective range of seventy-five yards. Thus, the only portion of Stansbury's force in range of the British in Bladensburg was three field guns—and Monroe had pushed these forces even farther away from the bridge.

The same could not be said of the British, who had both riflemen in their front lines and a wonder weapon called Congreve rockets. Congreve rockets were a new development for the British army with several variants in service. The most common had a twenty-four-pound warhead, while thirty-two-pound versions were used against Fort McHenry during the Chesapeake campaign. The larger rockets had a maximum range of about three thousand yards, and the smaller rocket could travel two thousand yards. Though inaccurate, these rockets gave the British the ability to bombard US forces while being safely out of range of retaliatory fire. In addition, the rockets didn't need hard ground or road access to set up for firing.

An example of this comes from the deployment of the Thirty-sixth Regiment's artillery when it arrived at Bladensburg. Behind the Thirty-sixth was to be a force of six artillery pieces placed on a commanding ravine. Unfortunately, the artillery could not be moved to the ravine because the ground around it was too soft for the gun carriages. A path to the top of the ravine was available, but it would take too long to move the guns along that route and into position. Thus the order was given to set up the artillery on a nearby position on the other side of the road. When the guns were in position, however, it was learned that the guns range placed the Thirty-sixth Regiment in the fire zone. The resulting shifting of troops placed the Thirty-sixth even farther from the bridge—and in line with the local militia under the command of Colonel Kramer. Thus, they were now on the Washington side of a small stream well over a thousand yards from the bridge they were defending.

As if the situation couldn't get any worse, at 12:00 the president arrived with Armstrong and several other cabinet members. Instead of taking up a position in the far rear of the battle, they had to set up directly behind Burch's cannons. Now the troops were watching their commander in chief and looking to him as to how the battle was going. They would soon learn the horrible lesson of why there cannot be multiple commanders in charge of a single army.

When the British arrived, Ross sent a brigade into Bladensburg to drive out any snipers left in the town. When the troops failed to find any snipers, they moved toward the bridge, believing they could cross unopposed. They were met by canister and round shot from Burch's three cannons, sending the first unit back in tatters. Surprisingly, no plans were implemented to destroy the bridge and force the British to ford the river.

Ross responded to this with the first salvo of what was to become a rolling barrage of rockets on US forces. These rockets were being fired by British sailors under the direction of Admiral Cockburn, who had come ashore just for this activity. The rockets disrupted the US front line but did not break it. What it did was prompt President Madison to withdraw in front of the entire force. This was the beginning of the morale breakdown that eventually resulted in the militia fleeing the battlefield.

With the rockets coming down, Ross then sent a second, stronger force across the bridge. This group moved rapidly and succeeded in getting across the bridge with few casualties. The battle was transitioning to infantry against infantry—and it was here that Monroe's changes proved fatal.

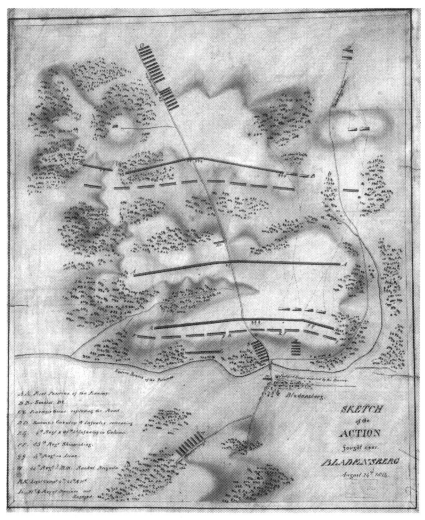

Figure 73: Map of the Battle for Bladensburg.

The placement of Pickney's riflemen on the right nearest the bridge in the redoubt was actually Stansbury's biggest mistake. When the British charged across the bridge, Pickney's units were the first to take the hit, and because his men were mostly riflemen, they had no bayonets. Only a single company, under the command of a Captain Doughty, actually had bayonets. Thus once the British were cresting the redoubt, the riflemen had no choice but to flee, their escape being covered by the one company of musket-armed riflemen placed in their unit.

As the riflemen were withdrawing, the Fifth Regiment was ordered forward to defend the cannons and throw back the British on the road. But because the Fifth was to the cannons' left and the road was to the cannons' right, their movement brought them right in front of their own artillery. Thus the cannons now had to cease fire to avoid hitting their own defending troops. If the troops had been left behind the guns, they could have moved against the British from behind and to the right of the cannons without masking their own artillery. Now it was one of Monroe's changes that proved costly.

The movement of the Fifth against the British did not last long. The moment they began moving, they became a target for Cockburn's rockets, which quickly rained down on them. The following comment expresses what the troops felt when these eighteenth-century wonder weapons began falling on them.

> It cleared the treetops, seemed to hang there for an instant before it plunged downward in its fiery arc. A man couldn't see a bullet coming; if his number wasn't on it, he heard only the hum of its passing. But this swooping thing was dreadfully personal. It appeared to be darting directly at each watching soldier, making him shake in his boots, turning his knees to water. Only when he saw it strike the ground some distances in front could he believe it was not headed straight for him.

The men of the Fifth wavered and then fired their muskets too early to be effective against the British troops. By this time, Stansbury had ordered Burch to withdraw his artillery. When the artillery began to retreat, so did the Fifth, followed by Stansbury's remaining brigade, which had not even engaged the enemy.

As the front line collapsed, the British pursued to the orchard, where they now used the cover of the trees to engage Ragen's and Schutz's regiments on the hill.[71] Caught in the open, these regiments were suddenly hard pressed, and when the rocket barrage advanced to their position, the troops had had enough. They had seen the president flee the field, and then the units in front of them. Now they were being shot at by British troops under cover and shelled by the terrifying rockets. The units turned and fled toward the Georgetown road.

In the middle of all this were the 260 horsemen Monroe had placed in the ravine. Totally under cover, they had no idea what was happening, and they were incapable of moving out to support or attack anyone. When stray rockets directed at the second line began falling into the ravine, Lavall had no choice but to withdraw. Thus, another US unit had left the field without even engaging the enemy. Monroe's changes had seriously weakened the first and second lines, virtually giving the British control of all the ground from the Bladensburg Bridge to the small stream that Kramer's militia and the Thirty-sixth Regiment stood behind.

Thus, at this point in the battle, all of Stansbury's 2,200 men, as well as three pieces of artillery, had been forced to leave the field. That left the remainder of the army under Smith just beyond the small stream. At this point the British formed up to cross the stream and push away Kramer's unit. The assault was quick, with Kramer's unit firing a few volleys before retiring toward Beall's unit and the navy artillery of Commodore Barney. Barney had come with his sailors and marines without orders from Winder (but on orders from Madison), and he had actually begun emplacing his guns while the British were storming the first line of US troops at the bridge.

It was at this point in the battle that the British came under extreme artillery fire from both the six cannons of General Smith on the left side of the road and the extremely large ship cannons Barney

---

[71] Being on the high ground, these two regiments were visible to the British commanders on Lowndes Hill from the moment the British arrived an hour earlier. There was plenty of time to plan the adjustment of the rocket bombardment.

brought with him (eighteen-pounders). Their first assault on Barney's position was repulsed, as was a second, forcing the British to give up a frontal attack and to move toward the US right flank. There it was shelled by three twelve-pound cannons and was repulsed again by the marines and sailors of Barney's flotilla. What Barney didn't know at the time was that General Winder had ordered a retreat.

Figure 74: Barney's marine gunners at Blandensburg.

Given the circumstances, the order to retreat opened the floodgates to a mad dash to the rear. In a short time, the only US units left at Bladensburg were Barney's marines and General Smith's artillery unit on the left side of the road. At this point in the battle, British riflemen began picking off Barney's men (and Barney's horse) while an infantry force moved against the guns on the US left. Having already been given the order to withdraw, they fled the field, leaving Barney's men without any support. Now wounded in the thigh, Barney finally had to order his men to leave him and retreat.

As for Colonel Minor and his six hundred Virginia militia, when they finally were able to move out, they ended up meeting the retreating Army at the turnpike. An aid to General Winder ordered them to cover the retreat from a nearby high point. After the troops had fled, Minor's unit withdrew to the capital and then followed the rest of the army to Tenlytown. They never saw any combat.

So ended the three-hour Battle of Bladensburg, but the story was not over. Before the day was out, the British had entered Washington and begun destroying government buildings. The White House was burned, as was a portion of the capitol. The next day a hurricane struck the Chesapeake, putting the fires out and forcing the British to flee the city. Where the troops of the United States had failed, the rage of nature prevailed, and Ross was forced to retreat back through Bladensburg and to Upper Marlbourgh. There, his battered troops boarded the boats of Cockburn's river force and sailed downriver to the bay and the main British fleet.

The damage to the United States was more than one could believe. In four days of action, from the twenty-second to the twenty-fifth, Ross had defeated over 6,000 troops and forced the majority of a city of 8,000 people to flee. On the twenty-second, when he took Marlbourgh, he had seized one six-pound cannon, and 156 muskets. On the twenty-fourth he took two eighteen-pound cannons, five twelve-pound cannons, three six-pound cannons, and 220 muskets. Then in Washington he seized 206 cannons of all types, some 2,000 muskets at the Federal ordnance laboratory, and 100,000 rounds of musket ammo in paper cartridges. Not counting the loss of a frigate under construction, the total loss in military arms and material for the United States was staggering.

Within a few days of having to abandon the capital, Madison was back in Washington. Congress was meeting in the post office, and Madison was in the patent office—the only government buildings spared by the British. Six days after the British withdrew from Washington, a British naval force, working its way up the Potomac since before the British landed at Benedict, landed at Alexandria and took the town without a shot fired. They remained there for three days, plundered it of food and other "exportables," and then sailed back downriver to rejoin Cochrane's fleet.[72] This second defeat within sight of the capital added fuel to the public's disgust with the Federal government.

Figure 75: Top: Depiction of the burning of the capital buildings. Bottom: Depiction of the burning of the Washington naval yard.

---

[72] During this withdrawal, the fleet was confronted every mile by American land forces.

Figure 76: Depiction of the burned presidential residence.

Baltimore

And yet the situation was turning rapidly in the government's favor. Cockburn thought the burning of the city would greatly demoralize the people of the United States. But like the burning of York the year before, the action did the exact opposite. Like York, following which there was even more resistance to the incursions of the United States into Canada, the burning of Washington prompted both anger and fear of the British. Within days of the burning, militia formed all over Maryland, Virginia, Delaware, and Pennsylvania. By the time Ross landed 4,700 troops at North Point on September 12, the militia around Baltimore had swelled to over 15,000 men.

At Baltimore there was no question as to who was in charge. It was General Samuel Smith, a completely different type of general than those who served at Bladensburg. He had worked with militia since the revolution, and he knew how to use them to their maximum. Thus, his defense of Baltimore had a completely different style then that employed by Winder at Washington.

Smith knew he could go behind his entrenchments and try to ride out a siege. But he knew he had to go on the offensive at the beginning and make Ross fight for every piece of ground he took. He sent out a force of three thousand men (the Third Brigade) to engage Ross as far from Baltimore as possible. Today historians say he was buying time to finish his entrenchments, but in reality he was tempering his troops.

One mistake Winder made at Washington was not engaging the British either before the British reached Marlborough or the next day. In truth he might have caused just as much of a panic in his own troops, but the British would not have been able to follow them any farther then the Anacostia River. Yet he would have also given his troops their baptism of fire. Thus in their next action, they would be less prone to run at the first crack of fire. If Winder had done this, by the time of Bladensburg his greatest handicap would have been the meddling of unwanted government officials.

Smith's active defense posture was also tempered with the knowledge he now had units under his command that wanted to redeem themselves for Bladensburg. The Fifth Regiment in the front line at Bladensburg was from Baltimore, and in the two weeks since that battle, they had returned to fight for their city. They had been under fire now as well as shelled by rockets. Thus, as Smith sent forward the Third Brigade of Maryland militia, he also sent forward the Fifth Regiment of the Third Brigade.

The Third Brigade, under General Stricker, left the city at 3:00 p.m. on September 11 for the Methodist meeting house, some seven miles from the city heading for North Point. The following morning at 3:00 a.m., Ross began landing his men at North Point. In less than four hours, he had landed his 4,700 men and was ready to march to Baltimore. By 9:00 Ross stopped his advanced force (a light brigade) at Gorsuch Farm, where he had breakfast. There he was said to have made two fateful statements, "I'll supp in Baltimore or in hell," and "I don't care if it rains militia."

By the time Ross had made these statements, Stricker had sent forward all his riflemen to harass the British troops. They did so for a short time until rumors of a British landing behind them (supplied by US cavalry) forced them to withdraw. Then Stricker sent a group of volunteers (about 250 men) forward to make contact with the enemy. This force included two companies of the Fifth Regiment and all the previously mentioned riflemen. At 1:00 p.m. the Fifth engaged Ross's advanced force at a place called Godley Wood. In the resulting skirmish, a rifle bullet mortally wounded Ross. The volunteer militia force then quickly retired, joining the main force at Bouldin's Farm.

With Ross dead, command shifted to Colonel Arthur Brooke, who engaged the US force with the intention of turning its left flank. Eventually this was accomplished, but not because of effective British leadership or training. The Fifty-first Regiment, positioned to prevent such a flanking maneuver, ran after firing only one salvo, taking with them some of the Thirty-ninth Regiment. The now seasoned Fifth held and made possible an orderly retreat back to Cooks Tavern, where the Sixth Regiment had been stationed. There, Stricker regrouped his forces, including the Fifty-first and Thirty-ninth Regiments.

The British had suffered over three hundred casualties, and the US had suffered just over two hundred. Though the forces of the United States had given ground, they had not run in panic. The British had stopped twice and lost their commander, and when they reached the edge of the Baltimore entrenchment, they realized they could not take the position without naval support. The defenders had a three to one superiority in men.

Figure 77: General John Stricker by Rembrandt Peale and the death of General Ross.

The next day, the British fleet began bombarding Fort McHenry with the plan to reduce the fort and then move close enough to the harbor side of the entrenchments to blow a hole in them for the British ground forces to pass through. The bombardment failed, sparing the city and giving the United States it national anthem. The following day the new commander of the British land forces received word he would get no support in his attack on the entrenchments. Thus, on September 14 the British began marching back to North Point. By September 17 the force had re-embarked and was leaving the Chesapeake. Its new targets: Mobile Bay, to be followed by the city of New Orleans.

The British Attack, Phase Two

As noted earlier, the attacks on Washington and Baltimore were a diversion to draw US forces away from the other two attacks that were being mounted. The second assault was now to come from Montreal, were an eleven-thousand-man British force under the command of General Prevost began marching south on September 1. Larger by almost three thousand men than Gentleman Johnny Burgoyne's

1777 assault during the revolution, this was the greatest threat the United States ever faced in the war because it threatened to split the northeastern states from the rest of the nation.

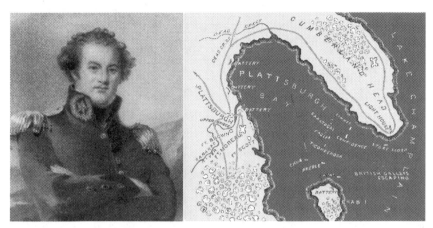

Figure 78: General Alexander Macomb by Thomas Sulley and the bay at Plattsburg.

Standing against Prevost was 3,400 men, of which only around 1,500 were fit for service under the command of General Alexander Macomb. Macomb was a combat engineer who had been building three forts, two redoubts, and two blockhouses along the Saranac River. Three days before Prevost began marching south under orders from Secretary of War Armstrong, General Izard and 4,000 men had left Plattsburg for Sackett's Harbor.[73]

Missing from all this was Colonel Forsyth and the First Rifle Regiment. On June 27 Forsyth and 70 of his riflemen had setup an ambush at Odelltown just south of Lacolle Mills. As the ambush was beginning, Forsyth broke cover and was promptly shot dead by an Indian scout. The ambush went off, leaving 17 British dead out of a force of 150.

---

[73] Izard is reported to have sent a message to Washington that within three days of his departure, everything in that section of New York would be in enemy hands.

Forsyth's men took it upon themselves to avenge their commander by killing the commander of the equivalent British force in that area, Captain Joseph St. Valer Mailloux. On August 10 Forsyth's men caught up with him, wounded him, and took him back to Champlain. Though a British surgeon worked on him, he died in custody one week later. The new commander of these riflemen, Major Appling, implemented severe punishment on the unit for this breach of military discipline. Forsyth had run a very lax unit, so this sudden change in policy destroyed morale, and by the time Prevost began his march south, these companies of the First Rifle Regiment had disintegrated, with many of the men deserting to Canada. Thus the United States was now blind to the movements of the British as they began their invasion.

On the first day of his invasion, Prevost took Champlain, New York, without any resistance. There he issued a proclamation along the same lines as the one General Hull had issued two years earlier when he'd entered Canada from Detroit. Three days later, he again began marching south toward the town of Chazy. There his forces began encountering American militia, who began burning bridges, felling trees, and performing the same delaying tactics they had administered to Burgoyne thirty-seven years earlier.

While the land force was moving south, a flotilla of gunboats was following on its left flank. On September 4 the gunboats landed on the Isle Le Motto and set up a gun battery. Isle Le Motto was not in New York but in Vermont, which until that moment was actually friendly to the British and definitely Federalist in politics. When the British came in without an invitation, the people of Vermont reacted as citizens of the United States and swarmed across Lake Champlain to Plattsburg, swelling the defense force.

On September 5 a force of one hundred riflemen, two hundred musketmen, and two field guns had taken up a strong position at Dead Creek. Supporting them from offshore were US Navy gunboats. Further inland, on the Beckman road leading from Chazy, was a second force of seven hundred militiamen. The following day, the

British arrived at both locations, Prevost's force being large enough to move in two columns (and this was after leaving garrisons at both Champlain and Chazy).

Whereas the force at Dead Creek was in a strong location, the force along the Beckman road was not. Worse, the New York State dragoons that were supporting them wore red coats like British troops. These units were constantly spooking the militia, who were afraid of being surrounded by the British. These same cavalry units would later cause endless trouble with friendly Vermont militia who also couldn't tell the difference.

Thus, when the British did arrive, the militia was too confused to make a good fight. There were two main attempts to check the British movement, but the size of the British force was too great, and in a short time US forces were in full retreat. The loss of this position made the defense at Dead Creek impossible, and now both forces withdrew back to Plattsburg.

The Battle of Plattsburg

On reaching Plattsburg, US forces crossed the Saranac River, destroying the bridge behind them. When the British arrived, Prevost surveyed the situation and decided not to mount a frontal attack. Instead, he sent word to the commander of his support fleet, Captain Downie, to move up and engage the enemy fleet in Plattsburg harbor. The plan was for Downie to defeat the US fleet and then give support to the British land troops in storming the fortifications.

Prevost had to remove the US fleet from Lake Champlain for two reasons. First, the US Navy was already attacking his forces moving along the river road, and the navy would support the forts closest to the lake during a British assault. Second, Prevost's army was one big eating machine. It was too big to live off the local food supplies and needed to be supplied by ship from Canada. Any threat to that supply line would force him to withdraw back to Canada.

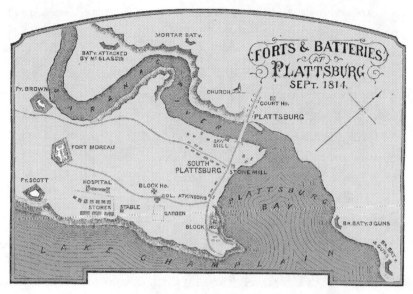

Figure 79: City and forts of Plattsburg, New York.

Of course the decision to not launch an attack didn't mean the British sat down and relaxed. Prevost sent his riflemen forward to the abandoned homes on the north side of the bridge. There they began sniping at the US troops across the river. Macomb countered this by firing heated cannon balls at the homes to set them ablaze. These back-and-forth skirmishes occurred for the next five days as Prevost awaited the arrival of his support fleet.

When the British fleet did arrive on September 11, the situation couldn't have been worse for the British. In just one week, the number of militiamen arrayed against the British had doubled. Adding insult to injury, the US militia had begun raiding the British lines at night, destroying a Congreve rocket unit[74] on September 9. Thus, the militia was losing their fear of the British, which made the militia even more effective. This was the situation as the battle of Plattsburg began.

---

[74] The commander of that attack was Captain McGlassin. He drove off three hundred veteran troops with only fifty men and destroyed the battery. Of course, it didn't hurt that that evening had been filled with rain, lightning, and wind.

When the British fleet was sighted, Prevost ordered his units to attack the US lines at three points: the Village Bridge, the Upper Bridge, and a ford three miles upstream. The British guns on shore began firing just as the sound of the naval battle reached the shore. At the bridges, regular US Army units met the British troops. At the ford, militia rifle fire from a nearby wood decimated the approaching British, destroying a company of the British Seventy-sixth Regiment. Then, as Prevost watched a British unit mount the breastworks of one of the enemy redoubts, he heard shouts of victory from the US positions. The flagship of the British fleet had struck its colors, and the British gunboats were running for safety.

Figure 80: Various depictions of the Battle of Plattsburg.

With the British fleet in retreat, there was no point to continuing the battle. Prevost sounded a recall and began preparations for a withdrawal. By his own numbers, he had only lost 37 men, 150 wounded, and 55 missing, for a total of 242 men. It was logistics that forced the withdrawal. Without control of the lake to ensure a regular supply line, he couldn't hope to maintain such a large force at Plattsburg through the winter. Within a few days, he was back in Canada.

Aftermath

Figure 81: Watercolor of the damaged Capitol Building.

Though both the victories at Plattsburg and Baltimore reached the ear of congress, the smoldering ruins of Washington were a constant reminder that the US military was in serious disrepair. Someone had to take the blame for all this, and the first name on the list was Secretary of War Armstrong. His unwillingness to even consider Washington as a target and his less than stellar performance when it became clear the city was endangered didn't help. Adding to this, his refusal to change his orders to Izard and reinforce Plattsburg ended all faith in his leadership. By September 23 he had resigned his office to be replace by James Monroe, the real architect of the defeat at Bladensburg.

Monroe then began the process of making his mark on the office of secretary of war. The first action was to increase the size of the army to make up for losses in battle and the growing strength of the enemy. In this regard, he inherited a September 23 congressional request of Armstrong to document the defects in the present military establishment and to determine what future provisions, by law, were deemed necessary to remedy such defects.

Granted that the situation may have looked bleak just outside of the Washington post office building, but the actual military situation wasn't a lack of men. The army now had about 40,000 men under arms and an authorized strength of 62,448 men, and for the year 1814 alone it had recruited over 10,000 men.[75] In addition, a significant amount of militia was also in the field in 1814, totaling 197,660 men according to records compiled after the war. The problem was where they were, how long they served, and how they were armed.

The fact was both the army and the militia was scattered throughout the country, and yet they were concentrated around the major cities and towns. As noted in chapter two, most of the Federal Army was concentrated at specific locations, forts, and cities. When Bladensburg occurred, of the 27,000 effective troops in the US Army, nearly 18,000 were assigned to the Ninth Military District out of Buffalo, Oswego, and Sacketts Harbor. In addition, over 50 percent of the militia was located in only five of the seventeen states in the union. To reposition any of these units meant long marches over poor roads, and moving the troops by water was nearly impossible given the British naval blockade. However, the British did not have this problem given their control of the St. Lawrence River up to Niagara and their Atlantic fleet. It was only when they didn't have water access that the British would not (or could not) mount a military action.

Because of the limited size of the army and its position on the New York frontier, the problem of coastal defense fell on the militia. The second problem the government had with the militia was that they served in short bursts. Having homes, businesses, and families back in their communities, the men in the militia couldn't leave them unsupported for extended periods. Six months was the regular maximum time of service, though Virginia held its men for only three months. Any extension of this service time was viewed as a major hardship to both the militiamen and their general community. This

---

[75] Bounties paid for recruits in the year 1814 totaled $2,012,439.33.

problem is no different today: members of the National Guard place their families under financial hardship when they serve overseas.

The third problem was what they were armed with. The government and its commanders expected the militia to be armed with the same caliber gun as the army, per the requirements of the Militia Act. Instead, given the data, there were only some 218,000 proper muskets to the 565,000 men required to carry it. There were other arms: in the returns alone there were 84,000 rifles of Federal caliber and some 60,000 pistols and carbines, making for 383,000 documented weapons. Outside of these were hundreds of thousands of muskets of various calibers in state arsenals and private hands, as well as a large number of rifled muskets. But these arms were not uniform in caliber, and thus supporting them in ammunition could prove difficult. As noted with the Federal call for militia from Virginia to defend Washington, a few States deliberately armed and organized their troops differently then that prescribed by federal law.

But what about arms in the Federal store? When the war began, the government had 135,000 arms fit for service and another 65,000 of the wrong caliber or in need of repair. Thus, as stated earlier there were well over 520,000 military weapons in country at the start of the war.

> Excerpt from Communication to the House of Representatives, July 8, 1813, Subject: Arming the Militia per the Act of 1808. "Would it have been wise, under these circumstances, to distribute 30,000 stands of arms equally among the 800,000 militia? Or would it have been wiser to consult the wants and exposure of particular portions?"

This comment is part of a larger letter explaining why nearly 8,500 muskets that the states had already paid for were not being distributed as required under the law of 1808. The Madison Administration had started the war with 135,000 muskets of proper caliber in Federal stores, and by the end of 1814, the two Federal arsenals and outside contractors had assembled 64,000 muskets. That should make for nearly 200,000 muskets to equip an army of 60,000 men. Yet suddenly the administration felt compelled to hold on to 8,500 muskets as an emergency measure. The answer is simple: they were running out of arms.

> Letter of Colonel Bomford, on ordnance duty, to the Secretary of War, relative to the number of arms required annually to supply the Militia of the West, February 24, 1823. "In reference to the expediency or inexpediency of establishing an additional armory, it may be proper to state, that muskets belonging to the United States, at the commencement of the late war, have been estimated at upwards of two hundred thousand stands, and that the number of muskets manufactured during the war was about sixty thousand. At the close of the year 1814, scarcely twenty thousand stands remained in the arsenals, and great efforts were made to procure an additional supply. Had the war continued another year, the deficiency of arms would have occasioned the most embarrassing consequences."

Yes, it was true: of the 191,000 guns that should have existed, by late 1814 there was only some 20,000 in federal store that were of the proper caliber and not already committed to combat. Add the numbers.

(1) 18,482 muskets loaned to the states prior to Jan 1816
(2) 13,700 muskets delivered to the states in accordance to the 1808 Act

(3) 21,000 muskets repaired in 1815 at Springfield Armory and Harpers Ferry
(4) Some 10,000 muskets lost in battle by this time
(5) 60,000 muskets just for the standing army
(6) 50,000 for the volunteers under the Act of 1812
Total: 173,182 of the 191,000 muskets

To put it bluntly, the real problem the government had wasn't an unarmed militia; it was how to keep the Federal army in arms. This situation would become even more acute as Monroe put forth his plan for the first national military draft—a conscription that, if implemented, would double the size of the United States Army

CHAPTER 7
Monroe's Proposal and the First Draft Law

Cover Letter

To; The Honorable William B. Giles, Chairman of the Committee of the Senate on Military Affairs

From: James Monroe, Secretary of War, October 17, 1814

Sir:

The great importance of the subject, and the other duties of the Department, which could not fail to be very sensibly felt, at so interesting a period, by a person who had just taken charge of it, are my apology for not answering your letter, of the 23rd of September, at an Earlier day, on the defects of the present military establishment.

Due consideration has been bestowed on the subject matter of the letter, and I have now the honor to submit to the committee the following report:

1. That the present military establishment, amounting to 62,448 men, be preserved and made complete, and that the most efficient means authorized by the constitution, and consistent with the equal rights of our fellow citizens, be adopted to fill the ranks, and with the least possible delay.

2. That a permanent force, consisting of not less than 40,000 men, in addition to the present military establishment, be raised, for the defense of our cities and frontiers, under an engagement by the Executive with each corps that it shall be employed in that service within certain specified limits. And that a proportional augmentation of general officers of each grade, and other staff, be provided for.
3. That the corps of engineers be enlarged.
4. That the ordnance department be amended.

Respecting the enlargement of the corps of engineers, I shall submit hereafter a more detailed communication.

For the proposed amendment of the ordnance department, I submit a report from the senior officer in that department, now in this city, which is approved.

I shall be ready and happy to communicate such further remarks and details on these subjects as the committee may desire, and shall request permission to suggest, hereafter, the result of further attention to, and reflection on, our military establishment generally, should anything occur which may be deemed worthy it attention.

I have the honor to be, with great respect, your very obedient servant,

James Monroe

Monroe's Proposal

Explanatory Observations

In providing a force necessary to bring this war to a happy termination, the nature of the crisis in which we are involved, and the extent of its dangers, claim particular attention. If the means are not fully adequate to the end, discomfiture must inevitably ensue.

It may fairly be presumed that it is the object of the British Government, by striking at the principal sources of our prosperity, to diminish the importance, if not to destroy the political existence, of the United States. If any doubt remained on this subject, it has been completely removed by the dispatches from our ministers at Ghent, which were lately laid before Congress.

A nation contending for its existence against an enemy powerful by land and sea, favored, in peculiar manner, by extraordinary events, must make great exertions, and suffer great sacrifices. Forced to contend again for our liberties and independence, we are called on for a display of all the patriotism which distinguished our fellow-citizens in the first great struggle. It may be fairly concluded that if the United States sacrifice any right, or make any dishonorable concession to the demands of the British Government, the spirit of the nation will be broken, and the foundations of their union and independence shaken. The United States must relinquish no right, or perish in the struggle. There is no intermediate ground to rest on. A concession on one-point leads directly to the surrender of every other, the result of the content cannot be doubtful. The highest confidence is entertained that the stronger the pressure, and the greater the danger, the more firm and vigorous will be the resistance, and the more successful and glorious the result.

It is the avowed purpose of the enemy to lay waste and destroy our cities and villages, and to desolate our coast, of which examples have already been afforded. It is evidently his intention to press the war along the whole extent of our seaboard, in the hope of exhausting equally the spirits of the people and the national resources. There is also reason to presume that it is the intention to press the war from Canada on the adjoining States, while attempts are made on the city of New York, and other important points, with a view to the vain project of dismemberment or subjugation. It may be inferred likewise, to be a part of the scheme, to continue to invade this part of the Union, while a separate force attacks the State of Louisiana, in the hope of taking possession of the City of New Orleans, and of the mouth of the Mississippi, that great inlet and key to commerce of all that portion of the United States lying westward of the Alleghany mountains. The peace in Europe having given to the enemy a large disposable force has essentially favored these objects.

The advantage which a great naval superiority gives the enemy, by enabling him to move troops from one quarter to another, from Maine to the Mississippi, a coast of two thousand miles extent, is very considerable. Even a small force, moved in this manner, for the purposes avowed by British commanders, cannot fail to be sensibly felt; more especially by those who are most exposed to it. It is obvious that, if the militia are to be relied on, principally, for the defense of our cities and coast against these predatory and desolating incursions, wherever they may be made, that, by interfering with their ordinary pursuits of industry, it must be attended with serious interruption and loss to them, and injury to the public, while it greatly increases the expense. It is an object, therefore, of the highest importance, to provide a regular force with the means of transporting it from one quarter to another, along our coast, thereby following the movements of the enemy, with the greatest possible rapidity, and repelling the attack wherever it may be made. These remarks are equally true as to the militia service generally, under the present organization of the militia, and the short terms of service prescribed by law. It may be stated with confidence, that at least three times the force, in militia, has been employed at our principal cities, along the coast and on the frontier, in marching to, and returning thence, that would have been necessary in regular troops; and that the expense attending it has been more than proportionably augmented, from the difficulty, if not the impossibility of preserving the same degree of system in the militia as in the regular service.

But it will not be sufficient to repel these predatory and desolating incursions. To bring the war to an honorable termination, we must not be contented with defending ourselves. Different feelings must be touched, and apprehensions excited, in the British Government. By pushing the war into Canada, we secure the friendship of the Indian tribes, and command their services, otherwise to be turned by the enemy against us; we relieve the coast from the desolation which is intended for it, and we keep in our hands a safe pledge for an honorable peace.

It follows, from this view of the subject, that it will be necessary to bring into the field, next campaign, not less than one hundred thousand regular troops. Such a force aided, in extraordinary emergencies, by volunteers and the militia, will place us above all inquietude as to the final result of this contest. It will fix on a solid and imperishable foundation, our union and independence, on which the liberties and happiness of our fellow-citizens so essentially depend. It will secure to the United States an early and advantageous peace. It will arrest, in the further prosecution of the war, the desolation of our cities and our coast, enabling us to retort on the enemy, those calamities which our citizens have been already doomed to suffer-a resort which self-defense alone, and a sacred regard for the rights and honor of the nation, could induce the United States to adopt.

The return of the regular force now in service, laid before you, will show how many men will be necessary to fill the present corps; and the return of the numerical force of the present military establishment will show how many are required to complete it to the number proposed. The next and most important inquiry is how shall these men be raised? Under existing circumstances, it is evident that the most prompt and efficient mode that can be devised, consistent with the equal rights of every citizen, ought to be adopted. The following plans are respectfully submitted to the consideration of the committee. Being distinct in their nature, I will present each separately with the considerations applicable to it.

Monroe's First Plan

Let the free male population of the United States, between eighteen and forty-five years, be formed into classes of one hundred men each, and let each class furnish four men for the war, within thirty days after the classification and replace them in the event of casualty.

The classification to be formed with a view to the equal distribution of property among the several classes.

If any class fails to provide the men required of it, within the time specified, they shall be raised by draught on the whole class, any person, thus draughted, being allowed to furnish a substitute.

The present bounty in land to be allowed to each recruit, and the present bounty in money, which is paid to each recruit by the United States, to be paid to each draught by all the inhabitants within the precinct of the class within which the draught may be made, equally, according to the value of the property which they may respectively possess; and if such bounty be not paid within- days, the same to be levied on all the taxable property of the said inhabitants; and, in like manner, the bounty, whatever it may be, which may be employed in raising a recruit, to avoid a draught, to be assessed on the taxable property of the whole precinct.

The recruits to be delivered over to the recruiting officer in each district, to be marched to such places of general rendezvous as may be designated by the Department of War.

That this plan will be efficient cannot be doubted. It is evident that the men contemplated may soon be raised by it. Three modes occur by which it may be carried into effect: 1st, By placing the execution of it in the hands of the county courts throughout the United States: 2nd, By relying on the militia officers in each county: 3rd, By appointing particular persons for that purpose in every county. It is believed that either of these modes would be found adequate.

Nor does there appear to be any well founded objection to the right of Congress to adopt this plan, or to its equality in its application to our fellow-citizens individually. Congress have a right, by the constitution, to raise regular armies, and no restraint is imposed on the exercise of it, except in the provisions which are intended to guard generally against the abuse of power, with none of which does this plan interfere. It is proposed that it shall operate on all alike; that none shall be exempted from it except the chief Magistrate of the United States, and the Governors of the several states.

It would be absurd to suppose that Congress could not carry this power into effect, otherwise that by accepting the voluntary service of individuals. It might happen that an army could not be raised in that mode, whence the power would have been granted in vain. The safety of the State might depend on such an army. Long continued invasions, conducted by regular, well disciplined troops, can best be repelled by troops kept constantly in the field, and equally well disciplined. Courage in an army is, in a great measure, mechanical. A small body, well trained, accustomed to action, gallantly led on, often breaks three or four times the number of more respectable and more brave, but raw and undisciplined troops. The sense of danger is diminished by frequent exposure to it, without harm; and confidence, even in the timid, is inspired by a knowledge that reliance may be placed on others, which can grow up only by service together. The grant to Congress to raise armies, was made with a knowledge of all these circumstances, and with an intention that it should take effect, The framers of the constitution, and the states who ratified it, knew the advantage which an enemy might have over us, by regular forces, and intended to place their country on an equal footing.

The idea that the United States cannot raise a regular army in any other mode than by accepting the voluntary service of individuals, is believed to be repugnant to the uniform construction of all grants of power, and equally so to the first principles and leading objects of the federal compact. An unqualified grant of power gives the means necessary to carry it into effect. This is a universal maxim, which admits of no exception. Equally true is it, that the conservation of the State is a duty paramount to all others. The commonwealth has a right to the service of all its citizens; or rather, the citizens composing the commonwealth have a right, collectively and individually, to the service of each other, to repel any danger which may be menaced. The manner in which the service is to be apportioned among the citizens, and rendered by them, are objects of legislation. All that is to be dreaded in such case, is, the abuse of power; and, happily, our constitution has provided ample security against that evil.

In support of this right in Congress, the militia service affords a conclusive proof and striking example. The organization of the militia is an act of public authority, not a voluntary association. The service required must be performed by all, under penalties, which delinquents pay. The generous and patriotic perform them cheerfully. In the alacrity with which the call of the government has been obeyed, and the cheerfulness with which the service has been performed throughout the United States, by the great body of the militia, there is abundant cause to rejoice in the strength of our republican institutions, and in the virtue of the people.

The plan proposed is not more compulsive than the militia service, while it is free from most of the objections to it. The militia service calls from home, for long terms, whole districts of country. None can elude the call. Few can avoid the service; and those who do are compelled to pay great sums for substitutes. This plan fixes on no one personally, and opens to all who choose it a chance of declining service. It is a principal object of this plan to engage in the defense of the State the unmarried and youthful, who can best defend it, and best be spared, and to secure to those who render this important service an adequate compensation from voluntary contributions of the more wealthy, in every class. Great confidence is entertained that such contribution will be made in time to avoid a draught. Indeed, it is believed to be the necessary and inevitable tendency of this plan to produce that effect.

The limited powers which the United States have in organizing the militia may be urged as an argument against their right to raise regular troops in the mode proposed. If any argument could be drawn from that circumstance, I should suppose that it would be in favor of an opposite conclusion. The power of the United States over the militia has been limited, and that for raising regular armies granted without limitation. That was doubtless some object in this arrangement. The fair interference seems to be, that it was made on great consideration; that the limitation, in the first instance, was intentional, the consequence of the unqualified grant in the second. But it is said, that, by drawing the men from the militia service into the regular army, and putting them under regular officers, you violate a principle of the constitution, which provides that the militia shall be commanded by their own officers, If this was the fact, the conclusion would follow. But it is not the fact. The men are not drawn from the militia, but from the population of the country. When they enlist voluntarily, it is not as militia men that they act, but as citizens. If they are draughted, it must be in the same sense. In both instances, they are enrolled in the militia corps; but that, as is presumed, cannot prevent the voluntary act in the one instance or the compulsive in the other. The whole population of the United States, within certain ages, belong to these corps. If the United States could not form regular armies from them, they could raise none.

In proposing a straight draught as one of the modes of raising men, in case of actual necessity, in the present great emergency of the country, I have though it my duty to examine such objections to it as occurred, particularly those of a constitutional nature. It is from my sacred regard for the principles of our constitution, that I have ventured to trouble the committee with my remarks on this part of the subject.

Should it appear that this mode of raising recruits was justly objectionable, on account of the tax on property, from difficulties which may be apprehended in the execution, or from other cases, it may be advisable to decline the tax, and for the Government to pay the whole bounty. In this case, it is proposed that, in lieu of the present bounty, the sum of fifty dollars be allowed to each recruit or draught, at the time of his engagement, and one hundred acres of land in addition to the present bounty in land, for every year that the war may continue.

It is impossible to state, with mathematical accuracy, the number which will be raised by the ratio of 4 to 100, or 1 to 25, nor is it necessary. It is probable that it will be rather more than sufficient to fill the present corps. The extra number, in that case, may form a part of the local force in contemplation, a power to that effect being given to the President.

No radical change in the present military establishment is proposed. Should any modification be found necessary, on further consideration, it will form the subject of a separate communication. It is thought advisable, in general, to preserve the corps in their present form, and to fill them with new recruits, in the manner stated. All these corps have already seen service, and many of them acquired in active scenes much experience and useful knowledge. By preserving them in their present form, and under their present officers, and filling them with new recruits, the improvement of the latter will be rapid. In two or three months, it will be difficult to distinguish between the new and the old levies.

The additional force to be provided amounts to forty thousand men. Of this it is proposed that local corps be raised, to consist party of infantry, partly of mounted men, and party of artillery. There is reason to believe that such corps may be raised in the principal cities, and even on the frontiers, to serve for the war, under an engagement as to the limit beyond which they should not be carried. Every able bodied citizen is willing and ready to fight for his home, his family, and his country, when invaded. Of this we have seen in the present year the most honorable and gratifying proofs, It does not suit all, however, to go great distances from home. This generous and patriotic spirit may be taken advantage of, under proper arrangements, with the happiest effects to the country, and without essential inconvenience to the parties.

The officers who may be appointed to command these corps should be charged with recruiting them. Local defense being their sole object, it may be presumed that the corps will soon be raised. Patriotism alone will furnish a very powerful motive. It seems reasonable, however, that some recompense should be made to those who relieve others from the burthen; one hundred acres of land and fifty dollars to each recruit will, it is presumed, be deemed sufficient.

It is proposed that this additional force shall form a part of any plan that may be adopted.

The Author's Analysis

To be blunt, Monroe is being a lawyer. He is trying to state that his military draft is not a draft of men out of the militia, but a draft from the body of the populace. Yet he then contradicts himself immediately by calling for the classification of the free male population between the ages of eighteen and forty-five years of age. That just happens to be the same part of the nation's populace that is enrolled in the militia by the 1792 Militia Act. "The men are not drawn from the militia, but from the population of the country. When they enlist voluntarily, it is not as militiamen that they act, but as citizens. If they are draughted, it must be in the same sense."

When men volunteer to be soldiers and to risk their lives, it is a voluntary or individual decision, not because they are citizens. At that time, as today, men who are not citizens of the United States have volunteered to join the United States Army. Further, to force a man to serve against his will is also not an act of citizenship. Hamilton said it best when he described being forced to do militia duty in Federalist No. 24. Though Federalist No. 24 is describing the term "provide for the common defense" in the preamble of the constitution, the subject we would be interested in was the garrisoning of forts on the Western Frontier.

> "Previous to the revolution, and ever since the peace, there has been a constant necessity for keeping small garrisons on our Western Frontier. No person can doubt that these will continue to be indispensable, if it should only be against the ravages and depredations of the Indians. These garrisons must either be furnished by occasional detachments from the militia, or by a permanent corps in the pay of the government. *The first is impracticable; and if practicable, would be pernicious. The militia would not long, if at all, submit*

to be dragged from their occupations and families to
perform that most disagreeable duty in times of profound
peace."

Hamilton went on to say, "It would be as burdensome and injurious to the public as ruinous to private citizen."

Now, granted Hamilton was talking about a time of peace while Monroe is talking during a war. But the problem is the same: the men would have to abandon their occupations, farms, and families for a period of two years (in Monroe's proposal). What they would get out of it was intermittent Federal pay and a bounty for their service paid by their local community, not the government. If they ever returned to their community they would be ostracized for the cost the community incurred for the required bounty, and so would their family.

The biggest problem with Monroe's proposal is that it makes no consideration of the problem the conscripts' community would be under to meet the financial requirements dictated by the legislation. The community not only would have to supply the man, but the bounty in both money and land, the uniform and field kit, and the musket. By 1814 the Federal bounty was $124 and 320 acres of land. The federal government controlled vast tracts of public land that it simply had to transfer ownership to the enlistee. The local community would most likely have to purchase the land from a resident owner or from the government at who knows what price. At fifty cents an acre, the local community could be out almost $290 for every man required from that community.

To sweeten the proposal, Monroe then states, "It is a principal object of this plan to engage in the defense of the State the unmarried and youthful, who can best defend it, and best be spared." Thus Monroe is trying to say that the community would actually not be losing much, just those men who have no connections to their community, no business or occupation they have to give up, and no family to leave behind. Of course, all these men have families, being the sons of the farmers, businessmen, shopkeepers, or widowed mothers. It's true they are not the owner of a business, but the owner will suffer greatly from the loss of their service. It's never true that when you take people into service, they are without families or loved ones—unless they are the last member of a family, one of the few reasons for exemption from service under the law.

Monroe said, "In both instances, they are enrolled in the militia corps." Thus, he is saying that whether a man is in the militia or in the regular army, he is enrolled in both the militia corps and in this special corps from which he is drafting the men for the army. That means that, in reverse, to be in Monroe's grand body populace one must also be enrolled in the militia corps.

Monroe stated, "The whole population of the United States, within certain ages, belong to these corps." Thus, the women did not belong to the corps because they are not part of the population. Neither were the African slaves in the southern states. Granted, anyone in congress was exempt from militia service, so they too did not belong to the whole population. Yet under Monroe's proposal, only the chief magistrate of the United States and the governors of the individual states were to be exempt from service.

Monroe's Second Plan

This plan consists of a classification of the militia, and the extension of their terms of service.

Let the whole militia of the United States be divided into the following classes, viz.

All free male persons, capable of service, between the ages of 18 and 25, into one class; all those between the ages of 25 and 32, into another class; and those between 32 and 45, into a third class.

It is proposed, also, that the President shall have power to call into service any portion of either of these classes which, in his judgement, the exigencies of the country may require, to remain in service two years from the time each corps shall be assembled at the appointed place of rendezvous.

It is believed that a shorter term than two years would not give to these corps the efficiency in military operations that is desired, and deemed indispensable; nor avoid the evils that are so sensibly felt, and generally complained of, under the present arrangement. It requires two campaigns to make a complete soldier, especially where the corps, officers', and men, are alike raw and inexperienced. In the interim, the numbers must be multiplied, to supply the defect of discipline; and it requires the extension of the term of service, to avoid the additional proportional augmentation of having so many in the field at the same time, in marching to the frontier, and returning from it. The inconvenience to the parties, and loss to the community, in other respects, need not be repeated. It is proper to add, only, that if substitutes are allowed in this service, it must put an end to the recruiting of men for the regular army, especially the old corps. Of the justice of this remark what has occurred in the present year had furnished full proof. It follows that, if this plan is adopted, the militia must be relied on principally, if not altogether, in the further prosecution of the war.

The additional force for local service, amounting to forty thousand men, will likewise form a part, as already observed, of this plan.

Analysis: His second proposal describes the classification of the militia in exactly the same way as his first proposal. He simply doesn't put as many descriptive words into it because he has already described what was happening in his first proposal. After that the purpose of this proposal is simply to propose conscripting men from the State militias for two years of service in the Army.

Monroe's Third Plan

It is proposed by this plan to exempt every five men from the militia service, who shall find one to serve for the war. It is probable that some recruits might be raised in this mode, in most or all of the states. But it is apprehended that it would prevent recruiting in every other mode, by the high bounty which some of the wealthy might give. The consequence would probably be very injurious, as it is not believed that any great number could be raised by this mode.

Monroe's Fourth Plan

Should all the proceeding plans be found objectionable, it remains that the present system of recruiting be adhered to, with an augmentation of the bounty of land. Should this be preferred, it is advised that, in addition to 160 acres of land now given, 100 be allowed annually for every year while the war lasts.

These plans are thought more deserving the attention of the committee than any that have occurred. The first, for reasons stated is preferred. It is believed that it will be found more efficient against the enemy, less expensive to the public, and less burdensome on our fellow-citizens.

It has likewise the venerable sanction of our revolution. In that great struggle, resort was had to this expedient for filling the ranks of our regular army, and with decisive effect.

It is not intended by these remarks, should the first plan be adopted, to dispense altogether with the service of the militia. Although the principal burden of the war may thereby be taken from the militia, reliance must still be placed on them for important aids, especially in cases of sudden invasion. For this purpose it will still be advisable that the men be classed according to age, and that their term of service be prolonged. Even should this plan be attended with all the advantages expected of it, such an arrangement could not fail to produce the happiest effect. The proof which it would afford of the impregnable strength of the country, of the patient virtue and invincible spirit of the people, would admonish the enemy how vain and fruitless his invasions must be, and might dispose him to a speedy, just, and honorable peace.

Of the very important services already rendered by the militia, even under the present organization, too much cannot be said. If the United States make the exertion, which is proposed, it is probable that the contest will soon be at an end. It cannot be doubted that it is in their power to expel the British forces from this continent, should the British Government, be persevering in its unjust demands, make that an object with the American people. Against our united and vigorous efforts, the resistance of the enemy will soon become light and feeble. Success in every fair and honorable claim is within our easy grasp. And surely the United States have every possible inducement to make the effort necessary to secure it. I should insult the understanding, and wound the feelings of the committee, if I touched on the calamities incident on defeat. Dangers which are remote, and can never be realized, excite no alarm with a gallant and generous people. But the advantages of success have a fair claim to their deliberate consideration. The effort which we have already made has attracted the attention and extorted the praise of other nations. Already have most of the absurd theories and idle speculations on our system of government been refuted and put down. We are now felt and respected as a Power, and it is the dread which the enemy entertains of our vast resources and growing importance, that has induced him to push the war against us, after its professed objects had ceased. Success by discomfiture of his schemes, and the attainment of an honorable peace, will place the United States on higher ground, in the opinion of the world, than they have held at any former period. In future wars, their commerce will be permitted to take its lawful range unmolested. Their remonstrance's to foreign Governments will not again be put aside unheeded. Few will be presented, because there will seldom be occasion for them. Our union, founded on interest and affection, will have acquired new strength by the proof it will have afforded of the important advantages attending it. Respected abroad, and happy at home, the United States will have accomplished the great objects for which they have so long contended. As a nation, they will have little to dread; as people, little to desire.

Extract from Marshall's *Life of Washington*, Volume 4, page 241

In general, the Assemblies of the States followed the example of Congress, and apportioned on the several counties or towns within the State, the quota to be furnished by each. This division of the State was again to be subdivided in classes, and each class was to furnish a man by contributions or taxes imposed on itself. In some instances, a draught was to be used in the last resort; in others, the man was to be recruited by persons appointed for that purpose, and the class to be taxed with the sum given for his bounty.

Extract from Ramsay's *Life of Washington,* Volume 2, page 246[76]

Where voluntary enlistments fell short of the proposed number, the deficiencies were, by the laws of several states, to be made up by draught on lots from the militia. The towns in New England, and the counties in the middle states, were respectively called on for a specified number of men. Such was the zeal of the people in New England, that neighbors would often elect together to engage one of their number to go into the army. Maryland directed her Lieutenants of counties to class all the property in their respective counties into as many equal classes as there were men wanted, and each class was by law obliged, within ten days thereafter, to furnish an able-bodied recruit during the war; and in case of their neglecting

---

[76] Two author's- David Ramsay and Chief Justice John Marshall- wrote separate biographies of George Washington using the same title. Ramsay's version was published just after Marshall's.

or refusing to do so, the county Lieutenants were authorized to procure men at their expense, at any rate not exceeding fifteen pounds in every hundred pounds worth of property classed agreeably by law. Virginia also classed her citizens, and called upon the respective classes for every fifteenth man for public service. Pennsylvania concentered the requisite power in the President, Mr. Reed, and authorized him to decree forth the resources of the State, under certain limitations, and, if necessary, to declare martial law over the State. The execution of these arrangements, although uncommonly vigorous, lagged far behind.

Section from Washington's letter to the governors, June 18, 1783

The militia of this country must be considered as the palladium of our security, and the first effectual resort in case of hostility. It is essential, therefore, that the same system should pervade the whole; that the formation and discipline of the militia of the continent should be absolutely uniform; and that the same species of arms, accoutrements, and military apparatus, should be introduced in every part of the United States. No one, who has not learned it from experience, can conceive the difficulty, expense, and confusion, which result from a contrary system, or the vague arrangements which have hitherto prevailed.

Analysis: these references to the drafting of men for Washington's army, taken from Washington's letters and biographies were in tended to legitimizes the conscription of men into the Army. But these references are to men drafted out of their states respective militia and not to this grand body populace Monroe proposes in the first plan.

Monroe tries to create a separate system while still maintaining that the men in it are a part of the first system, but the new system is not a part of the old system and thus is not limited in its powers by the constitution.

In the end, Monroe's first proposal was never accepted. The Senate, in its infinite wisdom, debated the issue for a month. Then it accepted the second proposal and produced the following bill for consideration of the House of Representatives.

November 22, 1814

An Act

> To authorize the President of the United States to call upon the several states and territories thereof, for their respective quotas of eighty thousand four hundred thirty militia, for the defense of the frontiers of the United States, against invasion

> Be it enacted by the Senate and the House of Representatives of the United States of America in Congress assembled, 'That the president of the United States be, and he is hereby authorized and required to call upon the executives of the several states and territories thereof, for their respective quotas of eighty thousand four hundred thirty militia, armed and equipped according to law, to serve for the term of two years, from the time of meeting at the place of rendezvous, unless sooner discharged; that is to say:

> From New Hampshire, two thousand five hundred eighty.
> From Massachusetts, eight thousand six hundred eighty.

From Vermont, two thousand five hundred eighty.

From Rhode Island, eight hundred sixty.

From Connecticut, three thousand ten.

From New York, eleven thousand six hundred fifteen.

From New Jersey, two thousand five hundred eighty.

From Pennsylvania, nine thousand eight hundred ninety five.

From Delaware, eight hundred sixty.

From Maryland, three thousand eight hundred seventy.

From Virginia, nine thousand eight hundred ninety five.

From North Carolina, five thousand five hundred ninety.

From South Carolina, three thousand eight hundred seventy.

From Georgia, two thousand five hundred eighty.

From Kentucky, four thousand three hundred.

From Ohio, two thousand five hundred eighty.

From Tennessee, two thousand five hundred eighty.

From Louisiana, four hundred thirty.

From the Mississippi territory, five hundred twenty-two.

From the Indiana territory, five hundred forty-nine.

From the Illinois territory, two hundred thirteen.

From Michigan territory, sixty.

From Missouri territory, three hundred seventy-six.

And from the territory of Columbia, four hundred thirty.

Sec 2. *And be it further enacted,* that the whole number of militia of each state and territory, shall be divided into classes, in such a manner, as that one man from each class, shall, in the whole, amount, as nearly as may be, to the number required from such state or territory; and after such classification, each class shall furnish, by draft or by contract, one effective able-bodied man, to serve in the militia detached for the term of two years as aforesaid, unless sooner discharged: provided nevertheless, That if any state or territory shall, within three months after passing of this act, furnish its quota of militia or any part thereof required by this act, or other troops in lieu of them for an equal or longer term of service, the same shall be received into the service of the United States in substitution of the same number of militia called for by this act; and in the case, the draft shall so far cease to take effect. And the draft shall also cease to take effect in every case in which any class shall furnish a militiaman by contract as aforesaid.

Sec 3. *And be it further enacted,* That for the purpose of carrying into effect the provisions of this act, with equality and justice to all descriptions of militia, it shall be the duty of every officer commanding a company of infantry, to enter upon his muster roll every person subject to militia duty within the beat or district comprehending his company, whether of artillery, cavalry, grenadiers, light infantry, volunteers, or by whatever other denomination distinguished, including all non-commissioned officers and musicians; which muster roll he shall make out, on oath, and return to the officer commanding the battalion, or regiment, to which he belongs; who shall, without delay, return the same to the brigade inspector of his brigade, and the brigade inspectors are hereby required to make out regular return of all the muster rolls aforesaid, and transmit the same, by mail, free of postage, or otherwise, to the adjutant general of the state or territory; whereupon, all militia of every description, entered upon such muster roll, shall, in like manner, be subject to classification, for the purposes of draft or contribution required by this act, and in all cases of making the draft, where the person drafted shall heretofore have faithfully performed any tour of duty in the militia since commencement of the war, either as a volunteer or drafted militiaman, whether upon the requisition of the United States, or of any state or territory, he shall be entitled to a deduction for the whole of his former term of service, as aforesaid, from the term of service required by this act; and it shall be the duty of the officer making such a draft, at the same time, to make s true and faithful report to the department of war, of all persons drafted by him, who shall previously have performed a tour of service as aforesaid, specifying the nature and duration of such service; whereupon it shall be the duty of the secretary for the department of war, to cause discharges to be granted to all such persons, according to the principles of the aforesaid provision.

Sec 4. *And be it further enacted,* That the adjutant general shall, on receiving such returns of muster rolls, as aforesaid, ascertain and determine the number of men which shall compose each class, so that one man detached there from will make the whole number of men required by this act from such state or territory; and after apportioning the classes and number of men to be detached from several brigades, regiments, or battalions, shall transmit a copy of the same by mail, free of postage, or otherwise, to the commanding officer of each brigade of infantry, who shall, on receiving the same, issue his order to the commanding officers of regiments or battalions composing his brigade, requiring them to cause the commanding officers of the several companies composing their regiments or battalions, to divide their respective companies into classes, as is required by this act, and each class formed as aforesaid, shall, within twenty days thereafter, furnish, by contract or draft, an able-bodied man, to serve for the term of two years, who shall be delivered over by the class to such officer as shall be appointed to receive and muster the men who are to compose such detachment. And for the purpose of equalizing, as much as possible, the contributions of the respective classes, in all cases where any class may furnish a militiaman by contract, it shall be the duty of such militia officer or officers, in laying off the respective districts comprehending each class, to apportion the same, as nearly as possible, according to the value of property and the numbers of militiamen subject to draft within each company.

Sec 5. *And be it further enacted,* That the president of the United States be, and he is hereby authorized and required to organize the militia of each state and territory, called forth in virtue of this act, into divisions, brigades, regiments, battalions and companies, as the numbers from each state and territory shall render necessary and proper, conformably to the laws and regulations respecting the organization of the militia of the United States, and the corps of militia aforesaid shall be officered out of the militia officers, at the option and discretion of the constitutional authority in the respective states and territories.

Sec 6. *And be it further enacted,* That every officer, non-commissioned officer, or private, of the militia, who shall fail to obey any order of the proper officer for carrying into effect any of the provisions of this act, shall forfeit and pay a sum not exceeding one year's pay, nor less than one month's pay; and such officer shall, moreover, be liable to be cashiered by sentence of a court martial, and be incapacited from holding a commission in the militia for a term not exceeding twelve months, at the discretion of said court; and such non-commissioned officer and private shall be liable to be imprisoned, by a like sentence, on failure to pay fines adjudged against them respectively, for one calendar month for every eight dollars of such fine.

Sec 7. *And be it further enacted,* That the militia, or any corps of state or territorial troops accepted in lieu thereof, while employed in the service of the United States in virtue of this act, shall not be compelled to serve beyond the limits of the state or territory furnishing the same, and the limits of an adjoining state or territory: except, that the militia, or any corps of state troops accepted in lieu thereof, from Kentucky and Tennessee, may be required to serve in the defense, and for the protection of Louisiana; and that the militia, or any corps of state troops accepted in lieu thereof, from Pennsylvania and Virginia, may be required to serve in the defense and protection of the Michigan territory.

Sec 8. *And be it further enacted,* That the militia detached as aforesaid, or any corps of state or territorial troops accepted in lieu thereof, whilst in the service of the United States, shall be subject to the same rules and articles of war, as the troops of the United States; and, in like manner, shall be allowed the same pay, clothing, rations, and forage, and entitled to the same privileges and immunities, in all respects, as the troops of the United States.

Sec 9. *And be it further enacted,* That after classification of the militias aforesaid, any three classes, within any state or territory, which shall furnish, according to law, two effective able-bodied recruits, to serve in the army of the United States during the war, shall thereafter be exempted from the militia service required by this act; and to aid them in this respect, such recruits shall be entitled, respectively, to receive the bounty in money and land, which is or may be allowed to other recruits, respectively, for the Army of the United States, and in all cases where recruits shall be furnished as aforesaid, the same shall be delivered to some recruiting officer in the service of the United States, who shall immediately give his receipt therefore, on account of the classes furnishing them, and shall forth with report the same to the department of war, specifying in such report, the names and description of such recruits respectively, and the description of the classes of the militia furnishing the same; whereupon it shall be the duty of the secretary for the department of war to grant, without delay, to such classes, a certificate of exemption from the militia service required by this act; which certificate shall, to all intents and purposes, be good and available to them for their absolute exemption there from.

Sec 10. *And be it further enacted,* That in case the recruits furnished under the provisions of this act, in addition to the recruits now authorized by law, should amount, in the whole, to a greater number than sufficient to fill the present military establishment, it shall be lawful for the president of the United States, notwithstanding such excess; and to form them into regiments, battalions, and companies, as the numbers of such excess may render necessary, comfortably to the regulations of the present military establishment; and the president of the United States is hereby authorized and required to nominate, and, by and with the advice of the Senate, appoint as many officers to command such recruits as may be necessary for the purpose, conforming, in all respects, to the laws and regulations respecting the organization of the present military establishment, and the appointment and relative rank of officers therein. And the officers hereby authorized to be appointed, shall be placed upon the same footing, in all respects, with the officers' of the same grade in the present military establishment.

1814, November 22

Passed the Senate.

Attest,   Charles Cutts, Sec'ry.

The Author's Analysis

This proposed law is nothing more than a variation of a Federal statute that was regularly invoked from 1794 to 1812. Back in the days of Little Turtle's War, many viewed that war with England was so imminent that an emergency militia statute was passed on May 9, 1794.[77] Titled "An Act Directing a Detachment from the Militia of the United States," it placed in readiness a force of eighty thousand militia scattered throughout the states. But this earlier law only required the men to serve three months when in active service. This law also expired in 1796 at the end of that session of the house.

In June 1797,[78] at the beginning of the Quasi War with France, a modified version of the 1794 act was passed. The modification was the addition of the State of Tennessee to the quota of troops, though the quota of troops stayed at eighty thousand men. The following year, an act was passed to raise a provisional army of ten thousand men on three-year tours of duty. After this the crisis ended, and the Act of 1797 expired without replacement in 1799.

In 1803,[79] a different crisis hit the Jefferson Administration, forcing resurrection of the act. But now there was no listed quota of troops from the states because the new act was to use the militia returns, first started in December 1802, to compute the number of troops each state was to send. The act was then replaced by a new act in 1806,[80] with the addition of sections dealing with volunteers who agreed to remain in service for an additional six months after their tours were completed. When this act was due to expire two years later, a revised act was passed in 1808.[81] But after that, the attempt at a broader law in 1810 failed, creating a two-year gap until reactivation in April 1812,[82] less than a month before Madison submitted his letter to congress for a declaration of war.

The difference between the draft law and the older acts was that the men would now be in active service in the army for a period

---

[77] Act of May 9, 1794, c. 27, 1 Stat. 367 & 368.

[78] Act of June 24, 1797, c. 4, 1 Stat. 522.

[79] Act of March 3, 1803, c. 32, 2 Stat. 241.

[80] Act of April 18, 1806, c. 32, 2 Stat. 383 & 384.

[81] Act of March 30, 1808, c. 39, 2 Stat. 478 & 479.

[82] Act of April 10, 1812, c. 55, 2 Stat. 705-707.

of two years. Because the militia returns during the war were as chaotic as any other Federal census, the old procedure of stating quotas was re-established. The men were also to be armed by their respective states—another throwback to the 1790 series of laws where the government didn't supply the arms.

Again, the states, not some Federal military officer, were required to see to it the quota of men was furnished and that the men came armed and ready. It also gave the states the right to provide volunteers in place of the militiamen, if the state could find them, and if the state could afford to pay the full bounty required for the service of these volunteers. This was in line with the earlier volunteer act from 1812.

Further, where in Monroe's proposal the men could be sent anywhere, the militia men conscripted under this act could only be used within the confines of the states that raised them, or the confines of an adjoining state (the exceptions being Kentucky and Tennessee militia sent to Louisiana, and Pennsylvania and Virginia sent to Michigan). Thus, as stated in the bill's title," for the defense of the frontiers of the United States," this would create a continuous argument against the senate bill by the war hawks, as these members of congress and Monroe wanted to press the war back to Canadian soil.

The surprising fact is that either proposal places the expense of arming, equipping and even acquiring the new conscripts on someone other than congress. If Monroe's grand body populace concept was used, the cost of the enlistment bounty, and all the arms and field gear of the draftee, would be borne by the community where the men lived. If the draft from the militia proposal is used, the cost of acquiring the men and equipping them is borne by the state's themselves, who are required to ensure the men are "effective." Given the question as to how many arms were actually in Federal store, by 1814 one would expect the government to try to find an alternative method of arming these military drafts.

The Militia Draft proposal was argued over for two months in congress, finally ending on December 27, 1814. There is little evidence that the grand body populace proposal ever reached the floor of the house for debate. As for the militia based bill, it was sent back to the senate for reconciliation. Somewhere in this process, a completely different bill came out that was approved on January 27, 1815: "Chap. XXV. An Act to Authorize the President of the United States to Accept the Services of State Troops and of Volunteers."

Unlike the Militia Based Draft Bill of 1814, this act was to raise only forty thousand troops. Furthermore only twenty thousand troops were to come from state militia draft while the remaining were to be volunteers. The quota for the states was simply a halving of the earlier quota; all the territories exempted,

1. In New Hampshire, one thousand three hundred and eighteen.
2. In Massachusetts, four thousand three hundred and ninety-five.
3. In Vermont, one thousand three hundred and eighteen.
4. In Rhode Island, four hundred and forty.
5. In Connecticut, one thousand five hundred and forty.
6. In New York, five thousand nine hundred and thirty-three.
7. In New Jersey, one thousand three hundred and eighteen.
8. In Pennsylvania, five thousand and fifty-five.
9. In Delaware, four hundred and forty.
10. In Maryland, one thousand nine hundred and eighty.
11. In Virginia, five thousand and fifty-five.
12. In North Carolina, two thousand eight hundred and fifty-eight.
13. In South Carolina, one thousand nine hundred and eighty.
14. In Georgia, one thousand three hundred and eighteen.
15. In Kentucky, two thousand one hundred and ninety-six.

16. In Ohio, one thousand three hundred and eighteen.
17. In Tennessee, one thousand three hundred and eighteen.
18. In Louisiana, two hundred and twenty.

Another major difference was that any deficiency in the quota of conscripts supplied by any state was to be filled with volunteers. Thus while there were only to be forty thousand Federally acquired volunteers, the state could substitute volunteers for conscripts. Thus it was possible that all the men raised by this act could actually be volunteers.

One other interesting feature was the armament clause.

> Sec 5. *And it be further enacted*, that the said volunteers may, at their option, be armed and equipped by the United States, or at their own expense; and in case they arm and equip themselves to the satisfaction of the President of the United States, they shall each be entitled to receive six and one quarter cents per day, while in actual service, for the use and risk of such arms and equipments: *Provided,* That the compensation thus allowed shall not in any case exceed twenty-four dollars: *And provided also*, that no rifle shall be received into service of the United States, whose caliber shall be formed to carry a ball of a smaller size than at the rate of seventy balls to a pound of weight.

After all this time, an act of congress not only allowed men to bring their own rifles for service to the United States Army but would also pay them per day of actual service. Even more interesting is the fact that the caliber of these rifles would compute to be 0.41 inches in diameter. In simple terms, any hunting rifles in use at that time were now acceptable for military service.

The Treaty of Ghent (December 24, 1814)

While congress was debating its first military draft, delegates were meeting in the city of Ghent, in the Netherlands. Talks had been underway since Napoleon's abdication, though a vocal portion of the British people wanted the war continued. British Prime Minister Lord Liverpool realized that with Napoleon cooling his heels on Elba, the time was right to put an end to what had otherwise become a never-ending period of conflict.

That being said, when news of the English victory at Washington and the seizure of Maine arrived, British diplomats began making strong demands against the United States to gain a peace. The situation turned completely around in November when news arrived of the combined defeats at Baltimore and Plattsburg. With the British assaults now repulsed, the British diplomats put forth terms they expected the United States to accept. After some additional negotiations, a treaty was then signed on December 24, 1814.

The agreement essentially put everything back the way it was before the conflict began, minus the war in Europe. England stopped supporting Indian tribes in the northwest, and the United States joined England in banning the slave trade from Africa. Other then this, there was little that was changed under this document. The major problem now was that it would take two months to reach North America, and there was no assurance that when it did arrive, either the congress or President Madison would approve of it.

Figure 82: *The Signing of the Treaty of Ghent, Christmas Eve, 1814*, By Amédée Forestier.1814

CHAPTER 8
The Final Year, 1815

Even though the treaty was signed, no one in North America would know this for several months. After the defeat at Baltimore, plus the defeat of the northern force at Plattsburgh, British commanders in the Chesapeake should have given up on the three-prong plan and either maintained the blockade of the Chesapeake or moved north to Nova Scotia for new orders. Instead, they went ahead with the plan in the name of their fallen commander, General Ross. For some, this is viewed as a tribute to the troops' regard for their lost commander. For others, however, it is an example of a command structure that had lost track of the goals of the campaign. In many ways it's also an indictment of Admiral Cochrane, who seemed unwilling to end his private conflict with the United States.[83]

To get to New Orleans would take time however. The fleet had to sail around Florida to get there. This would give the city's defenders time to prepare their defenses, and devising and implementing these plans was General Andrew Jackson.

---

[83] Cochrane's view may have been tainted by the monetary value of the stores at New Orleans. As the senior officer, a portion of the spoils in sugar, cotton, and other goods would be his. The estimated value of the stores at New Orleans was fifteen million dollars.

Figure 83: Major General Andrew Jackson.

After he defeated the Red Sticks at the Battle of Horseshoe Bend, Jackson went home to Tennessee. The surviving Red Sticks fled to Spanish Florida, where they joined the Seminole Indian tribe. Months later, Jackson was recalled to duty, promoted to major general, and given command of the Seventh Military District centered at Mobile. On his way to Mobile, he stopped at Fort Jackson on August 9 to sign a new treaty with the Creek nation. Called the Treaty of Fort Jackson, it ceded half of Alabama and Creek-owned southern Georgia to the United States. With the Creeks now broken, the only threat to the Southern United States was from the British and Spanish forces in Spanish Florida.

Unfortunately for Jackson, he had to wait for reinforcements before he could do anything. When news of the battles in the Chesapeake reached him, it only added resolve to his plans to move against Pensacola. Then in September, a force of 130 British troops and 300 Indians attacked the recently built Fort Bowyer at the mouth of Mobile Bay. Though repulsed, a second attack from the sea occurred two days later, confirming British interest in taking the city and the port of Mobile. Convinced that the attacking forces were operating out of Pensacola, in late October Jackson began assembling a force of four thousand men at Fort Montgomery just two miles from Fort Mims, Alabama. On November 3 he then began his march to Pensacola, arriving on November 7.

Though he outnumbered the British forces almost ten to one, Jackson tried to convince the Spanish governor to surrender without a fight. Jackson's terms were simple: the British would evacuate the forts and harbor, and the forces of the United States would occupy said forts until Spanish troops arrived to take custody. The United States would recognize Spanish authority in the city, and the land would not be annexed to the United States. The negotiations got off to a bad start when the initial messenger, under a flag of truce, was fired on by the British troops at Fort St. Michael.

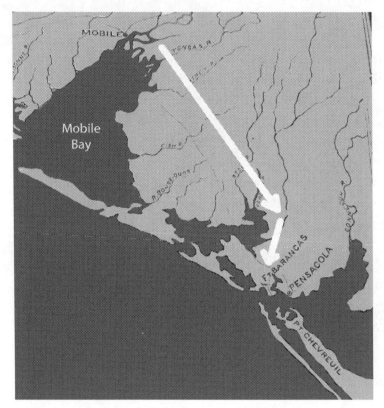

Figure 84: Spanish Fort Barancas and its proximity to Mobile Bay.

Eventually Jackson gave up his attempts at a nonviolent solution, and on November 9 he sent his forces against the eastern side of the city. The British sent a troop to confront Jackson, but this was quickly dispersed. The quick withdrawal of the British troops left the Spanish governor with a great distrust of the British and effectively ensured the British would get no further support from the Spanish in Florida. Jackson had no time to relax, however, because he was now concerned that the British fleet would move against Mobile in his absence. New Orleans wasn't even on the general's mind.

Jackson returned to Mobile within a few days to await developments. There he learned from Jean Lafitte that the British were planning an attack on New Orleans, and Lafitte had been approached to supply troops and pilots for the British forces. Armed with this information, on November 22 Jackson began marching his troops to New Orleans. He arrived on December 1 and immediately began working on the city's defenses.

First on his list was the reinforcing of Fort St. Philip, which guarded the entrance to the Mississippi from the Gulf of Mexico. It was a strong position, literally an island almost surrounded by the Mississippi and impassable swamps. Jackson did little here other then order the addition of a single thirty-two-pounder cannon to the fortifications and the placing of one battery across the river in the remains of the old Spanish Fort Bourbon. Jackson had more to do at Fort St. Leon, at English Turn. This fort had been allowed to decay, and Jackson ordered the building of new earthworks and batteries. In addition, he inspected the defenses at Fort Coquilles, which guarded the entrance to Lake Pontchartrain and ordered that Fort St. John on the edge of the lake along bayou St. John be reinforced. He even placed a battery along the Chef Menteur road to block that route to the city. All this kept Jackson busy until December 12, the day Cochrane's fleet was spotted in the Gulf waters.

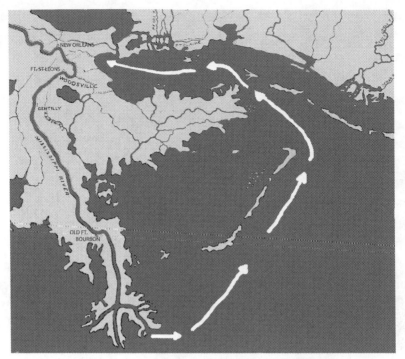

Figure 85: British fleet movement to bypass Jackson's defenses.

The following day, Cochrane defeated a US Navy gunboat unit at the entrance to Lake Borgne. These gunboats were the first line of defense against the British either landing on the west side of Lake Borgne and moving along the east bank of the river to New Orleans, or entering Lake Pontchartrain and landing on its east shore within two miles of the city. Thus, on day one Cochrane began demolishing Jackson's defenses against a ground invasion.

Cochrane would have invaded right then, but he had a problem. The death of Ross had forced the British high command to send a replacement in the form of Sir Edward M. Pakenham, the brother-in-law of the Duke of Wellington. Though he was not quite as well liked by the troops as his brother-in-law, he was an experienced general. Cochrane, being an admiral, might still have been the senior officer present, but he couldn't command troops on shore. Thus the invasion troops were landed on Pea Island, thirty miles from New Orleans, while Cochrane sent two navy officers to spy on Jackson's defenses and determine the best way into the city.

Figure 86: *The Battle of Lake Borgne,* by Thomas Lyle Hornbrook.

Waiting on Pea Island was probably the worst mistake Cochrane could have done. With no shelter from the incessant rains or the nightly frosts, the British troops suffered dearly. It is said that many of the men in the East Indies Regiment (one thousand freed African slaves from Jamaica), unaccustomed to the frost, died in the night from hypothermia.

While the British froze, Jackson went into overdrive. On the fourteenth he received word that 3,000 Tennessee militia under the command of General Carroll had arrived from Natchez with a keelboat loaded with ammunition[84] and 1,400 guns. Jackson quickly

---

[84] It is reported that blacksmiths in the keelboat were making paper cartridges all the way down the river. By the time they arrived at New Orleans, they had assembled fifty thousand rounds.

sent word to Carroll of the defeat of the gunboats, adding that he should increase his pace. He also sent a message to Baton Rouge, ordering General Coffee and his 1,200 men to move to New Orleans. By December 21, Jackson had increased his force from 1,500 men to over 4,000 men.

In addition to these troops, Jackson also requested an additional 2,300 troops from Kentucky, but he didn't actually have the authority to call for them. Jackson even contacted the captain of the Steamboat Enterprise on the Ohio River to pick up a shipment of ammunition at Pittsburg. This cargo began heading south on December 21.

By this time, the spies had returned and informed the admiral that there was a way into the city that was essentially unguarded. The route went through a fishing village on Lake Borgne, up Bayou Bienvenu, and into Bayou Mazant. By choosing this route, they avoided all of Jackson's forts, and once they were clear of the cypress swamps, they had a clean march to the city. Thus on December 21 General Keane, (the senior British general present, issued the order to land. By the twenty-third approximately 1,600 troops had landed and taken the Villeré plantation as their headquarters.

On hearing that the British had landed, Jackson rushed troops into position to block their advance. He then ordered the schooner *Carolina* to sail downriver until it was alongside the British positions. At 7:30 p.m., the *Carolina* was to begin shelling the British camp with all its cannons. Under the cover of this barrage, Jackson would then move up and attack the British position with 2,100 men, a mixed force of Baratarian pirates (on the *Carolina*), Choctaw Indians, free blacks, New Orleans French and Spanish militia, and Tennessean militia.

Figure 87: Depiction of an early confrontation between Jackson's militia and the British at New Orleans. US Army image

The Battle of New Orleans

When the Battle began, it looked as if Jackson's plan would work. In a short time, however, the battle degenerated into chaos. After over eight hours of fighting, Jackson withdrew to the Rodriquez Canal. He had lost 213 men, of which 24 were killed and 74 were missing. Of the missing were 24 of the 64 members of Beale's rifle unit; this was a force of lawyers in their late thirties and early forties who were the best shots in New Orleans. The British fared far worse: 276 casualties, of which 46 were killed and 64 were missing.

Pakenham arrived with the British fleet just as the land fighting began. What his response was to the news has been the subject of debate for over a century but the fact is he waited. His arrival at the British camp was on December 25, over a day after Jackson's withdrawal back to Rodriquez Canal. By this time, Jackson had been able to bring down the river the sloop *Louisiana* to bombard the British camp with its sixteen-pound cannons.

Pakenham realized that before he could deal with Jackson, he had to defeat the *Carolina* and the *Louisiana*. If he did not, they would simply bombard his troops on the shore without mercy. Thus he ordered additional cannons brought in from the fleet and the building of emplacements along the shore. Then, on the morning of December 27, the larger cannons would be loaded with hot shot to set fire to the *Carolina*. So effective was the initial bombardment that the ship was soon abandoned. The British kept up the bombardment anyway until the *Carolina* exploded sometime between 9:30 and 10:00 that morning.

Figure 88: Upper Picture: Depiction of the final British attack by Henry Bryan Hall, 1861
Lower Picture: The bombardment of January 1, 1815, showing the cotton bales used by Jackson in his defenses.

With the *Carolina* gone, that left the *Louisiana*. But the crew of the *Louisiana* manned their boats and towed their ship back upriver to safety. Thus ended the December 27 river battle. Pakenham now moved against Jackson's forward positions in order to clear the way for a full assault on Rodriquez Canal. Initially the British were successful, but eventually the fire from Jackson's batteries, and the cannons of the *Louisiana*, forced them to halt. Jackson added to the situation by having the plantation buildings forward of his position burned and destroyed. Thus, Pakenham's troops would have no cover for close to two thousand yards as they advanced on Jackson's main defense line.

To deal with these obstacles, Pakenham again halted his advance to build cannon positions. For three days he built his defenses; Jackson did the same, which included removing the cannon unit from the Chef Menteur road. Further, every night Jackson's Tennessee riflemen were showing their skill by regularly engaging the British pickets at distance. The *Louisiana* would be rowed downriver to bombard the British positions, only to be withdrawn by daybreak. Pakenham was thus subjected to the kind of combat modern armies used to prevent their opponents from sleeping and create fatigue throughout the ranks. By New Year's Day, Pakenham's troops were in a sorry state.

On that day, Pakenham began an artillery bombardment of Jackson's line. For three hours British and US guns exchanged fire. Then the British cannons suddenly stopped, much to the surprise of Jackson. The British had run out of ammunition and had to withdraw from their positions. Jackson had won another victory in what was becoming the longest run battle of the war.

It took six days for Pakenham to receive enough ammunition from the fleet to resume the battle. Thus, on January 7, 1815, Pakenham put forward his plan to remove Jackson and take the city beyond. First he would land a force under the command of Colonel Thornton across the river to move against Jackson's cannons on that side of the river. These guns, commanded by General Morgan, could rake the entire British assault from the flank. Once these guns were taken, the British could then use them against Jackson's right flank. At this point the British assault would begin in three columns.

The three columns were as follows: First was to be a movement of about eight hundred troops through the swamp toward Jackson's left flank. This was a diversion intended to draw as many of Jackson's forces as possible away from the center of Jackson's defense line. The second column, under the commands of Majors Rennie, Henry, and King, was to move along the public river road against first a forward redoubt and then Battery One across the canal. It was this group that was to be supported by the cannons Col. Thornton was to capture across the river. Then would come the final column, six thousand men assaulting Jackson's center and two gun batteries (numbers seven and eight). In total, eight thousand British troops went against Jackson's four thousand.

The British movement across the river was the first major mistake. First, getting the boats into the water proved more difficult than imagined and prevented the force from leaving for several hours. Then came the revelation that the river's current prevented the boats from going directly across the river. Instead of landing some three miles from the battery, they landed over half a mile further south. This additional distance was compounded by the fact that when the boats went back to pick up the remaining troops, they would again be taken farther downstream to arrive over a mile from where the remaining British troops were. In short, Thornton had to make do with the troops he landed in the first wave.

No one informed Pakenham that the river force was both late and half strength. Also, no one took the time to inform Pakenham that one key unit of the main attack, the Forty-fourth, was out of position. They had moved to their jump-off location without the ladders they needed to scale Jackson's defenses. They had thus returned to camp to pick them up, placing them at the rear of the attacking column instead of the front. It was without these facts that General Pakenham gave the order to attack on the morning of January 8, 1815.

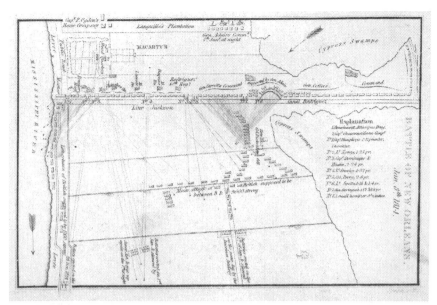

Figure 89: Upper: Battle map of the British final assault.
Lower: Depiction of the British assault at the river batteries.

The assault up the river road was fast and almost decisive. Even
without the support of the guns across the river, the British quickly
overran the forward redoubt and drove the defenders across the canal

into Jackson's main line. But that was as far as they got. Engaged by batteries one, two and three, plus the guns of General Morgan across the river, the river force was repulsed with decent casualties. This was the only part of the British force that actually reached the US defense line.

The force that was to attack through the swamp never got started and instead moved into the center column as that force approached Jackson's line. The morning was foggy, providing natural cover for the troops. But before the British where within one thousand yards of the line, the fog lifted and the approaching redcoats became visible. For a brief moment the center assault had all the imagery of a military parade. Then the first of Jackson's cannonballs fell among the British ranks.

Jackson's batteries mowed down whole sections of the British force, and yet the British continued to approach. When the British reached two hundred yards, the Kentucky and Tennessee riflemen that made up the center began firing in rotation: one line would fire, and then while it was withdrawing to reload, another line would move forward take aim and fire. Adding to the lethality of the US fire was the fact that the great range of the Kentucky rifle allowed units all along the center to concentrate their fire on the approaching British column. Further, the Americans were shooting from behind the rampart, resting their arms against the embankment for added accuracy while only exposing their heads to the British fire. The result was a wall of lead shot cutting through the British lines.

Figure 90: A representation of the battle near the center of Jackson's line. The British officer depicted is General John Keane, who was seriously wounded in the assault.

Many historians list musketmen and riflemen in the Tennessee and Kentucky militia serving under Jackson. Although it is true that musketmen are listed in the militia returns for these states, Tennessee had twice the number of rifles as muskets listed in their return, whereas Kentucky had over three times the number of rifles to muskets. These two states alone had twenty thousand of the seventy thousand rifles listed in the 1812 militia return. Add to this the already noted Tennessee State policy of sending riflemen, and the odds are very high it was American riflemen who faced off against the British at this point in the defense line.

And yet the British troops still came on, regardless of the volume of fire. They only stopped when they reached the canal they needed the ladders to cross—and the ladders were in the back of the column because they had been forgotten earlier. Thus the British stopped, becoming perfect targets for the rifles, muskets, and cannons of Jackson's force. It was at this point that General Gibbs was mortally wounded.

Figure 91: The death of General Pakenham, Battle of New Orleans By F.O.C. Darley

Seeing what was happening, Pakenham rode forward to rally the men. His horse was shot out from under him by a blast of grapeshot. Himself wounded in the knee by the event, Pakenham tried to remount using the horse of his aide. As he raised himself on top of the horse, a rifle bullet hit him in the chest. He died within minutes, but only after uttering an order that the battle must be renewed. The new British commander, General John Lambert, decided against such an action.

As the British center was withdrawing, across the river Colonel Thornton's force had just finished driving off the US militia unit defending General Morgan's cannons. Though victorious and more than capable of repelling any US counterstrike, Colonel Thornton's success was an hour too late to have helped the main British attack.

All he could now do was withdraw to the boats and ferry his men back to the British camp.

The British had lost some two thousand of the eight thousand men they had started the day with. Most were in the center force, which included General Keane's Ninety-third Sutherland that was badly mauled by American fire as they marched across the battlefield to reinforce the center force.

As for Jackson, his casualties numbered less than one hundred men killed, wounded, or missing. Most of these men could be accounted for by the loss of the redoubt at the beginning of the battle. Thus Jackson had caused the British to lose one-fourth of their force as well as expend large amounts of ammunition for no gain of ground. Jackson had won by every sense of the word. Yet Jackson also knew the British force was still a threat to the city. He thus made no move against them, allowing the British to remain unmolested in their camp for ten days. During that time, the British completely withdrew back to their ships and set sail for Mobile Bay.

On February 11, 1815, the British force under Lambert attacked Fort Bowyer at the entrance to Mobile Bay. The fort and the port city were essentially unguarded due to the fact that most of Jackson's forces were still in New Orleans. While at Fort Bowyer, on February 13 the British fleet received word that the Treaty of Ghent had been signed, ending the War of 1812. The United States Congress would learn of the treaty at about the same time, within days of hearing of Jackson's victory at New Orleans. Thus, they quickly ratified the agreement on February 17, 1815, viewing themselves the victors in the conflict. Ten days later, on February 27, 1815, congress repealed without replacement "Chap. XXV. An Act to Authorize the President of the United States to Accept the Services of State Troops and of Volunteers."

England really didn't care how the United States viewed itself after the treaty was signed. Before they even heard that congress had ratified the treaty, on February 26, 1815, Napoleon escaped Elba and threatened to plunge Europe into another decade of conflict. By the end of March, he was again in complete control of France with 140,000 troops and 200,000 volunteers at his disposal. England had no time anymore for North America as it quickly repositioned its troops to put Napoleon down once and for all at Waterloo on June 18, 1815.

So ended the war. In the years to come, the government would document the conflict with the goal of learning what went wrong. Thus, within ten years they had determined how many militia they had actually fielded, how much equipment was lost, how many homes were destroyed—essentially, the cost of war. In that regard, 1822 estimates of militia serving in 1814 reached 190,000 men, and the estimated loss in arms was put at 240,000 from the federal arsenals. Most of this information was quickly forgotten as new issues and conflicts came forth. The first Seminole War would begin within a few years, followed by the second Barbary War, disputes with Canada over Maine, and more.

The Change

The end of the war also marked a massive increase in federally funded rifle production. Production of the Model 1803, resurrected at Harpers Ferry in June 1814, would continue until 15,703 additional examples were completed in 1819.[85] In addition, the firm of Deringer and Tyron of Philadelphia produced several thousand Model 1814 rifles under federal contract. In 1817 a further contract for 40,000 rifles was issued to four outside contractors (Deringer, Johnson, North, and Starr). Thus within six years of the end of the war, the United States had produced some 70,000 new rifles for army service.

When production of the Model 1803 was completed at Harpers Ferry, production began on a new breech-loading rifle called the Model 1819 Hall. A development of a design Hall patented in 1811, it

---

[85] Three thousand of these rifles were assembled from parts made at Springfield Armory following an order from James Monroe in October 1814.

was the second truly successful breech-loading military rifle. The Hall Breechloader was also the first firearm made using interchangeable parts, laying the foundation for all later mass-production methods and the development of standard parts. Unfortunately, like its predecessor the British Ferguson rifle, the Hall was too new for the US military, and production was limited to only 4,200 examples by 1830.

And of course, domestic production of rifles for civilians increased as people began moving westward into the new territories broken out of the Louisiana Territory. By 1823 there were twenty-four states in the union and three major territories. The population also exploded with the white male population increasing from three million in 1810 to nine million in 1820. Many of these men would seek their fortunes in the new territories, and many would go armed with civilian rifled muskets made in various states, but nearly all were generically called the Kentucky rifle. It was these civilian manufacturers that would be the first to incorporate the percussion cap firing system into their products years before the first army weapon would have it.

These changes prompted the following discussion in congress on December 20, 1822.

History of Congress: December 20, 1822- Pages 434 and 435

Arming Militia with Rifles

Mr. Wright submitted the following:

Resolved, That the Committee on the Militia be instructed to inquire into the expediency of arming the militia with rifles, except those residing in cities, towns, and villages, and report thereon by bill or otherwise.

In offering this resolution, Mr. Wright said he had submitted it in confidence of the attention of the House to the subject, it being one of the first importance, the protection of the liberties of the people, and from his own experience in the use of firearms, having taken a hand in two wars, he hoped for the attention of the house to his remarks.

The militia in the country, said Mr. Wright, in their dispersed situation, can never be taught the use of the musket, and maneuvers necessary to fit them to contend with a regular foreign army. The labor they undergo in their periodical meetings, their marchings and counter-marches; their lugging their rusty muskets five or six miles, is truly painful to a spectator skilled in arms, I know vastly distressing the country militia.

They, sir, have such disgust to this business, and such antipathy to the duties of militiamen, have so little confidence in their fitness to contend with a regular army, that they consider themselves as sacrifices to the liberties of their country, when thus compelled to fight.

But, sir, arm the country militia with rifles, and possess each of them with a rifle, compel them to meet as often as may be necessary, and distribute the fines and forfeitures into premiums for sharp shooting- taking care to have the fourth day of July, perpetual; one of those days; and, sir, you will relieve the militia from an intolerable burden, give them a perfect confidence in their strength and power, and make them, as I have always though they were, the real bulwark of the liberties of their country.

They fight for themselves, and not like mercenaries for pay; they in a little time, a hundred or two hundred yards, would be sure of their object; and riflemen need not be told of the vast certainty to which the use of the rifle may be brought.

The havoc made at New Orleans, near the close of the last war, leaves no doubt on this subject. I have been told of a case, of two riflemen there, who shot at the same officer, and each claimed him- one said that he shot to hit him under the left eye; the other that he shot at his head; he was found to have been shot just under the left eye, and also in the head; so that he would have been killed by either.

The immense carnage at New Orleans seals the truth of all I have said. I have been told, further, that, after the battle, a bet of a supper was made between officers of two rifle corps from Georgia and Tennessee, of six shots aside, and hundred yards; that they shot at a paper on the mouth of a musket, that the Tennesseans shot their six balls into the musket, on which the Georgians gave up the bet.

When the British took possession of Kent Island there were said to be three rifles in the hands of the militia of the island, and though concealed to avoid their getting them, kept them in a constant state of caution, for fear of being taken off, and which they were anxious to buy.

Besides, the economy in the supply of rifles is of great consequence; the rifle barrels can be kept good for a long time; can be rebored; and by constant use of oil in their patches, are not liable to rust- when muskets, with the greatest care, are liable to rust, and may be bent, and thereby destroyed.

Sir, I have no doubt if our militia shall be thus armed and thus prepared, and their feats of sharp shooting published to the world, that all the Powers of Europe would not be able to press their officers to land on our coasts; but, sir, if they shall, notwithstanding,

have their hardihood, I have no doubt they will pay
for their temerity.

I ask that the resolution may lie on the table, that
the subject thus broke, may be acted on at an early
day, understandingly, and the liberties of this country
be thus preserved till the last trump.

Without further debate, the motion of Mr. Wright
was ordered to lie on the table.

There is no record of whether congress accepted this proposal.
However, there is an interesting statistic: in the 1823 Militia Return,
the number of rifles was reported as 80,000. Three years later in 1826,
the number of rifles was reported at 117,000 for a 37,000 increase.
Though the number of men did increase by 69,600 men, the number
of muskets actually decreased by 6,400. Thus in three years the rifle
had gone from 23 percent of militia arms to 30 percent. Of course,
five states didn't even submit ordnance reports for both years.

Figure 92: During his 1827 visit, Lafayette inspects a
volunteer militia unit. US National Guard Image

The change lasted for another decade, following which the 1792 militia system collapsed under its own political weight. By the mid-1800s, early labor unions wanted the act repealed to remove an obstacle to poor and lower-middle-class men in the acquisition of land. As noted earlier, many states only required landowners to serve in the militia. This meant that acquiring property also meant buying all the militia equipment required under the law. To avoid this, men remained landless, renting property from wealthier people. And yes, they also sold themselves as substitutes for the required militia service of their landlord.

Early labor unions also noted that militia service cost men the equivalent of four day's wages, lost by attending the quarterly musters. Some groups reportedly estimated that mustering the entire national militia for one day cost the nation one million dollars.[86] It should be noted that in those days, there were few national holidays, and Saturday was not a day of rest for most US citizens.

Another group that attacked the militia system was the American Peace Society. They felt the militia, and the military as a whole, represented an outdated method of solving problems. Their goal was that the government should use only diplomacy to solve both its internal and external problems. Following the start of the Texas War for Independence in 1836 and the subsequent war with Mexico in 1843, peace groups claimed that these conflicts were solely caused by the existence of the 1792 militia system.

The Peace Society was joined in their opposition to the militia system by organized religious groups who took issue with the musters because of their religious stands against war. One of the largest of these groups was the Quakers, who claimed the right of conscientious objector. To them, the musters were illegal, and so was the fines levied on them for noncompliance. The liberal use of alcohol at the musters,

---

[86] A national force of one million men losing one dollar (a day's wages) each. Stated by Secretary of War Joel R. Poinsett on March 20, 1840.

and other immoral behavior, were others reasons why religious groups attacked the militia system.

The use of alcohol at the musters would also bring out the temperance groups, who one hundred years later would bring forth alcohol prohibition. Musters in the early 1800s were a cross between a military battle and the county fair. It would start with the men drilling, shooting at targets, or practicing with an old cannon. While this was going on, their wives and children were setting out food and drink. By noon the men were eating, drinking, and (if young enough) flirting with young women. Finally, the now reasonably intoxicated men would do a battle reenactment with plenty of blank rounds, bayonet charges, cavalry movements, and cannon blasts. After that, the whole crowd would leave for home, quite exhausted.[87]

The first state to withdraw from the Militia Act was Delaware, who abolished its militia law in 1831. It hadn't sent a militia return for four years, and attendance had been spotty going back before the War of 1812, so it was hardly unexpected.[88] Vermont also hadn't sent in a return since 1824, which is shown in the 1833 Militia Return. By 1836 the national numbers had gotten worse, with two million men on the roll but only 360,000 rifles and muskets. The last militia return was 1838, after which a form of open rebellion began in the states.

In 1840 Indiana passed a new law creating an active militia and a reserve militia similar to the system the United States has had since 1903. In the same year, Massachusetts abolished its militia laws and ended militia musters. When one of the strongest militia states abolishes its law, other states take notice, and in 1844 Maine, Vermont, and Ohio ended militia musters. Connecticut and New

---

[87] One of the quarterly musters was July 4.

[88] On February 2, 1816, Delaware legislature passed a law removing all fines for nonattendance of militia musters. It essentially caused the whole militia of the state to vanish.

York followed in 1846 with Missouri in 1847. New Hampshire then withdrew in 1851.[89]

Some states didn't abolish their militia in its entirety. Two states simply ended militia fines during time of peace: New Jersey in 1844 and Michigan in 1850. Iowa and California never administered militia fines as states; though militia service by every able-bodied male was still required, on statehood these states implemented a system similar to Indiana.

In all these states, the primary militia duty now fell on a picked group of volunteers, much like the volunteer units that were created by the Act of 1812. No longer a rich men's sons club that cost the community nothing, the states now would pay for the uniforms and arms—and then pay the men for time spent in what today is known as drill money. The cost for that service was to be paid by a general tax on the public, called a commutation charge.

Thus the states now restricted the Federal government to only the standing Federal army and those volunteer militia the states were willing to part with in an emergency. The old quota system, where states supplied a certain number of militiamen for Federal service based on their population, was abolished with the abandonment of the militia system. Of course, the government was getting in return an all-volunteer militia that looked really good on the parade ground and on paper.

---

[89] New Hampshire actually did abolish its militia law in 1845, but the governor didn't sign it before the session ended. Thus, it didn't become law.

Figure 93: The Mississippi Rifles (the Volunteer 155th Infantry Regiment) at the Battle of Buena Vista. US National Guard Image

For all their discipline, state-paid-for uniforms and weapons, these volunteer units were nothing more than parade ground troops. They could not march any real distance with their weapons (in the Mexican American War, volunteers demanded horses to ride), and there was no standard for marksmanship. Having thrown off the shackles of the Militia Act, they armed themselves as they saw fit; some used British arms, some used French, and some opted for German. Caliber uniformity or even a standard uniform color was now history; units wore British bearskin hats, Irish shamrocks, kilts (parade uniforms of units made up entirely of Scotch or Irish immigrants), German spiked helmets, and even French Zouave uniforms (which were based on Arabic outfits worn by Turkish troops). At the Battle of Bull Run, these units showed how impossible it was for them to operate with regular troops. Within a few months of the start of the Civil War, both the Federal Army, and the Confederate Army, found conscripts far more effective.

Why were the civilian conscripts more effective? Because they were familiar with the rifle! The end of the militia returns did not mean an end to firearm ownership in the United States. It simply meant that there was no longer any registry of weapons for potential militia service. As they had for the previous fifty years, men still owned guns! But now instead of a weapon they personally had little use for, they owned what they needed for their farms, their homes, or their hobbies. As new technology came out, the privately owned guns were the first to incorporate them.

One such technology was the previously mentioned percussion cap, developed by an English priest to help in his duck hunting. Civilian hunters were using this technology throughout the 1830s, and it was probably on the Kentucky style rifles fired by the defenders of the Alamo in 1836. In 1841 the US Ordnance Department finally approved of the percussion cap with the introduction of the Model 1841 rifle.

This new federal rifle would become legendary in the Mexican American War as the Mississippi Rifle.[90] In an ironic twist, however, the next year a new percussion musket was fielded and produced in such numbers it would be the primary musket seen on the battlefields of the Civil War.

The army bias against the rifle would continue until the advent of the 0.58 caliber Minie ball. Created in France in 1840, this conical bullet allowed for effective use of rifling without the tight patch required by the earlier rifles. Adoption by the United States Army occurred in 1855, corresponding with the introduction of the

---

[90] General of the Army Winfield Scott tried to forestall fielding of the percussion cap, believing it was unreliable.

Model 1855 rifle.[91] Of course by then civilian hunters, farmers, and sportsmen were using the newest thing in rifles, including Sharps breechloaders (patented in 1846). Following the Civil War, not only was the bias gone but even the memory of it had disappeared. Also gone was the idea of the bayonet charge, shattered at Civil War battlefields throughout the United States.

Figure 94: The American Civil War.

But the Militia Act, and its requirements, still remained on the Federal books. Its arms requirements were completely obsolete, and even its method of distinguishing caliber was no longer valid since the advent of the conical bullet. The act was used during the Civil War as the law under which the states supplied quotas of men. In fact, in order to support the war, the Northern states reactivated the very 1792-based militia codes they'd repealed in the 1840s. Yet once the Civil War was over, the volunteer militias that had so obviously failed were not replaced or even modified. The political organization that the volunteers had founded, the National Guard Association, had too much clout in congress.

For those concerned over the decline in the shooting skills among the men of the East Coast, the only solution was the creation of the American Rifle Association (later called the National Rifle

---

[91] Some in the army fought the introduction of the Model 1855, saying that it was wrong to abandon the tried and true buck and ball ammunition system. They argued for retention of a few muskets for use in close-quarters fighting.

Association), with General Ambrose Burnside as its first president. Formed in New York in 1871, it began the first national rifle matches in 1872. Two decades later, a pacifist New York governor drove the organization to New Jersey as part of a general political attack on the Spanish American War.

Following the Spanish American War, the effort to promote rifle practice gained a tremendous supporter in President Theodore Roosevelt. In 1903 he succeeded in the creation of a new Militia Act, incorporating both the National Guard and the common (now called unorganized) militia. He then established the National Board for the Promotion of Rifle Practice, followed two years later by the signing of Public Law #149 authorizing the first sale of surplus arms and ammunition to US civilians since 1824. Then in 1916, a new National Defense Act established the Office of Civilian Marksmanship and ordered the creation of rifles ranges for use by civilians. The program is still in existence today.

Figure 95: Left: General Ambrose Burnside, first NRA president. Right: President Theodore Roosevelt, who created the Civilian Marksmanship Program to promote rifle practice.

APPENDIX ONE
The 1792 Militia Act
with Amendments

Chap. XXXIII. *An Act More Effectually to Provide for the National Defense by Establishing an Uniform Militia throughout the United States.* (a)

Section 1 *Be it enacted by the Senate and House of Representatives of the United States of America in Congress assembled;* That each and every free able-bodied white male citizen of the respective states, resident therein, who is or shall be of the age of eighteen years, and under the age of forty-five years (except as is herein after excepted) shall severally and respectively be enrolled in the militia by the captain or commanding officer of the company, within whose bounds such citizen shall reside, and within twelve months after the passing of this act. And it shall at all times hereafter be the duty of every such captain or commanding officer of a company to enroll every such citizen, as aforesaid, and also those who shall, from time to time, arrive at the age of eighteen years, or being of the age of eighteen years and under the age of forty-five years (except as before excepted) shall come to reside within his bounds; and shall without delay notify such citizen of the said enrollment, by a proper non-commissioned officer of the company whom such notice may be proved. That every citizen so enrolled and notified, shall, within six months thereafter, provide himself with a good musket or firelock, a sufficient bayonet and belt, two spare flints, and a knapsack, a pouch with a box therein to contain not less than twenty-four cartridges, suited to the bore of his musket or firelock, each cartridge to contain a proper quantity of powder and ball: or with a good rifle, knapsack, shot-pouch and powder-horn, twenty balls suited to the bore of his rifle, and a quarter of a pound of powder; and shall appear, so armed, accoutered and provided, when called out to exercise, or into service, except, that when called out on company days to exercise only, he may appear without a knapsack. That the commissioned officers shall severally be armed with a sword or hanger and espontoon, and that from and after five years from the passage of this act, all muskets for arming the militia as herein required, shall be of bores sufficient for balls of the eighteenth part of a pound. And every citizen so enrolled and providing himself with the arms, ammunition and accouterments as required as aforesaid, shall hold the same exempted from all suits, distresses, executions or sales, for debt or for the payment of taxes.

Section 2. *And be it further enacted*, That the Vice President of the United States; the officers judicial and executive of the government of the United States; the members of both Houses of Congress, and their respective officers; all custom-house officers with their clerks; all post-officers, and stage drivers, who are employed in the care and conveyance of the mail of the post-office of the United States; all ferry men employed at any ferry on the post road; all inspectors of exports; all pilots; all mariners actually employed in the sea service of any citizen or merchant within the United States; and all persons who now are or may hereafter be exempted by the laws of the respective states, shall be, and are hereby exempted from militia duty, notwithstanding their being above the age of eighteen, and under the age of forty-five years.

Section 3. *And be it further enacted*, That within one year after the passing of this act, the militia of the respective states shall be arranged into divisions, brigades, regiments, battalions and companies, as the legislature of each state shall direct; and each division, brigade, and regiment, shall be numbered at the formation thereof; and a record made of such numbers in the adjutant-general's office in the state; and when in the field, or in service in the state, each division, brigade and regiment shall respectively take rank according to their numbers, reckoning the first or lowest number highest in rank. That if the same be convenient, each brigade shall consist of four regiments; each regiment of two battalions, each battalion of five companies; each company of sixty-four privates. That said militia shall be officered by the respective states as follows: to each division, one major-general and two aids-de-camp, with the rank of major; to each brigade, one brigadier general, with one brigade inspector, to serve also as brigade major, with the rank of a major; to each regiment, one lieutenant colonel commandant; and to each battalion one major; to each company one captain, one lieutenant, one ensign, four sergeants, four corporals, one drummer and one fifer or bugler. That there shall be a regimental staff, to consist of one adjutant and one quartermaster, to rank as lieutenants; one paymaster; one surgeon, and one surgeon's mate; one sergeant-major; one drum-major, and one fife-major.

Section 4. *And be it further enacted*, That out of the militia enrolled, as is herein directed, there shall be formed for each battalion at least one company of grenadiers, light infantry or riflemen; and that to each division there shall be at least one company of artillery, one captain, two lieutenants, four sergeants, four corporals, six gunners, six bombardiers, one drummer, and one fifer. The officers to be armed with a sword or hanger, a fusee, bayonet and belt, with cartridge-box to contain twelve cartridges; and each private or matross shall furnish himself with all the equipements of a private in the infantry, until proper ordnance and field artillery is provided. There shall be to each troop of horse, one captain, two lieutenants, one cornet, four sergeants, four corporals, one saddler, one farrier, and one trumpeter. The commissioned officers to furnish themselves with good horses of at least fourteen hands and a half high, and to be armed with a sword and pair of pistols, the holsters of which to be covered with bearskin caps. Each dragoon to furnish himself with a serviceable horse, at least fourteen hands and a half high, a good saddle, bridle, mailpillion and valise, bolsters, and a breast-plate and crupper, a pair of boots and spurs, a pair of pistols, a saber, and a cartridge-box, to contain twelve cartridges for pistols. That each company of artillery and troop of horse shall be formed of volunteers from the brigade, at the discretion of the commander-in chief of the state, not exceeding one company of each to a regiment, nor more in number than one eleventh part of the infantry, and shall be uniformly clothed in regimentals, to be furnished at their own expense; the color and fashion to be determined by the brigadier commanding the brigade to which they belong.

Section 5. *And be it further enacted*, That each battalion and regiment shall be provided with the state and regimental colors by the field officers, and each company with a drum and fife, or bugle-horn, by the commissioned officers of the company, in such manner as the legislature of the respective states shall direct.

Section 6. *And be it further enacted*, That there shall be an adjutant-general appointed in each state, whose duty it shall be to distribute all orders from the commander-in chief of the state to the several corps; to attend all public reviews when the commander-in chief of the state shall review the militia; or any part thereof; to obey all orders from him relative to carrying into execution and perfecting the system of military discipline established by this act; to furnish blank forms of different returns that may be required, and explain the principles on which they should be made; to receive from the several officers of the different corps throughout the state, returns of the militia under their command, reporting the actual situation of their arms, accoutrements, and ammunition, their delinquencies, and every other thing which relates to the general advancement of good order and discipline: all which the several officers of the divisions, brigades, regiments, and battalions, are hereby required to make in the usual manner, so that the said adjutant-general may be duly furnished therewith: from all which returns he shall make proper abstracts and lay the same annually before the commander-in-chief of the state.

Section 7. *And be it further enacted*, That the rules of discipline, approved and established by Congress in their resolution of the twenty-ninth of March, one thousand seven hundred and seventy-nine, shall be the rules of discipline to be observed by the militia throughout the United States, except such deviations from the said rules as may be rendered necessary by the requisitions of this act, or by some other unavoidable circumstances. It shall be the duty of the commanding officer at every muster, whether by battalion, regiment, or single company, to cause the militia to be exercised and trained agreeably to said rules of discipline.

Section 8. *And be it further enacted*, That all commissioned officers shall take rank according to the date of their commissions; and when two of the same grade bear an equal date, then their rank to be determined by lot, to be drawn by them before the commanding officer of the brigade, regiment, battalion, company, or detachment.

Section 9. *And be it further enacted*, That if any person, whether officer or soldier, belonging to the militia of any state, and called out into the service of the United States, be wounded or disabled while in actual service, he shall be taken care of and provided for at the public expense.

Section 10. *And be it further enacted*, That it shall be the duty of the brigade-inspector to attend the regimental and battalion meetings of the militia composing their several brigades, during the time of their being under arms, to inspect their arms, ammunition, accoutrements;

superintend their exercise and maneuvers, and introduce the system of military discipline before described throughout the brigade, agreeable to law, and such orders as they shall from time to time receive from the commander-in-chief of the state; to make returns to the adjutant-general of the state, at least once in every year, of the militia of the brigade to which he belongs, reporting therein the actual situation of the arms, accoutrements, and ammunition of the several corps, and every other thing which, in his judgement, may relate to their government and the general advancement of good order and military discipline; and the adjutant-general shall make a return of all the militia of the state to the commander-in-chief of the said state, and a duplicate of the same to the president of the United States.

And whereas sundry corps of artillery, cavalry, and infantry now exist in several of the said states, which by the laws, customs, or usages thereof have not been incorporated with, or subject to the general regulations of the militia:

Section 11. *Be it further enacted*, That such corps retain their accustomed privileges, subject, nevertheless, to all other duties required by this act, in like manner with the other militia.
Approved, May 8, 1792

Statute I, Chap. XXIII, Sec. 27. *And be it further enacted*, that the deputy postmasters, and the persons employed in the transportation of the mail, shall be exempted from militia duties, or any fine or penalty for neglect thereof.
APPROVED, May 8,1794

Chap. XV. *An Act in addition to an act, intituled "An act more effectually to provide for the National defence, by establishing an uniform Militia throughout the United States."*

Be it enacted by the Senate and House of Representatives of the United States of America in Congress assembled, That it shall be the duty of the adjutant-general of the militia in each state, to make return of the militia of the state to which he belongs, with their arms, accoutrements, and ammunition, agreeably to the directions of the act, to which this is an addition, to the President of the United States annually, on or before the first Monday in January in each year: and it shall be the duty of the Secretary of War, from time to time, to give such directions to the adjutant-generals of the militia, as shall, in his opinion, be necessary to produce an uniformity in the said returns, and he shall lay an abstract of the same before Congress, on or before the first Monday of February, annually.

SEC. 2. *And be it further enacted,* That every citizen duly enrolled in the militia, shall be constantly provided with arms, accoutrements, and ammunition, agreeably to the direction of the said act, from and after he shall be duly notified of his enrolment; and any notice or warning to the citizens so enrolled, to attend a company, battalion, or regimental muster, or training, which shall be according to the laws of the state in which it is given for that purpose, shall be deemed a legal notice of his enrolment.

SEC. 3. *And be it further enacted,* That in addition to the officers provided for by the said act, there shall be, to the militia of each state one quartermaster-general, to each brigade one quartermaster of brigade, and to each regiment one chaplain.
APPROVED, March 2, 1803.

Chap. LXXX. *An Act in further addition to an Act, entitled "An Act more effectually to provide for the National Defense by establishing an Uniform Militia throughout the United States."*

Be it enacted by the Senate and House of Representatives of the United States of America in Congress assembled, That in addition to the officers of the militia provided for by the act, entitled "An act more effectually to provide for the national defence by establishing an uniform militia throughout the United States," approved May the eighth, one thousand seven hundred and ninety-two, and by an act in addition to the said recited act, approved March the second, one thousand eight hundred and three, there shall be to each division, one Division Inspector, with the rank of Lieutenant Colonel, and one Division Quartermaster, with the rank of Major; to each brigade one Aid-de-camp, with the rank of Captain; and the Quartermasters of brigade heretofore provided for by law, shall have the rank of Captain. And it shall be incumbent on the said officers to do. and perform all the duties which by law and military principles are attached to their offices respectively.

APPROVED, April 18, 1814.

Chap. LXIV. *An Act concerning field officers of the militia.*

Be it enacted by the Senate and House of representatives of the United States of America, in Congress assembled, That from and after the first day of May next, instead of one lieutenant colonel commandant to each regiment, and one major to each battalion of the militia, as is provided by the act entitled "An act more effectually to provide for the national defence, by establishing an uniform militia throughout the United States," approved May the eighth, one thousand seven hundred and ninety-two, there shall be one colonel, one lieutenant colonel and one major to each regiment of the militia, consisting of two battalions. "Where there shall be only one battalion, it shall be commanded by a major: *Provided,* that nothing contained herein shall be construed to annul any commission in the militia which may be in force, as granted by authority of any state or territory, in pursuance of the act herein recited, and hearing date prior to the said first day of May next.

APPROVED, April 20, 1816.

Chap. XCVII. *An Act to establish an uniform mode if discipline and field exercises for the militia of the United States.*

Be it enacted by the Senate and House of Representatives of the United States of America, in Congress assembled, That the system of discipline and field exercise which is and shall be ordered to be observed by the regular army of the United States, all the different corps of infantry, artillery, and riflemen, shall also be observed by the militia, in the exercises and discipline of the said corps, respectively, throughout the United States.

SEC. 2. And be it further enacted, That so much of the act of Congress, approved the eighth of May, one thousand seven hundred and ninety-two, as approves and establishes the rules and discipline of the Baron de Steuben, and requires them to be observed by the militia throughout the United States, be, and the same is hereby, repealed. **APPROVED, May 12, 1820.**

APPENDIX TWO
From the Congressional Record, June 1798: Arms for Militia

The House then resolved itself into a Committee of the Whole on the bill providing arms for the militia throughout the United States, Mr. SITGREAVES in the Chair; when.

Mr. Coit, not seeing any necessity for passing this bill, moved to strike out the first section.

Mr. Dayton (the Speaker) could not give his assent to the first section, and was rather in favor of striking it out, because it would be found in practice very inconvenient for the United States to become the retailers of arms to the extent therein proposed. He called upon gentlemen to reflect for a moment upon the expense of transporting them to every division of the militia, which in many cases would require a land carriage of two or three hundred miles. And let it be also taken, into consideration how many of the muskets must be injured materially by such transportation, and rendered utterly unfit for service until repaired. Armorers must, therefore, be sent with every parcel of arms into the interior of the United States, and held in constant pay, not merely to repair the damages sustained by transportation, but to expose them frequently to the air, and to keep them free from rust, to which they must be constantly exposed. If they should be scattered abroad in parcels throughout the country, as this section required, it was very uncertain whether the militia would buy the arms, with the additional expense laid on them for transportation, and those thus unsold would consequently be useless both to the public and individuals, or must after some time be brought back to the public armories, with an expense equal to their first cost. The plan contained in the first section was, therefore, the worst that could be proposed, and ought to be essentially altered or struck out.

Mr. McDowell hoped the section would not be struck out. He supposed it must be the wish of every gentleman that the militia throughout the country should be well armed. In some parts of the Union it is well known that this is not the case at present, and some provision ought to be made for supplying the deficiency. The gentleman from New Jersey, had said that the States or individuals ought themselves to procure arms from the manufacturers; but, in those parts of the country where these arms are chiefly wanted, there are no manufactories from which they can be purchased; therefore it would be well for the Government to undertake to supply them. The expense of transportation by land would certainly be great; but it ought to be encountered, because if it is not done in the first instance, if the service of the militia is wanted, they must have arms sent to them, where arms are wanting. Besides, the expense of transportation would be added to the price of the arms. As to the difficulty which would attend the keeping of arms in order, though it would be attended with some trouble, he could not think it would be so great as it had been represented.

Mr. Shepard said the Committee who reported this bill were induced do to it from a persuasion that the Southern States are in want of arms, and have not an opportunity of purchasing them. In the Eastern States, Mr. S. said, they had sufficient manufactories of arms, from whence Government might purchase, and furnish the desired supply. The committee did not forget the inconveniences mentioned by the gentleman from New Jersey, but, notwithstanding these, they were of opinion that Government ought to undertake the business, especially since it would be attended with little or no expense in the end, as the money laid out (or lent for a time) would be returned, when the arms shall be sold.

Mr. S. Smith felt some of the inconveniences pointed out by the gentleman from New Jersey; but when it is recollected that all the manufactories of small arms either are, or doubtless will be, engaged in public service, the necessity and propriety of Government undertaking this business will appear evident; for, if it be desirable that the militia should be well armed and it undoubtedly is so, Government ought to aid the people in the purchase. Mr. S. asked what was done in the late insurrection? One part of the militia called upon were not completely armed, and Government was obliged to transport arms from the arsenals of the United States; and it would be better to do this while we are at peace, than after we shall be engaged in war, especially as the people would now purchase their own arms; but, if they were supplied by Government in case of emergency, it would be at public expense. Mr. S. was, therefore, decidedly in favor of the measure.

Mr. Harrison said that a little time ago it was dangerous for gentlemen to' speak about saving expense, as any man who did so, was immediately charged with wishing to give up his country to a foreign enemy. But now, when a plan is on foot to supply the Southern States with arms, though no expense will eventually attend it, a loud cry is made against the expense which will be incurred. Though gentlemen are perfectly willing to incur the expense of a standing army; they are unwilling to risk a small loss which may accrue from carrying into effect the proposed measure for supplying such of the militia as want them with arms. For what purpose are these arms wanted? For the defense of the liberty and independence of the country; and yet gentlemen now speak of expense. At the present crisis of danger, when all allow that the Southern States are most likely to be attacked, and the militia of those States want arms, and asked for them, when it is proposed to accommodate them, expense is held up as an objection. He trusted, when gentlemen considered the situation of the Southern

States, and that they contain within their own bosom a dangerous enemy, they will not persist in their opposition to a measure calculated to remedy this defect; that they will not exhibit to the world a strange inconsistency in a free country, viz: that the General Government insists upon sending hired standing troops into the Southern States, against the will of the people, but at the same time refuses to give them an opportunity of purchasing arms for their own defense!

Mr. Harper believed that most, if not all of the inconveniences set forth by the gentleman from New Jersey, might be avoided, and the object of the bill attained. These inconveniences were supposed to arise chiefly from a lengthy transportation of those arms by land. Whatever inconvenience and loss, however, might attend this supply he thought, with the gentleman from Maryland, that the difficulty ought to be encountered now rather than in a state of war. Besides, if this supply is withheld until the arms are wanted, the same inconvenience would not only be encountered, but the arms would come too late for the people to use them in training. But are we, said Mr. H., obliged to incur the expense of land carriage? He believed not, except in very few instances. Let be recollected that every State, except two, borders upon the sea, and that they are penetrated by rivers, which are to a certain extent navigable by boats; and if these arms were sent into some town in every State, where the people could get supplied, though they might have to ride fifty or one hundred miles for the supply, they would readily depute a person to go and make a purchase of all that might be wanted in a neighborhood. There were to be sure, a few exceptions, in which cases the expense of land carriage must be incurred.

Mr. Dayton said that, if the motion to strike out the second section was withdrawn, he should not object to their proceeding with the bill, and endeavoring to make it as unexceptionable as possible. He had been opposed to the general project of it, because he believed it would rather prevent than promote the general arming of the militia, and would remove from use, as well as put out of repair, many thousand stands of the public arms.

Mr. D. declared that he was not willing to do more than to authorize the increase of the number of armories and arsenals, so that there might be one in every State, where it might be deemed safe and practicable. He hoped that each State would take measures to procure arms for their citizens. It was known than the United States had no surplus of this important instrument of war, but, on the contrary, were deficient.

Mr. Harper knew that the section as it stands, without amendment, would produce great inconvenience; but he also knew that this section is capable of a very simple amendment, which would bring the bill to what the gentleman from New Jersey wished.

Mr. Coit withdrew his motion.

Mr. S. Smith moved to strike out the words, "in due proportion," which was immediately agreed to.

Mr. Harper moved to strike out the words, "within each division of the militia of the State."

Mr. Varnum wished a division of the question.

Mr. Rutledge said, as some of the States could easily supply themselves, they did not, of course, stand in need of the assistance of Government; though in other States, where arms cannot be got, it will be proper to send them. In the State from which he came, (South Carolina,) though the citizens in the lower part of the country are well armed, the inhabitants of the back country are in want of arms; and, in order to furnish a supply for that part of the country, the Legislature of that State had appropriated a sum of money for the purchase of ten thousand stands of arms. This money now lies in the Treasury, and if the General Government could send this quantity of arms to that State, they would be immediately paid for. He had himself applied to the Executive Department on account of these arms, but had received for answer, that, though Government had arms in their arsenals, they had no authority to sell them, but, if this law passed they might be forwarded.

Mr. R. said, if the United States were asked to supply the militia at their own expense with arms, some objection might be made to the request; but as they were only requested to be instrumental in affording the supply, without bearing ultimately any part of the expense, he thought the proposition could not reasonably be objected to.

Mr. Varnum did not believe that the militia of any of the States are completely armed; and many of the arms which they have are of *different calibres*. In the State of Massachusetts, he believed those persons who had not proper arms could not get them. He hoped, therefore, the arms would be distributed among the several States.

Mr. Brooks did not think the gentleman from Massachusetts had any reason to be uneasy on this subject. If the words are struck out, the President would, doubtless, distribute them where they are most wanted, and where the people will be willing to purchase them.

Mr. Macon said, that he had supposed, since the words "due proportion," were struck out, that the words now moved to be dispensed with, would have gone out of course. This, he said, was one of those kind of bills which are calculated to benefit the whole Union. Those States which manufacture arms, will be benefited by the sale of them to other States which want them, and they will be benefited by the supply. There was very little chance of the State of North Carolina, from whence he came, being invaded; but if either of the neighboring States were attacked he supposed the people of his State would be called upon for assistance; and when they were so called upon, he was desirous that they should be well armed, and ready to obey the call.

Questions on both parts of the amendment were put, and carried.

Mr. S. Smith wished, from what had fallen from the gentleman from South Carolina, (Mr. Rutledge,) to strike out the word "out," and to insert "to the Government of the respective States, or."

Mr. Thatcher did not know why the General Government should be put to the trouble and expense of providing arms for the State Governments. The original object was to provide arms for such individuals of the States as should choose to purchase them, and he thought that object ought not to be extended to the State Governments.

Mr. T. Claiborne said, the gentleman from Massachusetts must have a very fertile imagination, indeed, if he could suppose that the State Governments could want arms for any other purpose besides that of distributing amongst the people; and, at this time, he thought it proper that arms should be put into the hands of the people, and that those who are not able to pay for them should have them given to them.

Mr. Bayard hoped this amendment would be agreed to. The object of the bill was to place arms in the hands of those who want them, and this object would be accomplished, whether they are sold to individuals, or to the State Governments. If gentlemen supposed the Governments of the States could readily get supplied, they are mistaken. He could speak with certainty as to the State from which he came. He knew money had been appropriated for purchasing arms for their quota of the militia. He knew the Governor of that State came to this city, to endeavor to make a contract for these arms, but he found all were engaged for the Government of the United States, and the money yet lies in the Treasury of the State. He hoped, therefore, no further opposition would be made to it.

Mr. Kittera said, the State of Pennsylvania had appropriated money for twenty thousand stand of arms; one half to be purchased within the United States, and the other half to be imported. Those which were ordered to be purchased within the United States had been purchased; *but the contracts abroad, he believed, had failed*; and he believed the State Government is anxious to complete the order.

Mr. Thatcher said, he did not oppose the amendment, because he wished to prevent the State Governments from purchasing any quantity of arms they pleased; but. he did not think this was the best way of bringing arms into the hands of the people. He thought the State Governments might as well go to the manufacturers, or send their orders abroad themselves, as to employ the General Government to do the business for them.

The question was put, and carried without a division.

Mr. Payton proposed a new section, authorizing the President, in case all or any part of the arms remain unsold, to cause them to be delivered to such of the militia as may want them when called into actual service; proper receipts and securities being taken for returning the same.

It was carried, 57 votes being for it.

The question on filling the blank containing the number of arms to be provided, being under consideration.

Mr. Harper hoped it would be filled with 100,000 stands. He thought that number might be well distributed throughout the United States. They were to serve a double purpose, it would be recollected, viz: they are not only to be sold, but to arm such of the militia as may stand in need of them whenever they shall be called into actual service

Mr. Rutledge thought this would be by far too large a number, they would require more money than could be well spared for the purpose; they would cost from 14,000 to 16,000 dollars. He believed 30,000 stands would be sufficient.

Mr. T. Clairborne thought 25,000 or 30,000 would be enough.

Mr. Otis was opinion that if such a number was agreed to, and the President of the United States was authorized to apply the money received from those which are unsold, in purchasing a fresh quantity, so as to keep the sum now appropriated as a fund to be constantly employed in the purchase of arms, until the people in all parts of the Union shall be well supplied with them, the provision would be sufficient.

Mr. Kittera was against 100,000. He believed that number would cost little less than $2,000,000.

Mr. Harper withdrew his motion for 100,000, and the sense of the House was taken on 50,000, and negatived, there being only twenty votes for it. 30,000 were then moved and carried 44 to 28.

Mr. Shepard believed they could be purchased for twelve dollars a stand, and therefore moved to fill the blank to contain the sum proposed to be applied for the purchase of those arms, $400,000. Agreed to.

APPENDIX THREE
Arms Production at Federal Armories

Springfield Armory Production (1795–1834)

Year	Muskets Per Year	Cumulative Total
1795	245	245
1796	838	1,083
1797	1,028	2,111
1798	1,044	3,155
1799	4,595	7,750
1800	4,862	12,612
1801	3,205	15,817
1802	4,358	20,175
1803	4,775	24,950
1804	3,566	28,516
1805	3,535	32,051
1806	2,018	34,069
1807	5,692	39,761
1808	5,870	45,631
1809	7,070	52,701
1810	9,700	62,401
1811	12,020	74,421
1812	10,140	84,561
1813	6,920	91,481
1814	9,585	101,066
1815	7,279	108,345
1816	7,199	115,544
1817	13,015	128,559
1818	12,000	140,559
1819	12,000	152,559
1820	13,200	165,759

1821	13,000	178,759
1822	13,200	191,959
1823	14,000	205,959
1824	14,000	219,959
1825	15,000	234,959
1826	15,000	249,959
1827	14,500	264,459
1828	15,500	279,959
1829	16,500	296,459
1830	16,500	312,959
1831	16,200	329,159
1832	13,600	342,759
1833	12,400	355,159
1834	14,000	369,159

Harpers Ferry Armory Production (1801–1834)

Year	Muskets	Rifles	Pistols	Cumulative Total
1801	293			293
1802	1,472			1,765
1803	1,048			2,813
1804	161	772		3,746
1805		1,716		5,462
1806	136	1,381		6,979
1807	50	146	2,892	10,067
1808	3,051		1,208	14,326
1809	7,348			21,674
1810	9,400			31,074
1811	10,000			41,074
1812	10,200			51,274
1813	9,000			60,274
1814	10,400	1,600		72,274
1815	5,239	1,508		79,021
1816	6,416	2,052		87,489
1817	8,513	2,726		98,728
1818	9,892	2,700		111,320
1819	7,020	3,324		121,664
1820	9,856	1,793		133,313
1821	10,320			143,633
1822	10,000			153,633
1823	12,200			165,833
1824	10,559			176,392
1825	14,000			190,392
1826	8,720			199,112
1827	12,020	1,000		212,132
1828	10,000			222,132
1829	8,915			231,047
1830	10,130			241,177
1831	11,160			252,337
1832	12,000			264,337
1833	12,000			276,337
1834	12,000			288,337

APPENDIX FOUR
Federal Arms Contracts to Civilian Manufacturers

Army Musket Contractors, 1798–1808		
Army	**State**	**Ordered**
Robert McCormick	PA	3000
Thomas Towsey & Samuel Chipman	VT	1000
Richard Falley	MA	1000
Eli Williams	MD	2000
Nicholas White, Thomas Crabb, Jacob Mitzger & Schristopher Barnhizle	MD	1000
Eli Whitney	CT	10000
Adijah Peck	CT	1000
Amasa Allen, Samuel Grant & Joseph Bernard	NH	1500
Thomas Bicknell		2000
Darius Chuipman, Royal Crafts, Thomas Hooker, and John Smith	VT	1000
Owen Evans	PA	1000
Ard Welton	CT	1000
Amos Stillman	CT	500
Alexander Clagett	MD	1000
Adam Kinsley & James Perkins	MA	2000
Daniel Gilbert	MA	2000
William Rhodes & William Tyler	RI	2000
Elisha Brown	RI	1000
Stephen Jenks Jr. & Hosea Humphries	RI	1500
Jonathan Nichols Jr.	VT	1000
William Henry	PA	500
Joseph Clark	CT	500

Nathan & Henry Cobb	CT	200
Mathew & Nathan Elliott	CT	500
Mathias Shroyer	MD	1000
Elijah Baggett	MA	500
Gurdon Huntington, John Livingston, Josiah Bellows, and David Stone	NH	500

Army Pistol and Rifle Contractors 1807–1808		
Contractor	**Pistols**	**Rifles**
Year 1807		
Molan & Finn	350p	700
Joseph Henry[92]	150p	300
W.W. Cox	150p	300
Henry Pickel		200
Henry De Huff & Co.		600
Abraham Henry	200p	200
William Henry	150p	
Jacob Cooke	25p	
Year 1808		
Abraham Henry	400p	200
Jacob Cooke	50p	
Joseph Henry	600p	600
William Calderwood	60p	
A & J Ansted	50p	
Adam Leitner	100p	
John Shuler	150p	

---

[92] A Joseph Henry, who had been contracted to make 300 rifles in 1807, is specially noted in the records of Tench Coxe because the 64 rifles he delivered in1809 were 0.32 pistol caliber.

Contractors, 1808–1810			Delivered per Year				Total	Outstanding	% Filled
Name	State	Ordered	1809	1810	1811	1812	Total	Outstanding	% Filled
W. & I. I. Henry	PA	10,000	573	1600	1225	848	4246	5754	42
F. Goetz & Westphall	PA	2,500	113	406	400	100	1019	1481	41
John Miles	NJ	9200	213	438	967	789	2407	6793	26
Winner, Nippes & Co.	PA	9000	1000	1700	800	400	3900	5100	43
Waters & Whitmore	MA	5000		1200	1000	800	3000	2000	60
Ethan Stillman	CT	2500		75	325	425	825	1675	33
Daniel Gilbert	MA	5000			550	325	875	4125	18
French, Blake, & Kinsley	MA	4000		500	1050	625	2175	1825	54
I. & C. C. Barstow	NH	2500		275	650	700	1625	875	65
Wheeler & Morrison	VA	2500			125		125	2375	5
Oliver Bidwell	CT	4000		125	350	275	750	3250	19
O. & E. Evans	PA	4000	274	601	634	451	1960	2040	49
Stephen Jenks & Sons	RI	4000		325	1000	975	2300	1700	58
R. & C. Leonard	MA	5000		200	1125	800	2125	2875	43
A. & P. Bartlett	MA	2500		475	950	75	1500	1000	60
Rufus Perkins	MA	2500		100	100		200	2300	8
I. I. & N. Brooke	PA	4000		605	472	180	1257	2743	31
W. & H. Shannon	PA	4000	198	504	351	48	1101	2899	28
Sweet, Jenks & Sons	RI	3000				250	250	2750	8

SOURCES

The Library of Congress, *The Congressional Record*- Years 1790 to 1830

Auchinleck, Gilbert, *A History of the War between Great Britain and the United States of America during the years 1812, 1813 & 1814.* Toronto: Thomas Maclear, 1855, reprint by: H.C. Campbell 1972

Elting John R., *Amateurs, to Arms!: A Military History of the War of 1812* Chapel Hill, N.C. : Algonquin Books of Chapel Hill, 1991

Pitch, Anthony S. *The Burning of Washington: The British Invasion of 1814* Annapolis. MD. : Naval Institute Press, 1998

Headquarters, Department of the Army, *American Military History 1607–1958* ROTCM 145-20, July 1959

Remini, Robert V. *The Battle of New Orleans* New York, N.Y. : Viking Press, 1999

Lossing Benson J. *The Pictorial Field-Book of the War of 1812* New York, N.Y.: Harper & Brothers, 1868

Brown, M. L. *Firearms in Colonial America: The Impact on History and Technology 1491–1792* Washington, D.C. : Smithsonian Institution Press, 1980.

Hicks, Capt James E. *Notes on United States Ordnance, Volume 1: Small Arms, 1776–1940*
Mt. Vernon, NY: James E. Hicks publisher, 1940

Bell, Augustus C. *History of Andrew Jackson: Pioneer, Soldier, Politician, President*
New York, N.Y.: C. Scribner's Sons, 19

INDEX

Printed in the United States
By Bookmasters